Practices for Engaging the 21st Century Workforce

Practices for Engaging the 21st Century Workforce

Challenges of Talent Management in a Changing Workplace

William G. Castellano, Ph.D.

Vice President, Publisher: Tim Moore
Associate Publisher and Director of Marketing: Amy Neidlinger
Executive Editor: Jeanne Glasser Levine
Operations Specialist: Jodi Kemper
Marketing Manager: Lisa Loftus
Cover Designer: Chuti Prasertsith
Managing Editor: Kristy Hart
Senior Project Editor: Betsy Gratner
Copy Editor: Apostrophe Editing Services
Proofreader: Anne Goebel
Indexer: Tim Wright
Senior Compositor: Gloria Schurick
Manufacturing Buyer: Dan Uhrig

© 2014 by William G. Castellano
Published by Pearson Education, Inc.
Upper Saddle River, New Jersey 07458

Pearson offers excellent discounts on this book when ordered in quantity for bulk purchases or special sales. For more information, please contact U.S. Corporate and Government Sales, 1-800-382-3419, corpsales@pearsontechgroup.com. For sales outside the U.S., please contact International Sales at international@pearsoned.com.

Company and product names mentioned herein are the trademarks or registered trademarks of their respective owners.

Printed in the United States of America

ISBN-10: 0-13-480751-0
ISBN-13: 978-0-13480751-5

Pearson Education LTD.
Pearson Education Australia PTY, Limited.
Pearson Education Singapore, Pte. Ltd.
Pearson Education Asia, Ltd.
Pearson Education Canada, Ltd.
Pearson Educación de Mexico, S.A. de C.V.
Pearson Education—Japan
Pearson Education Malaysia, Pte. Ltd.

Library of Congress Control Number: 2013943657

I dedicate this book to my parents,
Anthony and Gladys,
and to my wife, MaryAnn, and son, Kevin.

Contents

Acknowledgments

This book would have been impossible to write without the support of many wonderful people. Given the extensive amount of research that was an important part of this book, I am very thankful to have worked with a number of outstanding research assistants including Ashley Hann, Monica Mackow, Mohammed Nazmussadad, and Maham Mukhtar. I am equally grateful to have collaborated and worked with outstanding scholars who have helped shape my thinking on managing talent in the 21st century and whose friendship I will forever value including Richard Beatty, Paula Caligiuri, Steve Director, Charles Fay, Stanley Gully, Mark Huselid, Susan Jackson, Barbara Lee, David Lepak, Jean Phillips, and Randall Schuler. I also thank Jeanne Glasser Levine, Executive Editor at Pearson, for all her support and patience helping me get my research into print.

Lastly, I am eternally grateful to my wife, MaryAnn, and son, Kevin, who have endured the long hours I spent alone writing this book. Their ongoing support and encouragement got me through many difficult periods putting words to paper.

About the Author

Dr. William G. Castellano is the Executive Director of the Joint Center for Management Development, a Clinical Associate Professor at the Rutgers Business School and School of Management and Labor Relations, and the former Director of the Center for HR Strategy and HRM Undergraduate Programs. His research, teaching, and consulting activities are focused on the effective management of contract human capital and strategic alliances, employee engagement, and aligning business and Human Resource (HR) strategies to enhance organizational effectiveness. Bill has more than 30 years of experience working in corporate Fortune 50, entrepreneurial, and research environments. Before joining Rutgers University, he was a Managing Partner at an executive search firm and a Chief Marketing Officer at a national HR outsourcing company. He also held senior HR management positions at Merrill Lynch and Manufacturers Hanover Trust where he was involved with HR strategies and practices that supported both individual business groups and the global enterprise. Bill is an accomplished researcher publishing his work in practitioner and academic journals and is a frequent speaker at national HR and business conferences.

1

Welcome to the New Normal

You truly live in interesting times. Change has been a constant in your life for some time now, and the pace of change is increasing at a dizzying rate. You are entering a new and challenging way of working as a result of unprecedented technological, global, economic, and demographic trends. Unlike previous tumultuous business cycles, you can now witness structural shifts in labor markets and the economy that are fundamentally changing the world of work. Many economists, business leaders, and commentators are describing this trend as the new normal.

This is a new era in which dazzling technological advances, new global competitors, and a new generation of workers can change the direction and fortunes of the old economic order. Every day new companies creating innovative products or services replace established, yet rapidly becoming obsolete, companies in a continuing process of creative destruction. In the United States and much of the developed world, the long-term trend is slower economic growth and higher unemployment, whereas in much of the developing world, it's faster economic growth and rising employment. Furthermore, you can witness dramatic labor force trends. In the United States, the workforce is growing at a much slower rate due to slower population growth and lower workforce participation rates. Even more alarming, there is a growing unsustainable gap between the supply and demand of high-skilled U.S. workers.

The world of work as a result of these trends has become increasingly more complex. An amazing amount of new information exists that must transform into knowledge, a greater degree of global interdependencies, and a need for much faster response times, all resulting in a much less predictable and chaotic workplace (see Table 1.1).

Table 1.1 Welcome to the New Normal

Seismic converging trends:
Technological
Globalization
Labor force
Economic
Creating:
Increasing complexity
Structural shifts

Technological Trends

Many people describe the new normal purely as a phenomenon of the impact of technological advances on every dimension of your life. Indeed, advances in computer and communication technologies transform how you work, live, and play (see Table 1.2).

Table 1.2 Technological Trends

Increasingly faster, powerful, and less expensive technologies
Transforming how you live and work
Reducing barriers of entry
Creating new industries

Increasingly Faster, Powerful, and Less Expensive Technologies

One reason why technology has been so ubiquitous is the seemingly impossible trend of simultaneously getting faster and more powerful while getting cheaper. In the 1960s, Gordon Moore, one of the cofounders of Intel, accurately predicted that the power and speed of computers would double approximately every 2 years. Unlike many predictions, this one was accurate, and today it is known as Moore's Law. You may be amazed about the stories that today's average home computer has more speed and power than the technology used to put a man on the moon.

Not too long ago you measured computer-generated information in kilobytes that equaled 1,000 bytes of information. Today, most home computers store gigabytes of information, which is the equivalent of billions of bytes of information, and have backup drives holding terabytes of information that equal 1,000 gigabytes. In 1 year, the entire world produces more than 800,000 petabytes of information. A petabyte is 1,000,000 gigabytes. To put this in perspective, the entire written works of mankind in recorded history in all languages equal 20 petabytes, which is equal to the amount of data processed by Google in one day. This is a true example of Parkinson's Law, which states that whatever information capacity you supply to humans, they will use it.

The competition for creating the world's most powerful computers is increasing more than ever. The United States, which was knocked from its top position by China in 2010 and Japan in 2011, once again is home to the world's most powerful computer according to the Top 500 list. Actually, the United States now holds the top two spots. The Department of Energy's Cray XK7, named Titan, has clocked in at 17.6 sustained petaflops or quadrillion floating-point operations per second (Top500, 2012).

You can witness a similar trend in the communications sector. The global mobile phone industry was launched on September 7, 1987, when 15 phone companies signed an agreement to build mobile networks based on the Global System for Mobile Communications (GSM). It took 12 years to reach 1 billion mobile connections, and only 30 months later there were more than 3.5 billion subscriptions globally. Today, there is an estimated 4.5 billion mobile subscriptions (Meister and Willyerd, 2010). The first commercial text message was sent in 1992; today, the number of text messages sent every day exceeds the total population of the planet. In addition to phone calls and text messages, advances in communication technologies enable massive amounts of digital data to be sent at light speed.

For example, fiber optic cables can now push 14 trillion bits of data per second, which is the equivalent of 2,660 CDs or 210 million phone calls.

Unlike any other industry, the fantastic advances in computer and communication technologies were accompanied by equally dramatic price decreases. Since the turn of the century, the cost of moving data across a network has dropped more than 90 percent, while over that same time period, data storage costs per unit fell from more than $500 to slightly more than 10 cents. Computing power measured in costs per 1 million transistors dropped from $222 in 1992 to $0.27 in 2008. Perhaps if the automobile industry advanced at a similar rate, everyone would drive cars that get 1,000 miles to the gallon and cost $500 (Benko and Anderson, 2010d).

At the dawn of the technology revolution, the costs to purchase and power a computer were so prohibitive only the government used the power of technology. As the speed of computers increased with a correspondingly decrease in price and the need for power, the transformative power of technology spread from governments to corporations to individuals. Actually, the average individual today has access to virtually an unlimited amount of information and computer power. In the past, companies spent millions of dollars on infrastructure and developing computer applications for their businesses. Today, individuals with a laptop computer literally have the world at their fingertips via search portals such as Google and Bing, have access to many free applications such as Gmail, Google Docs, and Picasa, and enjoy free online content from newspapers, magazines, and blogs.

More transformational than the power of technology is the impact on behavior that it engenders. Today, more than 65 percent of adults in Organization for Economic Cooperation and Development (OECD) countries use the Internet to send more than 9 trillion emails a year; perform more than 1 billion Google searches a day; and form countless communities and relationships that were previously unimaginable (OECD, 2011). Today, technology is a ubiquitous and integral part of our lives, and the pace of innovation and its scope is increasing at an accelerating rate. It took 75 years for the telephone to reach 50 million, 38 years for the radio, 13 years for television, 4 years for the World Wide Web, 3 years for the iPod, and only 2 years for Facebook.

Transforming How You Live and Work

Technology has been transforming how you live and work for decades. When access to technology is equalized, technology becomes a commodity, and companies can no longer differentiate by just having technology. Companies need to start viewing innovation as the true enabler and technology as the means to drive innovation. "In the last twenty years, becoming digital was a competitive advantage. In the next twenty years, in the New Normal, we have to focus on how to be clever with digital" (Hinssen, 2010 pg. 174). Companies use technology such as social media and digital marketing to improve their communication and collaboration within and beyond their boundaries.

In addition to fostering better collaboration among employees and gathering invaluable market intelligence from a significantly expanded audience, companies are doing so in faster and more efficient ways. Social media is shifting the older one-to-one communication channels via emails and phone calls to many-to-many communication channels via an array of social media platforms. These social channels enable employees to find information more readily within the organization and have access to communities of experts that facilitate knowledge sharing. As a result, they can connect with suppliers and customers and gain insights for improving customer service, as well as marketing and product development.

For example, innovative companies such as Inuit use technology to forge stronger customer relationships by creating online customer support communities to help monitor and resolve customer issues that enable more experienced customers to give their personal advice to those who need it. They monitor the questions and responses to help drive product upgrades and fixes without paying for costly customer surveys (Bughin et al., 2010). Procter & Gamble (P&G) created a customer network called Vocalpoint where mothers share their experiences using P&G's products with other members of their social circle. In markets in which Vocalpoint influencers are active, product revenues have significantly outpaced those markets without online customer networks.

Technology also transforms customer intimacy companies such as Nordstrom. In an interview published in *USA Today*, Blake Nordstrom noted how technology changes customers' shopping experiences

(Malcolm, 2012). Think digital fitting rooms, where parametric technology simulates a shopper's body type to show how a garment might look or fit. Soon 3-D printers will enable consumers to make products in their own homes. Intel has recently designed a mirror that shows shoppers how clothes look on them, enabling them to avoid having to use fitting rooms. Increasingly, where customers shop will not matter. People could shop from their homes, cars, or wherever they have access to mobile networks using a multitude of mobile devices. According to a 2012 survey of C-level executives conducted by McKinsey & Company, the top digital trends transforming business are big data and analytics, digital marketing and social media, and cloud computing (McKinsey & Co., 2012b).

Advances in technology have long been transforming where, when, and how work gets done. The idea of a workplace that is a fixed, physical location is obsolete. Today, there are millions of individuals working remotely from home and distributive workplaces. Going to work for many employees means walking to a home office where they are instantly connected to their managers and coworkers or can join a videoconference with team members around the globe. It's estimated that there are more than 13 million workers in the United States who work outside a traditional office space almost daily and another 10 million who telecommute at least one day per week (Benko and Anderson, 2010d).

Social networks such as Facebook, LinkedIn, and Twitter create new ways for employees to collaborate, share information, and get to know each other better. There is now a "virtual water cooler" at the workplace where employees spread out across vast distances can converse with one another. Companies such as Cisco and IBM utilize social networks as well as videoconferencing technology to help dismantle silos and increase collaboration and knowledge sharing across their organizations (Bisson et al., 2010). These new technologies transform and reduce the costs of how knowledge is created and shared, as well as increase the speed to access external experts.

Venture capitalist firms in Silicon Valley use advances in mobile technology to create what is often called the distributed workforce. Companies such as TaskRabbit have taken the on-demand workforce to a new level by organizing and auctioning tedious and time-consuming chores. According to Rob Coneybeer, managing director of Shasta Ventures, which has invested in several of these new companies, the goal is to build a new kind of labor market "where people end up getting paid more per hour than they would have otherwise and find it easier to do jobs they are good at" (Stone, 2012 pg. 1). What makes these companies different than the traditional job boards is the innovative use of smartphones and the supervisory services they provide.

Workers can load an app on their phone and can bid on jobs any time of day. Employers can monitor the whereabouts of workers, evaluate each job after it's completed, and make payments on their phones or via the Internet. In an interview with *Bloomberg Businessweek*, Leah Busque, the founder of TaskRabbit, says thousands of workers make a living (up to $60,000 a year) on her site. She goes on to say, "We are enabling micro-entrepreneurs to build their own business on top of TaskRabbit, set their own schedule, specify how much they want to get paid, say what they are good at, and then incorporate the work into their lifestyle" (Stone, 2012 pg. 2).

Crowdsourcing is another example of how advances in technology can transform how work is done. This innovation provides companies access to a potentially unlimited pool of talent in which Internet users over a common platform contribute to a project without necessarily getting paid. For example, in 2006, Netflix famously offered a $1 million prize to anyone who could increase the accuracy of its movie recommendation system by 10 percent. It openly provided access to its data set of more than 100 million customer movie ratings. In September 2009, it awarded $1 million in equity to the best-submitted recommendation. Meanwhile, social networking sites, blogs, and wikis offer many ways to tap the wisdom of many experts. Facebook regularly taps into its growing number of power users to translate its site into different languages, which for example took only 1 day to translate into French.

Reducing Barriers of Entry

Technological advances significantly lower the cost of entry for many businesses. One of the most revolutionary technological developments for start-up businesses is *cloud computing*. Today, companies have access to sophisticated business applications they can run over the Internet and pay only for what they use. Instead of investing large sums of money to buy hardware and servers and employ highly skilled and expensive teams of technologists to manage their business systems, they now have better and more economical options provided by specialized providers in the cloud. The shift to the cloud has also fundamentally transformed corporate information technology (IT) departments. Today, companies need people with technical skills who understand business and customer needs and focus on innovating with technology instead of managing technology.

Cloud computing also increases the computing capacity for many organizations while reducing costs, which is having a significant, positive impact on productivity. In a hypercompetitive work environment with an ever-growing number of new competitors entering markets due to reduced barriers of entry, it is imperative for organizations to continue increasing productivity to remain competitive. This is particularly the case in Western economies where there is slow workforce growth and thus a reliance on productivity increases to fuel future growth.

The reduction of barriers has also enabled more companies to compete on a global scale. You can now witness organizations that are literally "born global." These firms have the capabilities to virtually manage all their functional operations. They electronically access and link an array of offshore partners for their design, research and development (R&D), manufacturing, marketing, selling, financial, and human capital needs.

Creating New Industries

Not only is technology lowering the cost of entry and increasing business competition, but it is also radically changing entire industries. Through a relentless process of creative destruction, entire industries have been altered or have vanished while new totally different ones have taken their place. Just when I finally replaced all my old albums with shiny new CDs, I replaced all of them on my iPod I can carry in my pocket. Overnight, the music industry was transformed when people could download, copy, and play music on an array of devices. Other industries such as print media are rapidly being replaced with online alternatives.

In a similar fashion, the travel industry had to quickly adapt to remain relevant. People no longer have to go to a travel agent for research or make their travel arrangements. All these options are available online. At one time, the travel industry produced two glossy print catalogs a year, one in the summer and one in winter. Today, it must constantly update its online content. According to Peter Hinssen, "Once the industry hit the New Normal, the rhythm of two releases per year evaporated and the operations of the companies became a 24/7, 365 days a year operation" (pg. 23).

These technological advances also impact the manufacturing industry, which for decades has been the one area in which a blue-collar worker could make a decent living. You can see this trend in the automobile industry in which robotics and computer-controlled lathes have altered production so significantly that fewer but more highly skilled workers are needed to produce a fixed number of automobiles. Today, nearly 90 percent of U.S. and European automotive original-equipment manufacturers (OEMs) use robots for welding and car assembly (Agrawal et al., 2003).

Globalization

The second trend that is often cited when describing the "new normal" is globalization (see Table 1.3). Massive global population and economic trends are fundamentally altering the world of business and work. On one hand, there are phenomenal opportunities for U.S. businesses and workers as the developing world advances economically, creating new markets for your products and services. On the other hand, the rapidly growing number of new global workers and businesses are major threats for U.S. businesses and workers as the competitive landscape significantly increases.

Table 1.3 Globalization Trends

Growing population/labor force trends
More global talent/offshoring
Growing markets
Increasing competition

Globalization is truly a double-edged sword for the U.S. economy. The cheap imports from developing countries have helped to keep inflation and interest rates down, benefiting consumers and businesses. At the same time, countries such as China, India, and Brazil create huge markets for U.S. multinationals. However, low-cost imports have put significant downward pressures on U.S. workers' wages and have put significant competitive pressure on manufacturers operating with higher costs. Furthermore, the global workforce is growing and getting much more educated, putting pressure on white-collar workers' wages and incentivizing many U.S. businesses to move operations overseas and offshore back office and IT functions.

Growing Population/Labor Force Trends

The seismic population trends sweeping across the globe will shape global labor markets for decades to come. The developed economies of the world are experiencing slowing and declining population growth rates, whereas the emerging economies are seeing their populations significantly grow. According to a United Nations (UN) population research report, the world population surpassed 7 billion in 2011 and is projected to reach 9 billion people by 2050 and exceed 10 billion in 2100 (UN, 2011). However, there is a huge divergence in population growth rates between the developed and developing regions of the world. The developing countries are on track to see their populations increase from 5.7 billion in 2011 to 8.8 billion in 2100. In contrast, the population of the developed world is expected to change minimally, rising from 1.24 billion in 2011 to 1.34 billion in 2100. Significantly, the developed nations' populations would have declined to 1.11 billion during this time period if it were not for the projected net migrations from developing to developed countries, which is expected to average 2.2 million people annually from 2011 to 2050 and 0.8 million from 2050 to 2100 (UN, 2011).

Europe and Japan are facing a devastating combination of rapidly aging populations and declining fertility rates. Over the next 40 years, countries like Germany, Italy, Spain, and Japan are projected to see population declines ranging from 15 to 25 percent (U.S. Census Bureau, 2008b). Other developed countries including the United States, Great Britain, Canada, and Australia, due to growth in immigration, will not experience declining populations but will have much slower population growth rates.

Growing populations present many unique challenges for developing countries. The population of the developing countries is young, with children under 15 accounting for 29 percent of the population and young persons aged 15 to 24 accounting for an additional 18 percent. The number of children and young people is at an all-time high (1.6 billion children and 1.0 billion young people). Typically having such a young population bodes well for a region because their labor force grows and dependency ratio falls. However, it also poses a major challenge for developing countries, which are faced with the necessity of providing education and employment to large cohorts of individuals.

The situation is quite different in the developed regions in which the issue is a rapidly aging population in which the population aged 60 and over is increasing at the fastest pace ever. Over the next 4 decades, the number of people 60 and over in developed nations will increase by more than 50 percent, rising from 274 million in 2011 to 418 million in 2050 and to 433 million in 2100. The percent of the population 60 years of age and older in developed nations will increase from 22 percent in 2011 to 32 percent in 2050. In time, the developing nations' older populations will also increase. The rate of growth is faster than the developed nations (3 percent and 2.4 percent annually, respectively); however, as a percentage of the population, it will increase from 9 percent in 2011 to 20 percent in 2050, which is significantly less than the developed nations. Globally, the median age of the population is projected to increase from 29 to 38 years between 2011 and 2050 and to 42 years by 2100. Europe has today the oldest population, with a median age of nearly 40 years, which is projected to reach 46 years in 2050 and slightly decline to 45 years by 2100 (UN, 2011).

Within the developing world, there has also been a significant movement toward urbanization as large segments of the population migrate from the countryside to the cities where there are greater economic opportunities. China has been witnessing the largest migration of people moving to cities with roughly 40 percent of its population now living in urban areas, which is projected to increase to 73 percent by 2050. India, which is less than 30 percent urbanized today, is expected to be 55 percent urbanized by 2050 (Goldstone, 2010). Large migrations of people in these countries put severe strains on infrastructure and resources as well as on the capability of the economy to provide housing and work.

Not surprisingly, as the world's population continues to grow, so too does the global workforce. One look at global population trends is all you need to see to understand where most of the world's talent will come from. In both the developed and developing regions of the world, the number of working people aged 25 to 50 years of age is at an all-time high: 606 million and 2.5 billion, respectively. However, whereas in the developed regions that number is projected to peak over the next decade and decline thereafter reaching 531 million in 2050 and 525 million in 2100, in the developing regions it will continue rising, reaching 3.6 billion in 2050 and 3.7 billion in 2100. Significantly, the developing countries labor force is projected to add nearly one-half billion workers over the next decade.

The rapid growth in world population beacons the age-old concern, going back to Thomas Malthus's famous 1798 "Essay on the Principle of Population," of whether rapid population growth will outstrip the world's resources creating widespread poverty and famine. These concerns were echoed in the 1972 Club of Rome's report on the limits of growth. However, the continued advancements in agricultural technology and the increased productivity and discovery of new energy sources have dampened these concerns. Nonetheless, the continued increase in demand for critical commodities including food, water, energy, and minerals has created shortages and huge price fluctuations.

More Global Talent/Offshoring

As the developing countries' populations and economies grow, the educational attainment of the global workforce has been significantly improving. As a result, the competition for the developed world worker has never been higher, particularly in the highly in-demand fields of science and engineering. When many people think about U.S. companies' offshoring work, they typically think of the millions of factory jobs and other low-cost work that was sent overseas so that companies can hire cheap labor. A more startling trend for U.S. workers is the offshoring of white-collar work. As the world becomes increasingly more connected and more educated, it is both feasible and economically prudent to have work performed where wages and benefit costs are much lower than in the United States.

Jobs that are not candidates for offshoring typically require customer contact or extensive interactions with colleagues, such as many retail, managerial, support staff, and generalists' type of work. The types of white-collar jobs amenable to offshoring include IT, engineering, finance, and accounting. The two largest sectors for offshoring are IT outsourcing (ITO) and business process outsourcing (BPO), which encompass a wide range of jobs including low-skilled back office operation positions to high-skilled IT positions. Many of these offshored jobs were previously filled by college graduates.

Nearly 50 percent of the Fortune Global 250 had offshored IT and business processes activities. In 2009, IT and business process outsourcing revenues exceeded $250 billion and $140 billion, respectively. India has dominated these markets, capturing 65 percent of the ITO and 43 percent of the BPO markets (Willcocks and Lacity, 2009). Forrester Research estimates that the number of U.S. legal jobs moved offshore will increase from 35,000 in 2010 to 79,000 by 2015 (Meister and Willyerd, 2010).

Today, India has more technology workers than any other country, and China is on track to pass the United States as the country with the largest number of R&D workers (Bisson et al., 2010). As the demand for high-skilled labor exceeds the supply in the United States, many U.S.-based multinationals have no choice but to tap into the growing number of educated workers globally. However, there is a significant variance in the quality of workers' education within developing nations. For example, for entry-level corporate positions spanning a number of occupations including engineers, finance, accounting, and healthcare, there is a growing mismatch between the sort of graduates many Chinese universities turn out and the type of candidates who would interest local and multinational companies doing business in China. There is also a growing Chinese managerial and executive talent gap (Lane and Pollner, 2008). In a study conducted by McKinsey, researchers found that although nearly 50 percent of the engineers in Eastern European countries such as Hungary and Poland are suitable to work for multinational companies, only 10 percent and 25 percent of those in China and India, respectively, could do so (Farrell and Grant, 2005).

For many multinational firms, setting up operations around the world is not just about gaining access to lower cost and needed talent. Given the slowing population and economic trends in the developed world, many organizations want to be closer to the economies that are growing the fastest and hire local talent who understand the culture and intricacies of doing business in these countries. Expanding into new markets also gives these multinational organizations access to local supply chains enabling them to efficiently distribute their products and services.

Growing Markets

As emerging-market economies grow, they will shift primarily from an export-driven economy to a more consumption-driven economy, making them prime markets for multinationals striving to increase revenues. As workers in India and China advance economically, their demand for U.S. products and services increases. By the end of this decade, China is expected to have 595 million middle-income consumers and 82 million upper-middle-income consumers (Laudicina, 2005). In a report by McKinsey and Company titled "The Great Rebalancing," it's projected that more than 70 million people mostly from emerging economies are moving into the middle class each year (Bisson et al., 2010). Middle-class consumers across a dozen emerging countries now number almost 2 billion people and spend an estimated $6.9 trillion annually.

These global trends are both a threat and an opportunity for U.S. companies. Clearly, there is more competition; however, there are many opportunities for U.S. companies to reach a growing number of consumers in maturing developing countries. In a global survey conducted by PricewaterhouseCoopers (PWC), nearly two-thirds of the CEOs surveyed were positive about the impact that globalization will have on their organizations in the upcoming years (PWC, 2006). These CEOs' primary motivation for going global was not to reduce costs but to access new customers and better service their existing ones. Over the next decade, nearly 80 percent of the world's middle-income consumers will reside in emerging economies. Not surprisingly, 71 percent of the CEOs surveyed by PWC indicated that they plan to do business in at least one of the BRIC (Brazil, Russia, India, and China) countries within the next few years.

Increasing Competition

There are tectonic shifts altering the global competitive landscape. Although the United States has the largest economy, 50 years ago the U.S. economy accounted for 53 percent of global gross domestic product (GDP), whereas today it accounts for less than 28 percent, or less than 20 percent in terms of global purchasing power parity (Central Intelligence Agency [CIA], 2010). The biggest competition has been from the BRICs, with China and India posing the greatest competitive threats. The headquarters' locations of the *Financial Times* Global 500 rankings highlight these global business trends. From 2005 to 2009, the number of U.S.-based multinationals showed a sharp decline with a net loss of 38 companies, whereas companies located in the BRICs witnessed a dramatic increase. Brazil saw a net gain of four companies; Russia had a net gain of two companies; India had a net gain of five; and China had the largest increase with a gain of 35 companies (Meister and Willyerd, 2010).

The UN estimates that in 2010 there were more than 82,000 large multinational companies employing more than 77 million people worldwide (UN, 2010). The rising number of multinational firms located outside the United States is not just competing with U.S. firms on cost, but a growing number are making significant advances in innovation. In particular, there has been an explosion of R&D

expenditures in Asia. The 10 largest economies in Asia (China, India, Indonesia, Japan, Malaysia, Philippines, Singapore, South Korea, Taiwan, and Thailand) in 2011 spent an estimated $399 billion on R&D, slightly less than the $400 billion spent in the United States, but well ahead of Europe's $300 billion (National Science Board, 2012).

The *Bloomberg Businessweek* ranking of the 50 most innovative global companies highlights just how quickly the rest of the world is catching up with the United States. In 2006, there were only 5 companies in the top 50 that were located in Asia; by 2010, the number of firms had grown to 15. For the first time since the rankings began in 2005, the majority of the top innovative companies on the list were based outside the United States. The pace of change in this competitive space is also accelerating, as more than one-half of these companies were not on the list in 2009 (Society for Human Resource Management, 2011).

Today there is an interdependent global economy that is getting larger and more sophisticated by the day. In the coming decades, emerging-market economies will rapidly evolve from being minor players on the global stage into economic powerhouses. No longer will they be viewed as the world's factory producing low-cost goods and services as they become large-scale providers of human capital and innovation.

U.S. Labor Force Trends

Since the 1950s, a critical driver of the United States' competitive advantage has been its growing and highly educated labor force. Immediately following the end of World War II, millions of servicemen returned home to start anew. The result was a rapid increase in births now referred to as the baby boom. Indeed, between 1946 and 1964, nearly 80 million babies were born. Growing up in an era of uncontested prosperity, the baby boomers became the most educated and affluent generation of its time. Significantly, during this time, the role of women was rapidly changing. Female baby boomers were well educated and highly independent. As a result, they entered the workforce at an unprecedented rate. The female participation rate, a measure of the percentage of working age women in the labor force, increased from 34 percent in 1950 to 60 percent by the year 2000 (Toossi, 2012).

Slowing Labor Force Growth

For decades, U.S. businesses had a growing pipeline of available talent that helped fuel their rapid economic growth. However, since 2000, there have been significant headwinds slowing the labor force growth rate that will have a negative impact on economic growth well into the foreseeable future. There are two forces negatively impacting the U.S. labor force growth rate: slowing population growth and declining labor force participation rates. Population growth is a product of fertility rates, which is the average number of children born to a woman over the course of her life and immigration. In the 1950s, the average number of births per woman was 3.5. Using the most recent U.S. Census Bureau data, the Bureau of Labor Statistics (BLS) projects the future fertility rate will remain close to the present level of 2.1, which is roughly the replacement level of the population (Toossi, 2012).

Thus, if it weren't for net immigration growth, the U.S. population, like most of the developed world, would decline over the next few decades. Thankfully, net immigration has had a positive impact on population growth and is expected to add 1.5 million persons annually to the U.S. resident population from 2010 to 2020. However, even with a net positive immigration rate, the U.S. population grew at an anemic 1.1 percent annual rate from 2000 to 2010 and is projected to grow at an even slower 0.98 annual growth rate from 2010 to 2020 (Toossi, 2012).

In addition to slowing population growth, the overall U.S. labor force participation rate (the percentage of the working age population in the labor force) for men and women is declining. After peaking at 67.1 percent in 2000, the overall labor force participation rate declined to 64.7 percent by 2010. Furthermore, as the labor force continues to get older due to aging baby boomers, the labor force participation rate is projected to decline even more. The prime age work group, those between the ages of 25 and 54 years old, has the highest labor force participation rate, which in 2010 stood at 82.2 percent, whereas the 55-years-and-older work group has a much lower participation rate, which in 2010 equaled 40.2 percent. The oldest of the baby boomers reached the age of 55 in 2001, and for each passing year thereafter, there has been downward pressure on the overall participation rate. Looking forward, the BLS estimates that during the 2010 to 2020 time period, the participation rate will keep falling, reaching 62.5 percent in 2020 (Toossi, 2012).

The one silver lining to this negative trend is aging baby boomers are expected to have a higher participation rate compared to previous generations, which is expected to keep the rate from declining further in the future. In 2000, the participation rate for the 55 and older work group was 32.4 percent. A decade later, the rate rose significantly to 40.2 percent and is projected to keep increasing to 43.0 percent by 2020. However, the result of a combined slowing population and declining overall labor force participation rate has been a dramatic slowing of the U.S. labor force growth rate. Between 1990 and 2000, the U.S. labor force grew only at a 1.3 percent annual rate, followed by an even slower growth rate of 0.8 percent from 2000 to 2010. Based on current projections, the labor force growth rate will continue to slow well into the future. It's projected to grow at a 0.7 percent annual rate during the 2010–2020 time period (Toossi, 2012) and an even slower 0.4 percent annual rate during the 2020–2050 time period (Toossi, 2002).

These massive population shifts impacting U.S. labor force trends portend difficult times for businesses trying to compete in a global economy. As their pipeline of talent continues to slow, U.S. businesses are simultaneously facing the fact that 80 million or so baby boomers (those born between 1946 and 1964) are rapidly approaching retirement. More than one-half of those aged 62 and older are already moving into retirement. Over the next 10 years, approximately 40 percent of the U.S. labor force will be eligible for retirement. Generation X (those born between 1965 and 1979) is only slightly more than one-half of the number of the baby boomers. Thus, from 2008 to 2018, the percentage of 25–54-year-olds in the labor force will decrease from 67.7 percent to 63.5 percent, whereas the percent of 55 plus year olds will increase from 18.1 percent to 23.9 percent (BLS, 2009).

The BLS is projecting that from 2008 to 2018, the number of job openings resulting from individuals retiring and leaving their jobs will be more than double the number of new job openings due to economic growth. The key question is whether there will be enough of a supply of talent with the range of skills necessary to both replace these workers and fill new positions (BLS, 2009).

Workforce Education Trends

The United States is witnessing a significant decline in the labor force growth rate, just when companies need human capital more than ever due to demands brought about by both technological and global trends. To make matters worse, the quality of the U.S. labor force is also declining. High school graduation rates peaked at 77 percent in 1969, declined to 70 percent in 1995, and have not improved since this time. A study conducted by the OECD ranked the United States 16th out of 21 OECD countries for high school graduation rates. The United States was ranked 24th out of 30 countries in science and 25th in math. National surveys of working age adults in the United States age 16 years of age and older indicate a large number lack sufficient literacy and numerical skills needed to fully participate in an increasingly competitive work environment (Kirsch et al., 2007, Educational Testing Service [ETS], 2007).

The U.S. Department of Education estimates that 60 percent of all new jobs created over the next two decades will require skills that only 20 percent of the current workforce possesses (Augustine, 2007). Yet the current educational system in the United States is ill prepared to meet this challenge. A 2011 report issued by American College Testing (ACT) Inc. shows only 45 percent of U.S. high-school graduates who took the ACT assessment exam were considered prepared for college-level math. Only 30 percent were prepared for college-level science. It is the deficiency of early education for U.S. students that has led high school graduates to be unprepared for highly quantitative majors in scientific, technological, mathematic, and engineering fields. As a result, a trend exists of students initially opting-out and dropping out of these highly in-demand majors (Light and Silverman, 2011).

In addition to being ill-prepared, students entering college are not putting in the time and effort needed to be successful. A study conducted by Richard Arum and Josipa Roska of New York University and the University of Virginia, respectively, discovered that American students study, on average, 12 to 13 hours per week. This is approximately one-half the time that students in 1960 spent studying (Light and Silverman, 2011). In a research paper sponsored by the ETS, the authors predict that by 2030 the average literacy and numeracy levels of the U.S. working-age population will decrease by approximately 7 percent (Kirsch et al., 2007).

In other words, over the next 20 years or so, as better educated individuals leave the workplace, they will be replaced by those who on average are expected to have lower levels of skills. During this same period of time, nearly one-half of the projected job growth will be in occupations that require complex skills (Kirsch et al., 2007, ETS, 2007). According to a 2008 study by the Society for Human Resource Management, 58 percent of HR professionals reported that a growing number of workers lack competencies needed to perform their jobs, up from 54 percent in 2005. Further, more than one-half of the respondents predicted that workers entering the job market in the next 10 years will lack the competencies necessary for them to be successful in the workplace (Society for Human Resource Management, 2008a). According to a 2009 McKinsey report, the growing educational achievement gap is the equivalent of a permanent recession. It continues that the U.S. GDP would have been approximately $2.3 trillion higher in 2008 had the United States succeeded in closing the international achievement gap 25 years earlier (McKinsey, April 2009).

If these trends continue, the outcome will be a continuing divide between the haves and have-nots based on skill level and job prospects. There will also be continuing upward pressure on wages for high-skilled jobs as the demand for talent for these jobs exceeds the supply. Conversely, there will be continuing downward pressure on wages for low-skilled jobs as the supply of immigrants and workers in low-wage economies exceeds the demand for this type of work. It is estimated that a worker with a bachelor's degree today will earn 1.73 times more in lifetime earnings than a high-school graduate. This ratio of lifetime earnings increases to 3.36 for individuals with a professional degree (Baum and Payea, 2004).

Economic Trends

The convergence of the tumultuous technological, global, and demographic trends is creating many challenges for the U.S. economy (see Table 1.4). An important driver of the United States' dominant position as the world's leading economic power for decades has been its growing and well-educated labor force. However, as the U.S. labor force growth rate continues to fall and as the imbalances of supply and demand of needed skills increase, the United States is facing severe pressures in maintaining its lofty position. To make matters even more difficult, the United States is dealing with these negative labor force trends at a time when the demand for high-skilled talent and global competition is intensifying.

Table 1.4 Economic Trends

Evolving knowledge economy
Slower consumption
New global economy

Evolving Knowledge Economy

Technological advances are fundamentally changing the economy and the underlying drivers of growth. Since the 1950s, the United States has been evolving from an industrial-based to a knowledge-based economy. From 1950 to 2003, manufacturing's share of total employment in the United States fell from 33.1 percent to 10.7 percent (ETS, 2007). Authors Pine and Gilmore say we are witnessing the beginning of a new economy following the service and knowledge economies called *The Experience Economy*, the title of their 1999 book on the subject. Products like the iPod, iPhone, and iPad that provide an intense experience for the end user and generate an enormous amount of consumer loyalty are prime examples of what is needed to succeed in this new economy (Pine and Gilmore, 1999). Amazon.com's desire to constantly improve the user experience and Google's "perpetual beta" site that is never finished because it is constantly being tested, improved, and fine-tuned for optimal user experience are other examples (Hinssen, 2010). As we compete in a knowledge-based and experience economy, the demand for tacit work that requires knowledge workers who possess complex skills will continue to increase. It's estimated that by 2015, knowledge workers will account for 44 percent of the U.S. workforce.

Throughout the 1990s and 2000s, the U.S. economy has been a beneficiary of strong productivity growth mainly as a result of large investments in computer and communication technologies. Labor productivity is a critical contributing factor to GDP growth resulting in greater output for a given level of employment. Higher output per worker in turn results in higher wages and more profits, which collectively contribute to overall improvements in living standards. During the 2000 to 2010 period, labor's productivity, as measured by output per hour, grew at a 2.5 percent annual growth rate nearly 25 percent higher than the historical average. Productivity growth actually spiked immediately after the 2007–2009 recession as businesses grew output with fewer workers. However, even with continued technology investments, the structural shifts in the labor force are putting a damper on labor productivity growth, which is projected to decline over the 2010 to 2020 period back to its historical average at a 2.0 percent annual growth rate (Byun and Frey, 2012).

Slower Consumption

Slowing labor force growth and participation rates as well as declining incomes for many workers are negatively impacting personal consumption growth rates. Baby boomers are also experiencing greater financial challenges. Due to low savings rates and increasing debt, nearly two-thirds of the oldest baby boomers have insufficient funds saved for retirement (Beinhocker et al., 2009). As a result, it's expected that there will be a significant increase in savings and a reduction in spending for a cohort that has been a huge a driver of consumption until now. When the baby boomers start to retire and begin drawing down on their savings, the negative impact on consumption will be significant. Given the smaller cohort waiting in the wings to replace the boomers, worker productivity will have to substantially increase to make up for this anticipated shortfall in GDP.

Median household income has been under pressure and actually declined from 2000 to 2010. Indeed, for the first time since World War II, incomes for middle-class families during the first decade of the 21st century are lower than what they were 10 years earlier. The median household income in 2010 was $50,046, down 8.9 percent from 2000 (Berube et al., 2011). By 2011, just more than one-half of the U.S. population was classified as middle class, defined as having annual incomes between $39,000 and $118,000 for a three-member household, which is down from 61 percent in the early 1970s (Pew Research Center, 2012).

As a result of these trends, personal consumption expenditures (PCE) are projected to grow at much slower rates compared to previous decades. Consumers were increasing their expenditures at a robust 3.6 percent annual growth rate from 1990 to 2000. During the 2000–2010 time period, the average PCE continued to grow at a high rate during the first several years and then fell dramatically during the recession resulting in a low 1.9 percent average annual rate. Looking forward to the 2010–2020 time period, the BLS predicts an average annual PCE growth rate of 2.7 percent, a modest increase but well below the growth rates of previous decades (Byun and Frey, 2012). Given that PCE comprise approximately 70 percent of the U.S. nominal gross national product (GNP), the impact on the future economic growth rate will be negative.

New Global Economy

The evidence is quite compelling that the United States' economy is experiencing a structural economic shift that will impact businesses' and workers' opportunities for many years to come. Following World War II, the United States was the uncontested largest economy. As Europe and Japan rebuilt and as the developing world invested in its institutions and infrastructure, it was only a matter of time before the rest of the world would catch up with the United States economically.

In just one generation, the United States went from being the world's largest creditor to the largest debtor. The U.S. trade deficit ballooned from $35.2 billion in 1992 to a peak of $729.4 billion in 2006. By 2010, the trade deficit stood at $658 billion. Most of the deficit was attributable to the trade of manufactured goods rising from $79 billion to $509 billion. The only sector that generated a trade surplus was in services, which saw a modest increase from $78 billion to $88 billion. It is estimated that the rising deficit translated to a net loss of approximately 3.8 million jobs in 2006 (McKinsey Global Institute, 2009b). Over the coming decade, export growth is expected to be larger than import growth, which will narrow an albeit high trade deficit from $421.8 billion in 2010 to $193.3 billion in 2020 (Byun and Frey, 2012).

It is impossible to talk about global economic trends without considering the BRIC countries. The prediction of the rise of the BRICs was quite accurate, as their combined annual growth rate over the past 20 years of 5.8% far exceeded the 2.5% annual growth rate of the developed countries. The growing emerging economies are often referred to as the E7, which in addition to the BRICs include Indonesia, Mexico, and Turkey (Hawksworth, 2006). By 2050, the E7 collectively is projected to have a larger economy than the current largest developed economies of the world called the G7, which includes the United States, Japan, Germany, United Kingdom, France, Italy, and Canada.

Today, the United States continues to have the undisputed largest economy in the world with a nominal GDP approaching $16 trillion as of the second quarter in 2012 (Bureau of Economic Analysis, 2012). However, its contribution to global output and its dominance dictating global economic affairs will continue to get smaller as the rest of the world continues to grow. Looking toward the future, the only country that is projected to challenge the U.S. position as the largest economy is China. Depending on how you measure GDP (using market exchange rates or purchasing power parity), there is debate on when China will eclipse the United States as the largest in the world. However, there are many risks in making long-term predictions because many unpredictable events can occur between now and then.

During the late 1980s, many people were predicting that Japan would overtake the United States as the largest economy; however, it's 2013, and Japan has not only failed to overtake the United States but also is now the third largest economy having fallen behind the United States and China. Though long-term forecasting is a dangerous profession, demographic trends are the most predictable, and it's indisputable that China's large and talented population will be an economic force to reckon with for many decades to come. Thus, many economists are predicting that China will have the largest economy in the world surpassing the United States sometime around 2050. However, in 2050, the United States is projected to still have the highest GDP per capita by far than any other country in the world at more than twice China's GDP per capita, which is projected to be 15th in the world.

This unprecedented situation, whereby a country has the second largest economy in the world but with a low GDP per capita, is likely to create an enormous amount of policy and business challenges for China well into the future. China is also witnessing a demographic crisis that may derail its hot growth rate in the near future. China's low fertility rates, rapidly aging population, and slowing population growth rate are creating significant supply and demand imbalances of young working-age people. Coupled with wage inflation and comparatively low productivity levels, China's dominant position as one of the world's lower-cost manufacturers is in jeopardy.

The other dominant emerging market, India, is on a quite different trajectory. By 2030, India is expected to replace China as the world's most populous country. India also has a much younger and growing population that will yield economic benefits for decades to come. By 2020, the average age in India is estimated to be 29 years, compared to 37 years in both China and the United States. The economic impact of projected demographic trends in Europe and Japan are much more negative as their populations get smaller and reach an average of 45 and 48, respectively, by 2020 (Mitchell et al., 2012).

The United States' other dominant partner in the developed world is the European Union (EU), which is also facing deep economic problems that are further diminishing the developed countries' slice of the global economic pie. The sovereign debt crisis infecting many European countries has dramatically increased borrowing costs resulting in draconian cuts in government expenditures and commercial lending. There is concern of another banking crisis as many of these institutions holding government debt are fearful of defaults, which can result in €billions of losses and create a collapse of the global financial system. Making matters worse, Europe must respond to these challenges while facing a demographic crisis of epic proportions.

Due to a declining population, the median age in the EU is projected to rise from 40.4 years in 2008 to 47.0 years in 2060 when the number of people age 65 and over will almost double. Critically, during this time, the working-age population is projected to decline by 15 percent, and the dependency ratio (ratio of people age 65 and above to working-age population) will double. As a result, the EU will move from having four workers to support every retiree to only two. Given that most European countries spend more on public pension benefits than other advanced countries, these negative demographic trends are creating an unfunded pension crisis that will put enormous stress on government treasuries (Lannquist, 2012).

The continuing decline of the United States' leading global economic standing is both a cause and a result of the structural shift in its labor force. The United States is facing hypercompetition at a time when its labor force growth rate is declining and skills gap is widening, creating significant headwinds for economic growth. At the same time, American workers are experiencing the effects of globalization. A large segment of the labor force finds itself in direct competition for jobs with lower-wage workers around the globe, and leading-edge scientific and engineering work is taking place in many parts of the world. As a result of advances in computer and communication technologies and a highly interdependent global economy, workers in virtually every sector must now face competitors who live just a plane ride or mouse-click away.

Increasing Complexity

Each of the technological, global, demographic, and economic trends reviewed has contributed to this sense of a new normal that seems to permeate every aspect of our lives. We seem to be at a tipping point within each of these trends that is fundamentally different than a normal extrapolation. What is also different is the greater interdependency of these trends and the resulting increase in complexity. Increasing complexity is a fact of life in the new normal, as shown in Table 1.5. It characterizes the world you live in, the jobs you perform, your relationships, and the decisions you make. You manage complexity all the time, even if you are unaware of doing so. You communicate with multiple sources of technology, pay your bills electronically, install software to protect your identity and computers, and shop online to avoid traffic jams. You are a master of multitasking.

Complexity also enriches your life. Pursuing an education, advancing in your career, and raising a family all increase complexity in positive ways. Being part of a global community increases complexity in both positive and negative ways. Living and working with diverse people enriches your life.

Table 1.5 Increasing Complexity

Greater interdependencies
More data, more information, more knowledge
Faster and faster response times
More intangibles
Less predictability

In a study conducted by PWC, 41 percent of the global CEOs that were surveyed agree strongly that complexity is an inevitable byproduct of doing business today (PWC, 2006). Furthermore, 77 percent of these CEOs noted that the level of complexity in their organizations is higher than it was 3 years ago. The challenges of managing global businesses were noted as contributing factors of business complexity. Entering new markets, meeting customers' needs, and developing new products and services that result from globalizing add layers of complexity that must be managed if the benefits of globalization are to be realized. Respondents cited overregulation as the chief challenge of globalization (64 percent), followed by trade barriers/protectionism (63 percent), and social issues (56 percent). Surprisingly, terrorism and the antiglobalization movement, two topics that dominate media headlines, were near the bottom of the list of perceived challenges at 48 and 21 percent, respectively. Other chief causes of increasing complexity were extending operations to new territories, forming strategic alliances, and outsourcing functions to third parties.

The capability to effectively manage complexity is an important strategic need for many organizations. The CEOs surveyed by PWC ranked employing highly capable people as the single most important way for managing complexity followed by effective communication. Other factors ranked highly included the ability to identify activities that are creating value, the ability to identify activities that are destroying value, the alignment of IT with business processes, the ability to measure complexity, and having a corporate-wide framework for managing complexity.

What's amazing is this PWC survey was in 2006. Predicting that the level of complexity is increasing was quite accurate. In the following years, the world experienced a financial collapse that resulted in a global recession. There has been the sovereign debt and banking crisis that swept across Europe that is increasing the probability of another recession. There has been a series of political upheavals throughout the resource-rich Middle East, and there is now a fear of slowing growth and structural challenges in the once hot economies of China, India, and Brazil.

According to the CEOs who responded to the 2012 edition of "The Conference Board CEO Challenge" survey, today's business environment is characterized by the race to innovate, the war for talent, "black swans," bad debts, the hunt for new markets, and increasing regulations and oversight. When you add to this the need for speed, an overwhelming flow of information and data (not all of it reliable), along with increased risk and uncertainty, the overall leadership challenge facing CEOs is managing complexity (Mitchell et al., 2012). The huge disparities of economic growth, the growing skills gap in many regions, and the peculiarities of regional cultures, customers, and government policies mean that organizations around the world face unique challenges that reflect the business realities they face both locally and globally.

Structural Shifts

Unlike previous business cycles, there have been significant structural changes in the economy due to technological advances, increased globalization, and unfavorable demographic trends (see Table 1.6). Aided by advances in computer and communication technologies, organizations have automated, reengineered, and outsourced numerous jobs that were once filled by onsite full-time employees. As a result, many standardized and transaction-based jobs have either been automated or sent overseas to low-wage countries. All this is occurring at a time when the global economic environment is creating significant competitive pressures for U.S. companies.

Furthermore, advances in technology are fundamentally changing how firms compete. There is pressure to be more innovative, more responsive to customer preferences, and more efficient. The result is a significantly greater need for highly skilled human capital at a time when there are severe constraints. The slow growth of the U.S. labor market due to a decline in birth rates and a plateauing of worker participation rates, coupled with a lackluster educational system, are creating a structural economic shift that will transform how we conduct business and the lives of workers for decades to come.

Table 1.6 Structural Shift: This Is Not Your Typical Business Cycle

Growing skills gap
Slower economic growth
Structural unemployment

Growing Skills Gap

A large part of the structural shift constraining economic growth is the growing skills gap due to the imbalance between the current supply of highly skilled workers and increasing demand for these

types of workers. Most of the developed world economies are optimized for 20th century industrial-based economies, whereas new jobs
being created are for 21st century knowledge-based economies. This
negative structural shift in the labor market is creating difficulties for
companies that require highly skilled workers to remain competitive
as well as immense difficulties for the millions of workers unable to
find work. Exacerbating this war for talent is an aging workforce soon
to be retiring and a rise of rapidly developing economies' increasing
demand for talent.

The demand for highly skilled labor is expected to increase significantly over the next decade. The BLS projects total employment
in the United States will rise 20.5 million (14.3 percent) between
2010 and 2020 from about 143.1 million to 163.5 million jobs. All the
occupations that require a college degree are projected to grow at
an above-average rate throughout this time period. Occupations that
require a master's degree will see the largest percent increase (21.7),
followed by those that require a doctoral or professional degree (19.9
percent), associate degree (18.0 percent), and bachelor's degree
(16.5 percent). In terms of typical on-the-job training, occupations
that typically require apprenticeships are projected to grow the fastest (22.5 percent). The occupations that will grow at a below-average
rate include those that require a high school diploma (12.2 percent)
and those that require less than a high school diploma (14.1 percent)
(Lockard and Wolf, 2012).

According to a study conducted by the National Science Foundation (NSF), the number of graduates entering the workforce trained
in science and engineering is declining, whereas the number of jobs
requiring these skills is increasing. As predicted in the 2004 study,
the number of science and engineering jobs increased approximately
three times as fast as all other occupations from 2001 to 2010. The
rate of growth in these highly skilled jobs is expected to increase over
the next decade. Exacerbating this imbalance in supply and demand is
the projected retirement of large numbers of scientists and engineers
(S&E). S&E workers who are part of the baby boom generation that
entered the workforce in the 1960s and 1970s will be retiring over the
next 20 years. The study also predicts that other supply and demand
imbalances are projected in the jobs within the health science, math,
and computer science fields (National Science Board, 2004).

The growing imbalance of the supply and demand for highly skilled workers is not just endemic to the United States, but is a global phenomenon. Research by the McKinsey Global Institute conducted in 2012 found that employers in advanced economies might soon be unable to find as many college-educated workers as they require. The gap in the United States could reach 1.5 million graduates by the end of the decade. In the rapidly growing economy in China, the shortfall can be as high as 23 million college-educated workers by 2020 (Lund et al., 2012).

Companies are not only concerned about finding new talent that have the complex skills in high demand, but are also concerned about the skills and capabilities of existing employees. A study conducted by IBM noted that more than one-third of companies thought their employees' skills were not aligned with current demand (Benko and Anderson, 2010a). These companies reported that "the inability to rapidly develop skills is the primary workforce challenge" (IBM, 2008). In a worldwide survey conducted by the Manpower Group, one in three (34 percent) employers experienced difficulties filling positions due to a lack of available talent, a nearly 10 percent increase from 2010. When asked why, over one-quarter of the respondents said candidates' lack of experience necessary for the position; another 22 percent cited a lack of technical competencies or "hard" skills; whereas 15 percent noted candidates' lack of business knowledge or formal qualifications (Manpower Group, 2011).

In the past, companies have relied on a flow of highly skilled talent who emigrated to the United States to pursue higher education and the many job opportunities at companies in need of their skills. In 2010, foreign students received 17 percent of bachelor's degrees, 29 percent of master's degrees, and 38 percent of Ph.D. degrees awarded in science and engineering (National Science Board, 2012). However, as the demand for highly skilled talent increases globally, the flow into the United States is expected to slow. Indeed, the number of science and engineering positions has increased by 23 percent over the last decade in OECD nations compared to an 11 percent increase in the United States (National Science Board, 2012). According to an OECD report on the mobility of highly skilled workers, as opportunities for these workers increase along with advances in information and communication technologies, a growing class of global in-demand workers is evolving that is highly mobile. These workers, many of whom are educated in the United States, are now returning to their home countries or to other developing countries where the demand for their skills continues to increase at a rapid pace (OECD, 2008).

To make matters worse, U.S. immigration policies desperately need to be updated to reflect the realities of the 21st century workplace. All too often, brilliant foreign students who are trained at our top research universities are forced to leave the country due to their inability to obtain permanent work visas. The need to hire these well-trained students has prompted more than 130 corporations, trade organizations, and chambers of commerce to send a letter to the U.S. Congress urging lawmakers to establish a program to make it easier for foreign-born students who receive advanced degrees in science, technology, engineering, and mathematics (STEM) fields to stay and work in the United States (Heyn, 2012). The letter, which has been signed by such noteworthy firms as Apple and Microsoft, stated that such a policy would enable American companies to retain many foreign students with advanced degrees in STEM fields to work in the United States, which in turn will spur the creation and retention of high-paying manufacturing and research jobs in America.

A number of industries are also facing the prospect of having to replace large numbers of retirees in professional and managerial positions. In a survey of managers at Fortune 1000 companies conducted by Ernst & Young, 27 percent anticipate an upcoming knowledge and skills gap in their organizations due to difficulty in replacing retiring talent. The talent deficit will primarily be in middle management, professional, and technical positions (Ernst & Young, 2010). It's also forecasted that nearly 60 percent of all government employees will be eligible to retire over the next decade (Barford and Hester, 2011).

Slower Economic Growth

The United States has a consumer-driven economy that for decades has benefited tremendously by a growing and well-educated population and worker participation rates that positively impacted income growth and consequently consumption and economic growth. Today, these engines of economic growth are beginning to stall. The slowing population growth rates and declining worker participation rates have negatively impacted the labor force and income growth rates. Furthermore, there are an unprecedented number of workers expected to leave the workforce over the next two decades.

The retiring baby boomers present a large economic problem for this country. During their working years, baby boomers were a huge force in economic output and consumption. Their exit from the workforce will negatively impact future growth. In addition to these headwinds, there is a tremendous amount of deleveraging at the consumer sector of the economy and pressure to reduce government debt that is further dampening growth. Lastly, though the United States has the largest economy in the world, its global economic dominance is declining, and it continues to generate large trade imbalances with the rest of the world.

As the U.S. population continues to get older, government spending on social security and healthcare has been increasing at an alarming rate. The leading edge of the baby-boom generation became eligible for limited Social Security benefits in 2008 and Medicare benefits in 2010. By 2011, total healthcare expenditures consumed 8.2 percent of GNP, a 600 percent increase from 50 years ago. Total Social Security and Medicare expenditures are projected to outpace GNP growth as this large cohort continues to get older and as the costs of sophisticated medical care, including new technologies, continue to rise. As a share of nominal federal government spending, these two programs grew from 27.9 percent in 1990 to 32.6 percent in 2010. Social Security and Medicare costs are expected to continue rising to approximately 40 percent of nominal federal government expenditures in 2021 (Byun and Frey, 2012). These rising costs will limit the amount of money the government has to invest in education, R&D, and infrastructure.

The *en masse* retirement of the baby boomers will also put severe economic pressure on the workers who will have to offset the societal financial drain of these retirees. Labor economists measure this support using the BLS's *economic dependency ratio*, defined as the number of people in the total population who are not working per 100 of those who are. As large numbers of baby boomers retire and live longer, this ratio is increasing from 90.3 in 2010 to a projected

106.4 in the year 2030 when the youngest of the baby boom generation reach 66 years of age (Toossi, 2002). As a result, either the payroll taxes for workers will be dramatically increased or benefits will need to be reduced.

In addition to growing government entitlement deficits impeding economic growth, many private pension funds are severely underfunded, requiring massive new capital that otherwise could be put to more productive use. In 2012, as noted in *The New York Times*, companies in the Standard & Poor's (S&P) 500 reported that their pension plans had obligations of $1.68 trillion and assets of only $1.32 trillion. The $355 billion shortfall was the largest unfunded amount ever reported according to the S&P. A number of companies reported that their plans were underfunded by more than $10 billion, with General Electric having the largest shortfall at $21.6 billion (Norris, 2012). The main cause of these shortfalls is the lackluster performance of investment markets that have not performed well for a sustained period of time. Over the last 15 years, the S&P stock index rose at an annual rate of less than 5 percent even when including dividend reinvestments. Not since 1945 had a 15-year period been so bleak for the stock market.

The United States and much of the developed world experienced a severe economic downturn as a result of the 2008 global financial crisis. Though the stock market has recouped much of its losses, the continued weakness in real estate and labor markets has wiped out the positive wealth effect that fueled much of the economic growth leading up to the recession. As of the end of 2012, the bull market in stocks that began in 2010 along with modest gains in home prices have helped Americans to regain the estimated $16 trillion they lost during the recession (Federal Reserve, 2013). However, most of the gains that resulted in higher stock prices have been flowing mainly to the wealthy. By contrast, middle class wealth that is mostly in the form of home equity has risen much less.

The disproportional gains to the wealthy will dampen the positive wealth effect on future economic growth. The wealthy are more likely to save these gains rather than increase spending that could help spur growth. In addition, any future gains in home equity are unlikely to result in the type of home equity loans bonanza that fueled consumer spending in the past. Much of the euphoria associated with continuing rising home prices has dissipated. The good news is the U.S. economy is slowly improving, albeit at a much slower rate compared to historical norms.

After experiencing the worst downturn since the Great Depression, the U.S. economy is experiencing a slower-than-average recovery more than 3 years later. Significantly, the recovery coming out of the recession is the lowest on record. It seems that this is not a typical downturn, but something that is fundamentally different than other recessions experienced in recent decades. There is a structural shift in the economy that is a restructuring of the old economic order.

In years past, the average GDP quarterly growth rate immediately following a recession averaged more than 4 percent. However, in 2011 there was no quarter in which GDP grew at a 4 percent rate, and the entire year averaged a 3.1 percent growth rate. Even worse, GDP fell in 2011, growing at an anemic 1.6 annual growth rate. During the first quarter of 2012, the GDP fell back to a 2.2 percent growth rate (it was 3.0 percent in the fourth quarter 2011) and fell further to a mere 0.1 percent growth rate in the fourth quarter of 2012 (Bureau of Economic Analysis, 2013). According to the U.S. Congressional Budget Office and the Bureau of Economic Analysis, the U.S. GDP is projected to grow at an annual rate of 2.7 percent during the 2010 to 2020 time period, which is higher than the 1.6 percent annual growth rate over the 2000 to 2010 period, but slower than the 3.4 percent growth rate from 1990 to 2000 (Bureau of Economic Analysis, 2012).

Another indicator of the structural changes of the economy is the growing divide between the haves and have-nots. These growing inequities have given rise and visibility to many groups around the world that are expressing concern about the future of the global economic and social fabric. The widening inequity within many countries is hindering the prospect of future economic growth. At issue is not only the huge disparity between the wealthiest and the poor, but also the weak growth in median income. Between 1979 and 2007, the average U.S. real pretax income per household grew at a 1.2 percent annual rate. However, during this time period, the bottom 99 percent saw their income grow at one-half that annual rate, at only 0.6 percent, whereas the top 1 percent's income grew at 4.4 percent annually, more than three times the average growth rate (van Ark, 2011).

Though the concentration of income at the top is a concern and the growing number of people falling into poverty distressing, the weak growth of middle-income earners creates the biggest problem for sustainable economic growth. For example, between 1979 and 2007, the median hourly compensation in the United States increased at a dismal 0.3 percent annual rate (van Ark, 2011). Given the size of this cohort, an income growth rate that fails to at least stay even with inflation significantly diminishes their purchasing power and overall economic demand.

Structural Unemployment

Compared to previous recessions, in terms of employment loss, the 2007–2009 recession was both severe and long. Regarding the 1973, 1981, and 1990 recessions, employment recovered to the level it had at the beginning of the recession in 25, 28, and 31 months, respectively, after the recession began. The 2001 recession took 47 months to recover all job losses. In sharp contrast to all these recessions, 5 years since the beginning of the 2007–2009 recession, employment has still not fully recovered and remains 5 percent below the level it had at the start of the recession (Sommers and Franklin, 2012).

Although the economy has been growing, albeit at a slow rate since 2010, there are still large numbers of unemployed individuals. From December 2007 to June 2009, the U.S. unemployment rate doubled from 5 percent to a peak of 10 percent. Since the Great Recession ended in the third quarter of 2009, the unemployment rate has remained at more than 8 percent for the longest period of time since the Great Depression. It wasn't until October 2012 that the unemployment rate finally fell below 8 percent. As of March 2013, the unemployment rate stood at 7.7 percent (BLS, 2013).

The concern is many of those jobs eliminated during the economic recession are not expected to return. Many positions have been lost due to technology, offshoring, and squeezing more productivity out of existing workers. The slow recovery in employment has also been accompanied by a severe decline in the labor force participation rate, with many long-term unemployed workers having grown discouraged and dropping out of the labor force. As of 2012, the labor force participation rate stood at 64 percent, the lowest rate since January 1984. The BLS posits that this is a structural decline and expects it will persist over the coming decade falling further to 62.5 percent in 2020 (Byun and Frey, 2012).

Labor economists debate whether the slow employment recovery is the result of structural changes in the economy or due to a severely slow recovery in cyclical demand. *Cyclical unemployment* typically results in workers being laid off due to weak demand, but who expect to be hired again in their same occupation either by their previous firm or within the same industry when demand picks up. *Structural unemployment* is the result of weak demand rooted in other causes that hinder a worker's ability to return to work as demand revives. For example, weak demand may motivate firms to outsource or offshore nonstrategic work or accelerate the adoption of new technologies and practices that result in work being eliminated or transformed (Sommers and Franklin, 2012).

Workers who are unemployed due to structural causes are likely to be out of work for a longer period of time than someone who is unemployed due to cyclical reasons. Some workers who lose their job due to structural causes might have to completely change occupations and might require retraining. Though there is some debate, we are experiencing significant structural changes in the labor force and economy that may result in a natural unemployment rate that is much higher than recent decades.

In addition to high unemployment, the United States is also witnessing high underemployment. *Underemployment* is defined as working in a job that is below one's full working capacity, such as a full-time worker who is forced to work in a part-time or temporary job or in a job that does not fully utilize the individual's skills and consequently pays a lower wage. In 2012, the BLS reported approximately 17% of the labor force (26 million workers) was underemployed (BLS, 2012).

As the economy starts to grow, more jobs become available and more workers enter the labor force, which ironically will temporarily increase the unemployment rate, but also increase worker participation rate. However, the continuing technological advances and interdependency of global markets are creating many difficulties for low-skilled workers. For example, many jobs in the manufacturing sector have been permanently eliminated due to technological advances, and many of the newly created manufacturing jobs require higher skills. If the United States cannot enhance the skills of the bottom half of the workforce soon, then those lower-skilled workers must accept the prevailing global wage levels. The result can be a massive decline in the standard of living. Echoing this sentiment, the National Academy of Sciences issued a report warning that the United States is "on a losing path" competing in the global economy if it does not start strengthening the national commitment to education and research (Galama and Hosek, 2008).

Indeed, in the 2012 World Economic report, the United States' global ranking among the most competitive economies fell for the fourth year in a row, from fifth to seventh. It listed government bureaucracy, high taxes, and an inadequately educated workforce among the biggest deterrents of doing business in the United States. Other factors contributing to the decline of U.S. competitiveness include the millions of manufacturing jobs outsourced to countries that have lower wages, the spread of capitalism to formerly closed economies, and advances in technology that have enabled companies to do business almost anywhere in the world. The nation's $16 trillion debt is also a deterrent to U.S. competitiveness because it diminishes government investments in education and infrastructure and increases uncertainty among businesses about taxes and interest rates (Schwab, 2012).

2

The 21st Century Workforce

Successfully navigating the forces shaping the new normal is a strategic challenge for many organizations. We've never had such a competitive, technically demanding, and rapidly changing business environment as we do today. If that weren't difficult enough, organizations must face these challenges with a workforce unlike any other in the history of management (see Table 2.1). The 21st century workforce is older, more diverse, more technologically savvy, and more mobile than ever before. Organizations are faced with managing multiple generations of workers who have different values and needs. In addition, there are more dual-income couples and working parents who pose many unique challenges for companies. And though there are many highly talented workers, there are huge disparities in educational attainment at a time when the demand for human and intellectual capital is outpacing the supply. Lastly, there is a growing number of nontraditional workers—contract human capital—which includes temporary employees, consultants, independent contractors, as well as employees of outsourced and offshore businesses and strategic partnerships. Many organizations are ill-equipped to manage these multiple employment relations due to antiquated management systems that were developed primarily for traditional workers.

Table 2.1 Characteristics of the 21st Century Workforce

Multigenerational
Changing social norms
Highly diverse
Educational disparities
Multiple employment relationships

Multigenerational

The increase in life expectancy coupled with the growing number of older workers postponing retirement portends there will be multiple generations working together well into the foreseeable future. In a survey conducted by McKinsey & Co., 84 percent of the baby boomers surveyed indicated they expected to work after they formally retire, and 63 percent said they couldn't see themselves ever completely retiring (Court et al., 2007). According to the Bureau of Labor Statistics (BLS), the number of workers aged 65 and older has doubled over the last 30 years (BLS, 2008). As a result, there are four generations of workers actively working including the traditionalists, baby boomers, generation X, and generation Y. In addition to age, there are vast differences among these generational cohorts because they all came of age in different times and had different influences, as shown in Table 2.2.

Table 2.2 Generational Influences

Generation	Defining Events	Influences
Traditionalists 1927–1945	Great Depression World War II The New Deal	Radio Big Band Era FDR GIs
Baby Boomers 1946–1964	Vietnam Civil Rights Movement Moon Landing Woodstock	Television Rock and Roll Kennedy Social Movements
Generation X 1965–1980	Oil Embargo Watergate Stagflation	Personal Computers MTV Nixon Corporate Layoffs
Generation Y 1981–1999	Fall of Berlin Wall Challenger Explosion Columbine Massacre	World Wide Web Alternative Music Clinton Multiculturalism

Traditionalists

Born between 1927 and 1945, as of 2013, the traditionalists workforce were those workers 68 years of age and older. Also known as the *silent generation*, they were heavily influenced by the Great Depression and World War II. This generation was straddled by two larger generations, between the greatest generation (WWII vets) and the baby boomers. Because there were only 46 million born in this generation, many demographers refer to this time as the *birth dearth*. Given the uncertainty that they experienced, they considered work a privilege and typically stayed with one employer until retirement. Many of the men served in the military, and both the men and women are highly patriotic. This generation benefited greatly from the New Deal and valued the security and safety nets it provided.

They are called *traditionalists* because of their traditional values. They are respectful of institutions and believe that duty comes before pleasure. The men of this generation were expected to be the primary breadwinners and took pride in working hard. Women were expected to stay home to raise children and be homemakers.

Baby Boomers

As the victorious GIs came home following WWII, the birth rate in the United States rose sharply. From 1946 to 1964, there were nearly 79 million births creating the largest generational cohort called the *baby boomers*. At the beginning of the baby boomer generation, they represented a greater percentage of the country's population than Gen X or Gen Y did at the start of their respective generations. Unlike the previous generation, this generation grew up experiencing immense prosperity and received a lot of attention from their parents. They earned high incomes and spent lavishly, stimulating the economy, but also saved little and ran up huge amounts of debt.

Due to the sheer size and influence of this generation, its impact on society and the workplace has been astounding. As teenagers, their impact on the music and fashion industries was transformative. Their taste in music was in stark contrast to the big band era of their parents. Their interest in the vast array of new rock bands coming on to the scene led by the British invasion was reflected in the millions of records they purchased. Highly independent, they dressed and thought differently and fought for multiple causes. They were actively involved in the women's and civil rights movements and vehemently protested against the Vietnam War.

As baby boomers entered the workplace in increasingly large numbers throughout the 1960s and 1970s, they were the most-educated generation at the time and well matched for the jobs that were in demand. As the baby boomers entered their peak earning years throughout the 1980s and 1990s, both the stock market and housing market soared. Suddenly, the nonconformist generation seemed to have "sold out" using a term they would have used when they were younger, reflecting that they were now part of the establishment. Now it was cool being over 30. According to the Pew Research Center, baby boomers are generally more accepting of social and cultural changes than adults over 65 but not as accepting as younger Gen Yers. This generation also tends to be more conservative than the younger generation and more liberal than the older traditionalists generation in their attitudes toward politics and society. Regarding matters related to personal finances, economic security, and retirement, baby boomers feel they have been hurt more by the recent Great Recession than the older generation (Cohn and Taylor, 2010).

In 2000, baby boomers comprised 48 percent of the U.S. labor force. In 2010, the boomers' percentage of the labor force was approximately 38 percent. The BLS predicts that by 2020, baby boomers will comprise 20 percent of the labor force equating to a drop of 30 million workers since 2000. As the baby boomers reach retirement age, they are once again having a significant impact on society and the workplace. The economic drag as a result of baby boomers drawing down their savings and downsizing their homes will be felt for decades to come.

Gen X

Generation X, born between 1965 and 1980, is also known as the *baby bust generation*. Totaling only 50 million, this generation came of age during the time of the Internet revolution, growing workplace diversity, the end of "jobs for life," and increasing parental divorce rates. As a result of divorced households or dual-income parents, this generation became independent at an early age. Growing up in an environment of social insecurity and turbulence has caused many in this generation to be distrustful of companies.

Some refer to this generation as the *lost generation*. Like the traditionalists, this generation was much smaller than its two strad-dling generations, the baby boomers and Generation Y. They grew up in the shadows of the baby boomers and were overtaken by the emerging Yers. Growing up in the tumultuous 1970s during a time of economic stagflation, as well as social and political upheavals, this generation developed an almost myopic sense of survival. Not surpris-ingly they are skeptical of authority and believe in being self-reliant.

Given that many Gen Xers came from broken families, they have a much broader sense of family than other generations. This genera-tion has relied on and values a close circle of friends. Seeing how many of their workaholic parents lost jobs after many years of loyal service, Gen Xers want more of a work-life balance.

Gen Y

The generation following Gen X, born between 1981 and 1999, goes by a number of names. Some researchers refer to them as *Gen Y* or *Generation Next*; others have called them the *millennials*, and in other contexts they are called the *echo boomers*. I prefer to call this cohort Gen Y and recommend calling the cohort born after 2000 the millennials. The name echo boomer describes the fact that this gen-eration is largely the progeny of baby boomers. Slightly larger than the baby boomers at 80 million though smaller based on a percentage of the population, like the baby boomers, this generation is having a significant impact on society and the workplace.

This generation also grew up in prosperous times and experi-enced immense attention from their parents. As a result of protective households and constant praise, this generation is characterized as confident and independent. However, as a parent of a Gen Yer and professor who has taught hundreds of undergraduates, in my experi-ence, this generation oftentimes is overly dependent on others to help them overcome difficult problems. Perhaps this is the result of being raised by doting parents. According to a 2007 Pew Research Center study, 64 percent of Gen Y rely on their families (mostly mothers) for advice, 64 percent have had their parents help with errands, 73 percent have received financial assistance from their parents over the last year, and 40 percent are currently living with their parents (Pew Research Center [Pew], 2007).

Gen Y's family life is different than previous generations. Compared to older generations, they are less likely to have been raised in intact households composed of a mother and father living together. Only 63 percent of Gen Y parents were married during the majority of their childhood, compared to 76 percent of Gen X, 83 percent of baby boomers, and 89 percent of traditionalists (Wang and Taylor, 2011). In 1960, more than two-thirds (68 percent) of all 20-somethings were married. In 2008, only 26 percent were married (Pew, 2010). Compared to other generations, Gen Y is much more likely to view cohabitation without marriage and other family arrangements, such as same-sex marriage and interracial marriage, in a positive light.

Gen Y is the first generation that has taken technology for granted because they grew up with technology in their play, homes, and now the workplace. Compared to older generations, they think differently about technology. They approach technology with bottom-up thinking (Wikipedia), and network thinking (Facebook), and have little rapport with the old top-down models (Hinssen, 2010). This generation spends more time on social networking sites and the Internet, and sends more text messages than any other generation (Pew, 2007).

Although this generation is far more technologically sophisticated than any other generation, according to authors Arthur Levine and Diane Dean in their book *Generation on a Tightrope: A Portrait of Today's College Student*, Gen Yers are woefully unprepared for the real world. The authors characterize this generation as coddled, entitled, and dependent. This generation may have hundreds of social media friends, yet they have trouble communicating in person (Levine and Dean, 2012).

Like the younger baby boomers who prided themselves to be unconventional, Gen Yers are quite unique. More than one-half of this generation has altered their appearance by tattoos, dyeing their hair an unusual color, or body piercings; whereas, only 21 percent of those over 40 years of age have altered their appearance in such a way (Pew, 2007). Not surprisingly, this generation more than any other embraces diversity.

Gen Y is entering the workplace with a different mindset concerning traditional organizational practices. They favor teams and networks over hierarchies. They know that the key to their success is the knowledge they accumulate and the experience they gain. Gen Y believes that compared to young adults from previous generations, they have better opportunities for education and a higher likelihood of getting a high-paying job (Pew, 2007). However, unlike previous generations, they realize that their career paths in the new normal will not entail lifelong engagement with a handful of corporations.

Although they are more optimistic about their career prospects compared to previous generations, they are less optimistic about their financial well-being. Less than half of Gen Y believes they will be as financially secure as older generations. Sixty-two percent believe it was easier for young adults in the 1980s to buy a house than it is for a young adult today. Given these financial concerns, 64 percent of Gen Yers believe getting rich is their generation's most important life goal (Pew, 2007).

Age Waves

As a result of these demographic trends, there are significant age waves sweeping across the labor force. The impact of the baby boomers has been quite significant on the median age of the U.S. labor force. At the time the baby boom generation entered the workplace, there was a steady decrease in the median age of the labor force until it bottomed at 34.6 years in 1980, when baby boomers were between the ages of 16 and 34. As the baby boomers got older, the median age of the labor force continued to increase, reaching 41.7 years old by 2010. By 2020, the median age is projected to increase to 42.8, at which time the baby boomers will be between 56 and 74 years old (Toossi, 2012).

Prime-age workers, those between the ages of 25 to 54 years old, numbered 101.4 million in 2000 and 102.9 million in 2010, an increase of only 1.5 million workers. By 2020, the size of this age group is expected to be only slightly larger at 104.6 million. Thus, prime-age workers, which composed 71.1 percent of the labor force in 2000, saw their share decrease to 66.9 percent in 2010 and are projected to fall further to 63.7 percent by 2020.

As prime-age workers continue to make up a smaller percent of the labor force, older workers' share of the labor force continues to rise. The 55-years-and-older work group totaled 18.7 million in 2000 and 30.0 million in 2010, a significant increase of 11.3 million workers. By 2020, the size of this age group is projected to be substantially higher totaling 41.4 million. In only 10 years, the 55-years-and-older age group's share of the labor force increased from 13.1 percent in 2000 to 19.5 percent in 2010. This age group will continue to comprise a larger share of the labor force, reaching an estimated 25.2 percent by 2020 (Toossi, 2012).

Changing Social Norms

Changing social norms are transforming the roles of individuals both at home and at work. The continuing decline in the institution of marriage has resulted in an increase in dual-income couples and single working parents. The needs of these individuals in the workplace are vastly different than previous generations when the traditional family was composed of a sole breadwinner (who typically was a man) and a married partner at home (who typically was a woman) to manage all the family responsibilities.

Transformation of Marriage and Family Life/Dual-Income Couples

Social institutions generally change slowly. However, yet another structural shift exists, this time in an institution that has been stable for thousands of years—the institution of marriage. Since the middle of the 20th century, marriage and family life have been utterly transformed. The basic architecture of these age-old institutions has changed more rapidly than in any time in history. In 1960, nearly three-quarters (72 percent) of the adult population 18 years of age and older was married. In 2008, about one-half (52 percent) of all adults were married, the lowest proportion since the government began collecting data on this measure more than a century ago (Cohn, 2010).

According to a 2010 Pew Research Center study on "the decline of marriage and the rise of new families," nearly 4-in-10 (39 percent) respondents said they believe that marriage is becoming obsolete. Moreover, the study found that there is a new "marriage gap" in the United States that is increasingly aligned with a growing income gap. Though marriage is declining among all demographic groups, it remains the norm for adults with a college education and good income and is markedly less prevalent among those on the lower rung of the socio-economic ladder (Pew, 2010). In 2008, the percentage of married adults with college degrees was 64 percent compared to 48 percent of adults with a high school diploma or less.

In the 1950s, nearly two-thirds (63%) of households in the United States were classified as "traditional families" composed of one spouse working (mostly the husband) and one staying home (usually the wife). Today, approximately 17 percent of households fit the traditional family mold. The typical U.S. family in the 21st century is composed of parents who both work, single parents, and a multitude of other family permutations. One startling fact is that mothers are now the primary breadwinners or co-breadwinners in more than 65 percent of American families (Benko and Anderson, 2010c). Today in the United States, for the first time in history, women make up nearly one-half of the working population and are outpacing men in educational attainment. Nearly 6-in-10 wives work, almost double the share in 1960 (Pew, 2010).

Partly out of necessity and partly as a result of changing social norms, there are more dual-income couples in the workplace today than at any other time in history. Many married and unmarried couples living together find it necessary to work to make ends meet in these difficult times in which median income has been stagnant for decades, and nearly 20 percent of the workforce is underemployed. Both the husband and wife were wage earners in 55 percent of married couples in 2009, up from 44 percent in 1967 (BLS, 2011). In many dual-income households, the woman now earns more than the man. A study conducted by the U.S. Census Bureau of dual-earners noted that women contributed an average of 44 percent of total family income in 2008, up from 24 percent in 1987 (U.S. Census Bureau, 2008a).

A parallel trend has been a rise in cohabitation. As the rate of marriages continues to decline, cohabitation is becoming more widespread, nearly doubling since 1990, according to the U.S. Census Bureau (Fry and Cohn, 2011). In a Pew Research Center survey, 44 percent of all adults (and more than one-half of adults ages 30 to 49) said they have cohabited at some point in their lives (Pew, 2010). Based on the National Survey of Family Growth, the number of cohabitating couples having children is also rising. The percentage of first births to women living with an unmarried male partner jumped from 12 percent in 2002 to 22 percent in 2010, a startling 83 percent increase in just 8 years (Martinez et al., 2012).

The lines between work and personal lives for both men and women are blurred in many 21st century households. Three-quarters of married working men live in dual-income households and are much more involved in taking care of children and household responsibilities. An increasingly large number of workers are also responsible for the care of elderly relatives. In 2007, approximately 25 percent of U.S. households cared for older relatives, and that number is projected to increase to 40 percent over the next two decades (Benko and Anderson, 2010b).

Single Parents

From 1960 to 2008, the share of births to unmarried women increased dramatically from 5 percent to 41 percent. There are notable differences by race: 72 percent of black women giving birth in 2008 were unmarried, compared to 53 percent of Hispanic women and 29 percent of white women (Pew, 2010). As of 2010, 18.6 percent of all working parents were single working mothers (BLS, 2010b).

As marriage rates continue to fall, the percentage of children living with an unmarried parent continues to increase. From 1960 to 2008, the percentage of children living with a single parent nearly tripled from 13 percent to 36 percent (Pew, 2010). In 2010, families led by single mothers represented 24.3 percent of all families with children; of these single mothers, 67 percent were employed. Families led by single fathers represented 6.7 percent of families with children; of these single fathers, 75.8 percent were employed.

Although 52 percent of Gen Y felt that parenthood is a priority, only 30 percent believed having a successful marriage was as important. Compared to all other generations, Gen Y are less likely to feel that single parenthood and parenthood of unmarried couples are a negative quality in society (Wang and Taylor, 2011). Not surprisingly, the out-of-wedlock birthrate has increased to 51 percent for Gen Y (in 2008) as compared to 39 percent for Gen X at the same age (in 1997).

Greater Diversity

The United States' population is becoming increasingly more diverse due to immigration flows and higher fertility rates among the foreign-born population. Between 1995 and 2007, the U.S. foreign-born population grew by approximately 13 million to 37.9 million or slightly more than 1 million a year. As a percentage of the U.S. population, the foreign-born population was at a peak of 14.7 percent during the first few decades of the 1900s. After World War I and as a result of changes in immigration law during the 1920s, the level of immigration fell significantly. In 1970, the percentage of the U.S. foreign-born population was at the lowest rate of 4.7 percent. Since 1970, the percentage of the foreign-born population has risen steadily, reaching 12.6 percent in 2007. During this time period, immigrant workers' share of the U.S. labor force increased from approximately 5.3 percent to 15.8 percent (Camarota, 2007). Significantly, according to the U.S. Census Bureau, as of 2006, there were an estimated 11.1 million unauthorized migrants living in the United States who are unaccounted for in these data.

Looking out over the next few decades, the projected U.S. population and labor force growth rates would be growing at much lower rates if it were not for immigration. Indeed, much of the developed world due to significantly low fertility rates will be witnessing declining population and labor force growth rates well into the foreseeable future. However, like the United States, much of the developed world is getting increasingly more diverse. Although the United States has the greatest number of immigrants, as of 2007, it had a smaller amount of immigrants as a percentage of the population compared to a number of developed countries. For example, in 2007, immigrants in Australia composed 20 percent of its population, and composed 19 percent of the population in Canada. France is approaching the United States, with immigrants accounting for 11 percent of its population, as is the United Kingdom, with immigrants representing 9 percent of its population (Passel and Cohn, 2008).

According to the U.S. Census Bureau, the growth in immigration rates along with higher birth rates for minorities will result in a significant increase in the racial/ethnic diversity of the U.S. population over the next 25 years. Today, an estimated 34 percent of the U.S. population is classified as nonwhite; in 1960, it was 10 percent. Sometime before 2050, those who are classified as Hispanic, African American, Asian, and Native American are projected to compose more than 50 percent of the population (U.S. Census Bureau, 2009). In 2005, 12 percent (1 in 8) of Americans were immigrants. In 2050, an estimated 19 percent (nearly 1 in 5) of Americans will be immigrants. By that time, the immigrant portion of the United States will be greater than any time in its history (Passel and Cohn, 2008).

Between 2010 and 2020, minorities and immigrants will account for most of the projected net growth in the workforce, especially for younger workers. During this timeframe, the number of workers under 24 is expected to grow by approximately 3 million, or 15 percent, of which 85 percent will be minorities and immigrants. As the workplace becomes more diverse, the share of the white non-Hispanic labor force is expected to decrease from 67.5 percent to 62.3 percent.

In this decade, the share of the African American labor force is expected to modestly increase from 11.6 percent to 12.0 percent. The increase in African Americans' share of the labor force mainly comes from higher birthrates, immigration, and high labor force participation rates of African American women. The share of Hispanic workers will increase rapidly from 14.8 percent to 18.6 percent due primarily to rapid population growth (immigration and fertility rates) and high labor force participation rates. Though their numbers are smaller, the

Asian labor force is expected to grow at a fast rate increasing from 4.7 percent to 5.7 percent of the labor force due to high immigration and participation rates (Toossi, 2012).

Educational Disparities

The best predictor of economic success in the United States is one's education. Rising educational levels have been driving economic growth for decades. The percentage of the U.S. workforce over the age of 25 with college degrees has been rising steadily, from 22 percent in 1980 to nearly 30 percent in 2012. Between 2001 and 2009, the number of college graduates increased 29 percent; however, those graduating with degrees in science and engineering only increased 19 percent, and the number of graduates with computer and information science degrees actually decreased by 14 percent. Based on the 2011 BLS Current Population Survey (U.S. Census Bureau, 2011), the educational attainment as a percentage of the U.S. population 18 years and over in 2011 is shown in Table 2.3.

Table 2.3 2011 U.S. Educational Attainment Rates

Less than a high school diploma	13.5 percent
High school graduate	30.4 percent
Some college (no degree)	19.6 percent
Associate's degree (both academic and occupational)	8.9 percent
Bachelor's degree	18.1 percent
Master's/professional degree	8.2 percent
Doctoral degree	1.3 percent

The wide variance in educational attainment contributes to the widening economic divide among U.S. workers. A contributing factor of the growing disparity of educational attainment rates in today's workforce is the disproportional educational attainment rates of foreign-born workers. A study of immigrants entering the United States noted that in 2007, approximately 32 percent of foreign-born workers had not completed high school compared to 12.4 percent of native-born workers. The percent of foreign-born workers with a bachelor's degree or higher was comparable to native-born workers equaling 26.9 percent and 27.5 percent, respectively (Wilson, 2009).

Though immigrants compose nearly 16 percent of the labor force, they compose more than 40 percent of adults in the labor force who have not completed high school. The large number of foreign-born workers with low levels of education means that the immigration policy of the United States has significantly increased the supply of low-skilled workers. Such a policy has put downward pressure on wages for low-skilled jobs and has disproportionately affected the economic prospects of all less-educated workers (Camarota, 2007).

Overall, the United States lags behind other advanced nations in educational performance. The Program of International Student Assessment (PISA) is a noted international comparison of 15-year-olds used by the Organization for Economic Cooperation and Development (OECD) to assess countries' educational achievement rankings. In 2006, the United States ranked 25th of 30 nations in math and 24th of 50 in science (McKinsey & Co., April 2009). These poor rankings show just how far the United States has fallen from its onetime leadership position in education. Forty years ago, the United States was the world's leader in high school graduation rates; today, it ranks 18th out of 24 developed nations. As recently as 1995, the United States was tied for first in college graduation rates; by 2006, its ranking dropped to 14th. There is also a worrisome trend between the performance of America's highest performing students and that of top students elsewhere. According to the OECD, the United States has among the smallest proportion of 15-year-olds performing at the highest levels of proficiency in math (McKinsey & Co., April 2009).

In addition to an achievement gap in education with other advanced nations, the United States is facing a severe racial achievement gap. Based on the average National Assessment of Educational Progress (NAEP) scores, black and Latino students are approximately 2 to 3 years of learning behind white students of the same age. For example, based on NAEP scores for math and reading across the fourth and eighth grades, 48 percent of blacks and 43 percent of Latinos are "below basic" compared to only 17 percent of white students (McKinsey & Co., April 2009). As noted in Chapter 1, "Welcome to the New Normal," the economic costs of these educational achievement gaps are staggering. The magnitude of this effect if not resolved will only get worse in the years ahead as blacks and Latinos become a larger proportion of the population (McKinsey & Co., April 2009).

Rise of Contract Human Capital

Many individuals now work in a multitude of nontraditional work arrangements. A large segment of these work arrangements is labeled *alternative work arrangements* by the BLS. Data on these work arrangements have been collected periodically by the BLS only as supplements to the Current Population Survey. Due to a lack of funding, the last time any in-depth reporting of these work arrangements was conducted was in 2005. Trying to report on these work arrangements is also difficult due to a lack of consistency in classifying them. Some workers may be hired for only short-term or contingent work; others may be employees of firms that contract out their services; and yet others may be self-employed and incorporated.

The 2005 BLS Current Population Survey estimated that nearly 15 million workers (10.7% of the labor force) are employed in alternative employment arrangements including independent contractors, temporary employees, on-call employees, and employees of contract firms. Within this trend, contingent work in professional and technical functions is growing the fastest. By all estimates, the number of individuals in these alternative employment arrangements is rapidly increasing. At current growth rates, it is estimated that alternative employment arrangements may reach between 30 and 40 percent of the workforce by 2020 (Oracle, 2010).

In the last BLS report on alternative work arrangements, temporary employees represented approximately 1.1 percent of the workforce. However, since the end of the last Great Recession in 2010, the number of temporary employees has increased considerably as companies are reluctant to hire permanent staff. Today, the staffing industry estimates that the percentage of temporary workers today is closer to 1.3 percent, totaling more than 2 million workers. Regarding occupational concentration, temporary employees are more likely to work in administrative support, transportation, material moving, and production positions. In terms of industry concentration, they are more likely to be employed in manufacturing and professional business services. Temporary employees are the least likely to prefer working in an alternative work arrangement and are the lowest paid group of alternative workers. A survey of temporary employees conducted by the BLS noted that 56 percent of these workers would prefer a traditional job (BLS, 2005).

On-call workers consist of workers who are "on call" to work only when needed. These arrangements can last for several days or weeks at a time. In the 2005 BLS report, these arrangements composed 1.8 percent of all employment, which today would total more than 2 million workers. There is little discrepancy between the characteristics of these workers and traditional employees. Many of these individuals work in construction and extraction positions. Forty-four percent of these workers are employed as part-time employees. A large percentage of these workers (45 percent) stated that they would prefer to work in a traditional position (BLS, 2005).

It's also estimated that independent contractors represent approximately 7.4 percent of the workforce totaling more than 10 million workers. However, none of these estimates capture the many independent contractors who are incorporated. Anyone today can spend a few hundred dollars to get incorporated and put out a shingle. This is a common strategy for highly skilled individuals who market their services to the highest bidder. Although there are no official estimates, based on my research, approximately 5 percent of individual independent contractors are incorporated.

As a whole, independent contractors are more highly educated than the traditional workforce. More than 35 percent of independent contractors have at least a bachelor's degree compared to 30 percent of the workforce. The majority of these individuals work in professional and business services, education, health services, and construction (BLS, 2005). Less than 10 percent of independent contractors would prefer to work in a traditional job.

According to the BLS (2005), workers who are employed by contract firms compose 0.6 percent of the workforce, totaling nearly 1 million workers. These are individuals whose services are contracted out to client companies typically as consultants. However, the BLS does not include a growing and much larger number of individuals who work in similar arrangements at outsourced businesses, firms, and strategic partnerships. As with contract firms, these individuals are typically employed by a firm that provides services to other organizations.

The one commonality among all these work arrangements is an increasing large number of individuals who work in situations as *non-employees*. Today, it is not uncommon for a manager working at a large organization to manage an array of work arrangements to accomplish the work objectives including traditional employees, consultants, temporary employees, independent contractors, as well as individuals who are employees of outsourced businesses and strategic partnerships. Throughout the rest of this book, all individuals working in non-employee work arrangements are classified as *contract human capital* (see Table 2.4).

Table 2.4 Contract Human Capital

Defined as any non-employee worker of an organization, including the following:
Temporary employees
Consultants
Independent contractors
Strategic partnerships
Outsourced/offshore employees

Outsourced/Offshore Relationships

The 21st century workforce extends far beyond any one country's boundaries. Advances in computer and communication technologies, liberalization of trade agreements, along with less expensive and faster travel options have enabled organizations to reach and manage workers all around the world. As the world's population grows and continues to be more affluent, the demand for goods and services, and consequently the demand for talent, will continue to rise. In countries whose populations are declining including many in Europe and Japan, organizations seeking talent will have no choice but to find talent outside their countries. Other countries such as the United States that are experiencing talent supply and demand imbalances are also forced to seek talent beyond their borders. Lastly, to meet culturally diverse customer needs and to adapt business strategies to local conditions, it's becoming a necessity for growing multinationals to find local talent in the markets they enter.

The largest multinational firms are commonly referred to as *transnational corporations.* These organizations have the advantages of scale and scope of operations by integrating resources globally, as well as being locally responsive in the markets they operate in. Employment at U.S.-based transnational corporations grew by 34 percent between 1991 and 2001, with 42 percent of their employees living in other countries (Walsh et al., 2006). Some of these organizations operate in more than 100 countries. Much of the growth has been accomplished through cross-border joint ventures, mergers and acquisition, and strategic alliances.

The first wave of offshore activity consisted of organizations looking to take advantage of a growing supply of low-cost workers predominately in manufacturing and production jobs. Though many of these offshore facilities located in developing countries were not as productive as similar facilities based in developed countries, the cost differentials were significant enough to justify moving the work. The second wave of offshore activity beginning around 2000 consisted of an increasing large number of white-collar jobs being sent overseas (Lee and Mather, 2008).

A 2005 study conducted by the McKinsey Global Institute of 28 low-wage countries found there were some 33 million young professionals, defined as university graduates with up to 7 years of work experience, who earn significantly less than their counterparts working in the developed world. However, in interviews conducted with 83 HR managers at multinationals operating in these low-wage countries report that, on average, only 13 percent of university graduates are suitable for the jobs in these companies (Farrell et al., 2005).

A study conducted by Alan Blinder of Princeton University in 2007 found that the jobs more likely to be offshored can often be performed remotely and have well-defined rules and procedures.

Conversely, jobs that require physical interaction with a client, or require a great deal of judgment and cultural understanding, are less likely to be easily offshored. Blinder's findings show that nearly 30 million U.S. jobs are vulnerable to offshoring, or just over one-fifth of the U.S. workforce. Many of these jobs require a high level of education and pay high incomes, including computer programmers, research scientists, actuaries, mathematicians, statisticians, mathematical science, and film and video editors (Lee and Mather, 2008).

Many commentators have cited offshoring as the solution to the increasing supply and demand imbalances facing the United States and other developed countries for highly skilled talent. However, future global projections for global talent portends there will be looming skills shortages as the demand for global talent exceeds the supply. On the demand side, the rapid growth of developing countries' economies will significantly increase the need for more educated workers. On the supply side, the raw numbers of projected college-educated workers is falling short of demand. And when you consider the huge variance in the quality of education of the global workforce, the projected talent shortages will be even larger.

Indeed, research conducted by the McKinsey Global Institute projects that by 2020, the shortfall in college-educated workers worldwide could approach 40 million (Dobbs et al., 2012). Currently, many organizations in the developed world look toward China where there is projected to be tens of millions of more highly skilled workers produced over the next few decades. Yet, given the rapid growth of China's economy coupled with an aging population, it's projected that by 2020 China will likely need 23 million more college-educated workers to meet growing demand.

India, the second most populous country in the world, is also the destination of many multinationals for high-skilled offshore work. India is a much younger country than China and has a rapidly growing population of university graduates. It's projected that by 2020, India will produce 36 million college graduates, which is approximately 6 million more than what its domestic industries can employ (Dobbs et al., 2012). However, as already noted, this surplus is not even enough to cover China's projected shortfall, never mind the projected developed world's shortfall. When you also consider that less than one-third of India's graduates have the level of skills needed by most multinationals, it is doubtful that India will generate a big enough surplus to meet global demand.

Many multinationals are setting their sights on Eastern Europe. Although significantly smaller in population, the Czech Republic, Hungary, Poland, and Russia collectively have as many suitable managers and engineers as does India. The Philippines is also quickly becoming a potential source of highly educated college graduates. Though China's population is 16 times greater than the Philippines, China's pool of qualified English-speaking engineers is only 3 times as big (Farrell et al., 2005). Like the rest of Europe, as Eastern Europe continues to expand its economy, the demand for highly skilled talent is outstripping supply.

The one bright spot today for finding global talent is looking to the young developing countries that include Bangladesh, Kenya, Morocco, and Nigeria that are projected to contribute up to one-third of the growth in the global labor force. The supply of college-educated workers in these countries exceeds demand, creating a surplus of talent. The poor economies of these countries have resulted in unemployment rates of 20 percent for highly educated workers. However, this surplus of talent will not last forever as their economies continue to grow at a much faster rate than the developed world. Amazingly, by 2030, there are projected to be significant talent shortages for highly skilled workers even in these countries (Farrell et al., 2005).

All in all, the labor force of the 21st century has no boundaries. Companies located in the developed world will have no choice but to look beyond their borders for the talent they need to meet future growth. However, as the rest of world continues to grow and develop, it will become increasingly more difficult to rely on outside sources for highly skilled labor. Furthermore, the projected labor shortages will significantly increase the wages for highly skilled talent, making it more difficult to offshore knowledge work. Indeed, the war for offshore talent will continue to be fierce for decades to come, making it imperative for the developed world to create, develop, and engage its own talent.

3

Challenges of Talent Management in the New Normal

The increased complexity and structural shifts of the economy and workplace create significant talent management challenges, as shown in Table 3.1. The old, one-size-fits-all way of managing and engaging employees no longer applies. Today, employers must respond quickly to fluctuating business demands and a changing competitive landscape. Employers change strategies, structures, and competencies continuously in response to customer demands, competitor innovations, and operational challenges.

Despite the slow and uneven global recovery and lingering high levels of unemployment, organizations are still finding it difficult to find the right talent when they need it. They feverishly reevaluate ineffective workforce planning models and seek talent with unique skills. They must compete in the "new normal" in which economic pressures have forced them to do more with less. At the same time, advances in technology are transforming the world as cutting-edge organizations create amazing things and accomplish the unthinkable. In today's global economy, talent is the key strategic differentiator for many organizations. As you've seen in previous chapters, the challenge is how to harness this talent that is so diverse and comes to the workplace with a wide range of skills, preferences, and values.

Table 3.1 Challenges of Talent Management in the New Normal

Talent Management Characteristic	Challenge
Uncertain HR Planning	Uncertain business and workforce needs, unreliable forecasts, internal development versus hiring on demand
Organizational Challenges	Greater need for new competencies, sustainable resources, and flatter/boundaryless structures
Evolving Social Contract	Lack of loyalty from both employees and employers, new employer–employee relationship
Changing Needs and Values of Workers	Understanding generational differences: different ways of working, different preferences, different drivers of motivation
Managing a Diverse and Global Workforce	Need to manage multiple dimensions of diversity and cultural differences
Increasing Corporate Social Responsibility	Need to manage multiple stakeholders including employees, shareholders, vendors, and the community
Managing Multiple Sources of Talent	Different work preferences: flexibility, short-term work, freelance work, skill development, a job
Expanding Globally	Navigating and expanding into new markets via multiple strategies including joint ventures, mergers and acquisitions (M&As), and managing global workers

Uncertain HR Planning

Many companies that came of age in a more stable and predictable economy find their models of forecasting and workforce planning are not as effective as they previously were. From the 1950s through the early 1970s, businesses relied on more stable and predictable economic and business forecasting that enabled them to develop workforce-planning programs well into the future (Capelli, 2008). During this time, product market forecasts looked out upwards of 5 to 10 years. By the mid-1960s, a study of personnel departments found that 96 percent had a dedicated talent planning function (Allen, 1966).

Today, companies face a continuing imbalance between talent supply and demand. On one hand, organizations may find themselves with too many employees leading to layoffs and restructurings, and on the other hand, companies may have too little talent resulting in talent shortages. The risk associated with this imbalance is high. There are significant costs associated with these imbalances that can put a company at a severe competitive disadvantage.

A critical challenge facing many organizations is the impending loss of intellectual capital as large numbers of experienced baby boomers retire. As corporate leaders retire, organizations need to create ways to keep the knowledge these employees possess. In a study conducted by Ernst & Young, corporate executives noted that maintaining intellectual capital was one of their most important management issues they faced (Ernst & Young, 2006). In a follow-up survey of 340 Fortune 1,000 companies, 27 percent said they anticipate an upcoming knowledge and skills gap in their organizations due to the retiring of experienced workers (Ernst & Young, 2010).

The ability to make such long-term forecasts today has, however, significantly shrunk due to changes in customer tastes, new competition, and technological innovations. As a result, there has been a corresponding inability to reliably forecast the talent needed to meet business demands. Exacerbating these uncertainties is the correspondingly insufficient internal talent pools available to meet future business needs. As companies scaled back on internal development programs to reduce costs after the 2008 global recession and as more employees develop a free-agent mentality, it's becoming more difficult for them to align staffing and business needs. Conversely, some companies have proprietary technology and competencies that require a greater investment in developing talent internally.

Though the future is getting increasingly more difficult to predict, demographic forecasting is quite reliable. If there are 4 million births this year, you can predict with high confidence there will be approximately 4 million 10-year-olds 10 years from now. HR planning models have been tracking demographic trends for some time; however, the interpretation of these trends has not always been accurate. One of the premises of the "war for talent" predictions in the late 1990s was the expectation there will be a large cohort of workers (baby boomers) retiring who would have to be replaced with a much smaller cohort of workers (Gen X). Thus, the expectation was companies will face a severe shortage of workers when the first of the baby boomers reach retirement age.

Fast-forward to today and you can witness the unfolding of a far different phenomenon. Interestingly, there is a war for talent, but the cause is the result of a shortage of skills not necessarily a shortage of workers. Conversely, some researchers suggest that the increasingly large number of baby boomers postponing retirement can lead to a "gray ceiling" that could limit career opportunities for younger workers (Society for Human Resource Management, 2011).

Organizational Challenges

The increasing complexities and structural shifts in the economy pose many challenges for organizations trying to compete in the new normal, as shown in Table 3.2.

Table 3.2 Organizational Challenges

New Competencies
Sustainable Resources
Flatter/Boundaryless Structures

New Competencies

In an interview with Gary Hamel and Lowell Bryan published in the *McKinsey Quarterly*, Hamel noted that instead of being built with the capacity to innovate and adapt, many management systems have been designed to create standardization and efficiency. This old management strategy does not lend itself to the needs of the 21st century work environment. Bryan added that because organizations are not equipped to address the new work environment, the opportunities created by globalization and increased technology are not being fully utilized (Barsh, 2008).

Today, nearly three-quarters of the U.S. economy is in the service and knowledge sectors. In a knowledge economy, intangible assets drive economic growth and innovation. The investments that drive firm value include research and development (R&D), brand equity, and human capital. The entire global economy is becoming more knowledge- and technology-intensive. Global R&D expenditures have grown faster than global gross domestic product (GDP) over the past decade. According to the National Science Foundation, total global R&D expenditures increased from $522 billion in 1996 to nearly $1.3 trillion in 2009, with the United States remaining the world's leader at $400 billion (National Science Board, 2012).

However, many organizations struggle to find talent that has the competencies required for competing in a highly competitive and constantly changing environment. In such an environment, innovation is a critical strategy to create sustainable growth for many organizations. In a 2010 global survey conducted by McKinsey & Company, 84 percent of executives said that innovation is extremely or very important to their companies' growth strategy. Some of the challenges facing these executives in pursuing an innovation strategy included finding the right talent and encouraging collaboration and risk taking (McKinsey & Co., 2010).

There is also a great need for organizations to find people who can transform the increasing amount of new data generated every day into knowledge. Although the volume of data is estimated to increase fivefold over the next 5 years, best-guess estimates suggest that less than 10 percent of the information created will be meaningfully organized or deployed (Bisson et al., 2010). In a *USA Today* interview, Marc Andreessen, coauthor of the Netscape browser, talked about how over the next 30 years "the spread of computers and the Internet will put jobs in two categories, people who tell computers what to do, and people who are told by computers what to do" (Mullaney, 2012 pg. 1). In his new book, *Automate This: How Algorithms Came to Rule Our World*, Christopher Steiner talks about how complex mathematical calculations powering computer programs that trade stocks, compose symphonies, and analyze legal documents are replacing old jobs with newer more complex jobs. "With a well-written algorithm and enough data, Steiner says, a skilled computer programmer can automate almost any human endeavor." He goes on to say that the future will belong to "those who can build, maintain, and improve upon [computer] code and algorithms" (Destro, 2012).

E.O. Wilson, a two-time Pulitzer Prize-winning biologist, noted that the world henceforth will be run by synthesizers and people who can put together the right information at the right time, think critically about it, and make important choices wisely (Wilson, 1998). Research by McKinsey refers to this trend as the "rise of the tacit workforce" (April 2009). Increasingly, organizations rely on their intellectual capital to gain a competitive advantage, which is composed of their human and social capital. *Human capital* consists of one's knowledge and experience that can be translated into economic value, whereas *social capital* consists of one's connections in a network of people. These jobs require knowledge workers who possess a range of complex skills such as data analysis, problem solving, team building, and communication skills.

In a 2012 survey of CEOs conducted by The Conference Board, the top two challenges facing organizations are developing innovation and human capital. In particular, the human side of innovation was mostly emphasized including the people, minds, alliances, and culture that can create and nurture new ideas. These executives cited the need to create a culture of innovation by promoting and rewarding entrepreneurship and risk taking; engage in strategic alliances with business partners, customers, and suppliers; and attract and engage top talent. To address their human capital challenge, three strategies were cited including growing talent internally, improving leadership development programs, and providing employee training and development programs (Mitchell et al., 2012).

Sustainable Resources

The rapid growth of world population and wealth is putting a tremendous strain on global resources. The demand for energy, commodities, food, and water will continue to increase throughout the 21st century. This will create many threats as well as opportunities for corporations. To meet these challenges, organizations and governments need to develop new technologies and capabilities. There will be a significant increase in demand for workers who possess unique skills in engineering, environmental and material science, chemistry, and genetics.

Entire new industries are being created to develop new sustainable sources of energy and food, whereas the traditional energy and food sectors are being radically transformed. Steady increases in hydropower and the rapid expansion of solar and wind power have solidified the position of renewable sources of energy as an indispensable part of the global energy mix. It's projected that renewables will account for nearly one-third the world's total electricity output by 2035 (International Energy Agency, 2012).

New technologies for extracting traditional energy sources are being developed, and advances in solar, wind, bio-energy, and hydropower are rapidly improving. Tremendous strides have been made in discovering and extracting new sources of oil and gas. Driven by upstream technologies, the United States is unlocking oil and shale resources to significantly increase production. According to a report published by the International Energy Agency, by 2030, the United States is projected to be the largest oil producer, overtaking Saudi Arabia. Advances in drilling techniques combined with hydraulic fracturing have led to the rapid development of shale gas to such an extent that by 2030 gas will overtake oil as the U.S.'s largest fuel production in the energy mix (International Energy Agency, 2012).

The increasing demand for food and water is creating tremendous opportunities for organizations that develop new technologies for expanding these vital resources. Land and water resources are becoming scarcer and diminished in quality due to a continued degradation of resources and competition from other uses other than for food production. Growth rates in production will be smaller than in the past but will rise significantly in absolute terms between now and 2050. New discoveries in genetic engineering are transforming agricultural productivity. For example, production yields per hectare for cereal crops are projected to increase from 3.3 tons per year to 4.3 tons in 2050 (International Energy Agency, 2012).

Water is quickly becoming a valuable resource not only for drinking but also mostly for irrigation. The amount of irrigable land has doubled since the 1960s due to advances in finding, processing, and delivering water supplies. However, the potential for further expansion is limited. Although there are abundant sources of water around the world, they are extremely scarce in the Near East, North Africa, and in northern China where the demand for water is significantly increasing (International Energy Agency, 2012).

All in all, the need for sustainable resources will create many challenges and opportunities for organizations and entire economies. To overcome these urgent challenges, organizations must develop new technologies and processes, which will require them to develop new competencies in an array of scientific, economic, engineering, and environmental areas.

Flatter/Boundaryless Structures

In the 21st century work environment, organizations need to have access to multiple sources of external talent and have the capability to develop and redeploy internal talent. Rapidly changing technology increasingly favors individuals who are new to the field and decreases the demand for more experienced technology workers. Rapidly changing product markets often require organizations to access new skills that do not exist internally and must be obtained in the open market. Changing strategic direction oftentimes requires companies to bring in outside talent to help change its culture. All these demands require organizations to be adaptable and innovative by creating flatter, more nimble organizational structures.

There is a growing awareness that collaboration with multiple sources of talent is a requirement for creating sustainable competitive advantage in highly complex and rapidly changing environments. These flatter organizations require self-directed knowledge workers who can collaborate within and across organizational boundaries. Organizations need collaborators who are comfortable with complexity and ambiguity and can understand and find common ground with the goals of multiple stakeholders.

Furthermore, as more and more work gets done remotely through collaborative work systems, the need for competencies for developing social relations including emotional intelligence, teamwork, negotiation, and conflict management is growing. Employers and HR professionals responding to a study sponsored by the Society for Human Resource Management and WSJ.com reported an increased need for talent that possess adaptability/flexibility, critical thinking, and problem-solving skills (Society for Human Resource Management and WSJ.com, 2008). However, you continually hear how many workers are ill-prepared to handle complex jobs. Even among 4-year college graduates representing the top 30 percent of the workforce, employers have indicated many of these workers lack these complex skills and only a few have skills they would rate at excellent proficiency levels (Casner-Lotto and Barrington, 2006).

These evolving new organizational structures also require a different management strategy. The old hierarchical, top-down approach to management has been turned upside down. In its place are new management systems utilizing cutting-edge technology that empower employees to think and make decisions on their own. Managing diverse and interdependent alliances that include business, governments, competitors, and even critics (such as nongovernmental organizations and labor unions) requires a high degree of trust and communication. Flattened hierarchies are also increasing the span of control of managers. In the past, managers typically had 6 direct reports. Today, the typical span of control of a manager is between 15 and 20 workers (Benko and Anderson, 2010a). However, in a recent survey of U.S. companies conducted by Manpower, 53 percent of respondents said there is a shortage of middle managers who can effectively manage these complex work systems (Manpower Group, 2011).

As hierarchies continue to shrink, the number of opportunities to climb the corporate ladder is also calling into question that up is the only path to success. Accepting that one's career is no longer hierarchical within a single organization, individuals must focus on enhancing competencies that span many organizations and jobs as well as employment arrangements. As a result, organizations need new management systems for hiring and engaging mobile talent both within and beyond their boundaries.

Evolving Social Contract

In this second decade of the 21st century, the forces propelling the new economy are significantly changing the employer–employee relationship. For some time, beginning in the 1980s, you have been hearing about a new social contract between workers and organizations. This new social contract is often nostalgically compared to the employer–employee relationship of a previous era following the end of World War II when the world and workplace was a much different place. The underlying tone is often a yearning for what some researchers have called the *golden age of talent management.*

However, what is often not acknowledged is that this golden age was truly an anomaly. Following the end of World War II, the United States was the world's sole economic power. Europe and Japan were rebuilding and China and India were decades away from being global players. Throughout the 1950s and 1960s, the United States was the dominant supplier of goods and services throughout the world and faced virtually no competition. During this time, government regulations further restricted the level and nature of competition for U.S. companies. Within a vast number of industries, government regulations restricted new entrants, price cutting, and other aspects of a competitive market.

With little competition, U.S. corporations grew and enjoyed high profit margins, which were passed on to employees in the form of high pay, comprehensive benefits packages, and lucrative pensions. At the same time, the passage of the GI Bill of Rights provided the impetus for a rapid expansion of college enrollments and graduates, enabling the United States to have a dominant position in human capital. The unique combination of a continuous supply of human capital along with practically no competition enabled the United States to achieve a preeminent position in the global economy.

In such a stable and predictable environment, organizations fostered a high-commitment workplace in which there was a greater reliance on long-tenured employees. This was the era of the "organization man" when companies invested in the development of employees and later secured the benefits through employees' enhanced performance extending over decades (Cappelli, 2008). The social contract between employees and employers at this time was an exchange of employee loyalty for job security. Robert Reich, former U.S. Labor Secretary, in his book *The Future of Success,* writes during this time people implicitly expected that a job would consist of steady work with predictably rising pay (Reich, 2001).

The golden age of talent management began to fall apart during the oil shocks of the 1970s, first in 1973 and then again in 1979. U.S. gross national product (GNP), which had been growing at approximately 5 to 6 percent in real terms during most of the 1960s, actually declined in 1974, 1975, and 1980 (Bureau of Economic Analysis, 2012). This was a period of "stagflation" (a toxic combination of high inflation and high unemployment) that caused massive imbalances, leaving many companies overstaffed, unproductive, and financially strapped. By 1981, the U.S. economy was in the worst recession since the Great Depression when the GNP declined by 2 percent. After another economic setback in 1983, massive downsizing ensued, beginning with the financial services industry in which top management's attention shifted to questions of strategy and restructuring (Cappelli, 2008).

Many U.S. organizations marred with bloated bureaucracies were ill-prepared for the global and technological challenges confronting them entering the 1990s. Throughout the 1990s, advances in technology and the dismantling of trade barriers further increased the competitive pressures on business. In these difficult economic times, organizations pursued a relentless strategy to become more efficient, utilizing business process reengineering methods, such as Six Sigma, to leverage technology, streamline processes, eliminate unnecessary tasks, and rationalize the layers of management.

Well before the Internet bubble burst in 2000, and the 2008–2009 Great Recession, which all resulted in massive layoffs, the old social contract had been null and void for decades. In its place, a new social contract evolved whereby employees and employers exchange job performance for employability. Realizing there are no guarantees for job security in a constantly changing work environment, employees seek opportunities that will provide them with marketable skills that they can bring to another employer when needed. Organizations that provide these developmental opportunities have the advantage of attracting and engaging employees who can help them achieve their business objectives.

Changing Needs and Values of Workers

Understanding the different needs, preferences, and values of workers is necessary for knowing how to motivate and engage them (see Table 3.3). When the workforce was more homogenous and the workplace more predictable, organizations mainly relied on a uniform set of "best practices" that for the most part was an effective way of managing employees. However, in today's highly diverse and unpredictable work environment, a one-size-fits-all way of managing workers is highly ill-advised. The 21st century workforce consists of a vast array of individuals as noted in Chapter 2, "The 21st Century Workforce," who come to the workplace with vastly different experiences, cultures, and socio-economic statuses.

Table 3.3 Generational Differences in the Workplace

Generation	Attributes and Values	Communication and Leadership Styles	Feedback and Rewards
Traditionalists Before 1946	Respect authority and rules Duty before pleasure Patriotic	Written and formal Face-to-face interactions Prefer direct leadership and clear goals	No need for feedback Work is a privilege Satisfaction in a job well done
Baby Boomers 1946–1964	Challenge the status quo Workaholics Achievement-oriented Believe you must pay your dues at work	Experienced it all from memos to emails to text messages Like in person interactions Prefer consensual and collegial leadership styles	Don't appreciate feedback Seek advancement and titles Monetary gains
Generation X 1965–1980	Skeptical of authority Self-reliant Want to be empowered to get work done Seek work–life balance	Cell phone and email Like in person and group interactions Dislike hierarchy power structures Prefer power-sharing leadership styles	Appreciate and seek feedback Want the freedom to make own rules Value flexibility

Generation	Attributes and Values	Communication and Leadership Styles	Feedback and Rewards
Generation Y 1981–1999	Confident and independent Expect work to fit with other life commitments Value community and connecting with others Impatient and will move on quickly to get what they want	Connected electronically with friends and colleagues 24/7 Avoid in person communication if possible Prefer mentors over leaders	Demand constant and instantaneous feedback Seek skill development and knowledge Value meaningful work

Given the diversity of today's workforce, it's nearly impossible to predict what may or may not motivate workers at any given point in time. Quite frankly, there are too many variables to consider. Whether you are a sole provider or part of a dual-income household, how marketable your skills are, life-cycle preferences, economic circumstances, and so on can all impact drivers of motivation. Baby boomers whose skills are becoming obsolete and who lose their jobs might have a completely different set of motivational drivers than baby boomers who are part of a successful dual-income couple. A Gen Y worker who is a single mom struggling to make ends meet may not have the same work preferences than her more free-spirited peers.

A popular management theme today that acknowledges these management challenges is to segment the labor force into generational cohorts. As a result of more workers living longer and postponing retirement, there are now four different generations working together (traditionalists, baby boomers, Gen X, and Gen Y), each with its distinct attitudes and beliefs. There may be ways to generalize the preferences of different generational cohorts by their common experiences or age, but those who make such generalizations are not always accurate. As previously noted, even among common cohorts there can be significant individual differences that influence their values, needs, and preferences. It may also be surprising that there are similarities that cut across multiple generations, such as a preference for flexible work arrangements.

Traditionalists

Given that the youngest person from this generation is now 68, their numbers in the workplace are rapidly declining. Many from this generation have been beneficiaries of defined pension plans that have enabled them to retire by age 65. Those who are still in the workforce are motivated to work for different reasons. Some have a need for financial security, others have a strong preference for social interactions, and yet others want to continue making a contribution. Clearly these workers have a wide range of work preferences, including financial benefits such as 401(k) contributions or other pension benefits, a work environment that encourages their involvement, and opportunities to mentor younger workers or be involved in meaningful work.

Baby Boomers

The baby boomers being the beneficiaries of a booming economy after World War II and beyond spent lavishly and saved little. Unlike the traditionalists generation who saved more and participated in defined benefit pension programs that provided a steady source of income in retirement, many baby boomers are not financially prepared for retirement. For example, a survey by the Employee Benefit Research Institute found that 47.2 percent of "early baby boomers" and 43.7 percent of "late baby boomers" were at risk of not having enough retirement savings to pay for basic expenditures. The looming retirement crisis is also impacting Gen X as 44.5 percent were also at risk of not having enough retirement savings (Employee Benefit Research Institute, 2010).

In addition to saving too little, baby boomers came of age when most organizations switched to defined contribution pension plans that often rise and fall with the stock market. The value of these pension plans was negatively impacted during the tumultuous 2000s that witnessed an Internet-bubble bust and financial collapse. Making matters worse, many workers in their 50s who have lost their jobs have defaulted on 401(k) loans, causing taxes and penalties to further deplete their retirement savings (Transamerica Center for Retirement Studies, 2012). As a result, many baby boomers are postponing retirement and saving more to ensure their future financial security.

In a survey conducted by the McKinsey Global Institute, 85 percent of baby boomers surveyed indicated they are somewhat likely to very likely to continue working beyond their traditional retirement age (Beinhocker et al., 2008). In another survey by the Transamerica Center for Retirement Studies, fewer than 1 in 10 baby boomers strongly agree that they are saving enough for retirement, with 43 percent indicating that they plan to work past age 70 or not retire at all (Transamerica, 2012). Given their lack of savings and looming retirement, it's not surprising that in a study researching what motivates workers, baby boomers ranked compensation much higher than the other younger generations (Barford & Hester, 2011).

Sometimes referred to as the "sandwich generation," many baby boomers are simultaneously responsible for school-aged children and aging parents. As a result, organizations that provide flexible work options as well as childcare and elder care services are attractive to these workers. Also known as the "me generation," baby boomers are interested in their looks and health. As this generation continues to get older, many are becoming increasingly health conscious and value organizations that provide wellness programs and access to health clubs.

No other generation has experienced the massive technological, social, and economic changes as the baby boomers experienced during their working lives. When the baby boomers entered the workplace, the old social contract of job security in exchange for loyalty was firmly intact. (As a baby boomer myself, I can remember going to a retirement party nearly once a month when I began my career in banking.) Although the old social contract is as obsolete as vinyl records, many baby boomers have traditional work values including putting in long hours in exchange for money and status (Gilbert, 2011). There has also been a great deal of research contrasting the management styles of baby boomers and younger workers. Unlike many younger workers, baby boomers have persevered and overcome a great deal of challenges throughout their careers and are commonly characterized as competitive micromanagers who are intolerant of laziness (Crumpacker and Crumpacker, 2007).

The results of a study of two large-scale national surveys sponsored by four companies—Booz Allen Hamilton, Ernst & Young, and Time Warner, as part of The Hidden Brain Drain Task Force, a group of 50 multinational organizations—published in the 2009 *Harvard Business Review (HBR)*—provide great insights into the different attitudes and behaviors of multiple generations (Hewlett et al., 2009). Regarding baby boomers:

- Forty-two percent expect they will continue working past the age of 65 with 14 percent saying they don't ever think they will retire. Key factors are concerns over having enough savings for retirement and wanting to continue working because their identities are linked to their jobs and they enjoy work.

- Forty-seven percent consider themselves to be in the middle of their careers. As life expectancies increase and people stay healthier longer, this generation is likely to work far more years than previous generations.

- Fifty-five percent are involved in external volunteer networks. Trying to recapture the idealism of their youth, many boomers volunteer their time on cultural, environmental, educational, and other causes.

- Eighty-seven percent value their autonomy and flexibility at work. Boomers like having a balance and being successful in both their work and personal lives.

- Seventy-one percent report having elder care responsibilities. Boomers are clearly the "sandwich generation," having responsibilities for both children and aging parents.

Gen X

Gen X became independent at a young age, as a result of divorced households or dual-income parents. This generation was raised in an environment of social insecurity and turbulence and is known to be detached and distrustful of companies. Upon entering the workforce during the tumultuous 1980s, they found themselves competing with baby boomers for jobs and are known to be somewhat cynical toward the older generation (Crumpacker and Crumpacker, 2007).

Gen X is not as motivated by money as are baby boomers and is more motivated by personal satisfaction with their jobs. They value training and development and have a strong desire to grow and develop (Smith, 2012). They believe that workplace benefits, particularly health insurance and retirement savings plans, are extremely important, yet many acknowledge they are not saving as much as they should. Both Gen X and Gen Y feel they do not have enough knowledge to properly invest and save. They primarily attribute their financial knowledge to their parents rather than formal education (American Savings Education Council and AARP, 2008). They are wise to be concerned, as they are twice as likely to have a defined contribution retirement plan that requires self-management than previous generations. And when you consider the bleak prospects of Social Security, learning how to save and invest will be critical to ensure their future quality of life.

This generation is highly independent and is not intimidated by authority. They consider a job just a job and will quickly leave if they are not content or if work interferes with their outside interests. They are adventurous and risk takers; it's not uncommon to hear them talk about their weekend rock-climbing and other adventures. It's not uncommon for baby boomers to think of Xers as slackers because boomers' approach and commitment to work is different than this generation. However, give Xers the right amount of flexibility and an informal work environment with minimal supervision and they can be productive. Growing up during the computer revolution, this generation is technologically savvy and performs well at multitasking. Given all these generalities, it's not surprising that many of them are attracted to creative work.

Gen Y

Gen Y has been characterized as being highly confident and independent as a result of protective households and extensive praise (Crumpacker and Crumpacker, 2007). These workers view the employer–employee contract differently than baby boomers and even Gen Xers. Gen Y employees are like free agents and have little expectations of staying with one firm for an extended period of time. To motivate these workers, the organization must provide interesting and challenging work. In return, Gen Yers will reciprocate and invest discretionary effort in the task and produce relevant results. When one or both sides of this equation are no longer possible (for whatever reasons), the relationship will end (Erickson, 2010). Gen Y is also known to value their freedom and chafe under excessive control and bureaucracy. They have high expectations for themselves, seek challenges, and want constant feedback (Gilbert, 2011).

Like Gen X, they also value traditional benefits like health insurance and savings plans. Although Gen Y acknowledges they need to save more, they strongly believe they are more financially independent than Gen X. They see themselves as hardworking, family-oriented, and optimistic. However, they feel that it is more difficult for them than their parents' generation to support a family, save money, pay for their children's education, and buy a home. The path to success for this generation is continuous learning and education, which they believe is more available to them as compared to their parents (American Savings Education Council and AARP, 2008).

Gen Y can be difficult to manage; they want work–life balance and flexibility while looking to advance quickly (Barford and Hester, 2011). They require clear direction and management assistance while simultaneously seeking freedom in their jobs to feel empowered.

This generation is split when it comes to how it views its relationship with employers. Half agree and half disagree that employers are concerned with their employees' best interest. There is also an equal split regarding whether their generation is loyal to employers. Once again, it's unwise to generalize how an entire generation thinks about loyalty. The media primarily highlights how disloyal this generation is and the number of jobs they are expected to have in their career. Actually, many in this generation would be loyal if their employer reciprocated.

The results of the study sponsored by Booz Allen Hamilton, Ernst & Young, and Time Warner, as part of The Hidden Brain Drain Task Force, published in the 2009 *HBR* (Hewlett et al., 2009) paint a unique portrait of this generation:

- Eighty-four percent say they are ambitious. Almost as many also say they are willing to put in the extra effort for their company's success.

- Forty-five percent expect to continue working for their current employer for their entire career. However, a clear majority say they seek a range of new experiences and challenges at work, putting in doubt the likelihood they will achieve these goals with one employer.

- Seventy-eight percent say they are comfortable working with diverse people from different ethnicities and cultures. Clearly, this generation embraces diversity, whereas only 27 percent of baby boomers have such a comfort level.

- Eighty-six percent feel it's important that the work they do makes a positive impact on the world. Gen Y workers seek companies that share their eco-awareness and social consciousness both in and out of the workplace.

- Forty-eight percent say it's important having a network of friends at work. This generation finds working in teams to be highly motivating. They enjoy connecting with others and seek workplaces that are open and conducive to socializing. They want coworkers and even bosses to be readily accessible.

Desire for Flexibility

Baby boomers have long been known to place work over personal needs. However, as baby boomers near retirement, many are looking to switch to work that better suits their changing lifestyles and is more fulfilling. A study conducted by Families and Work Institute found all three generations want to balance their work and personal lives. Only 13 percent of Generations X and Y and 22 percent of baby boomers say they consistently place work over family needs (Benko and Anderson, 2010c). Another study sponsored by The Hidden Brain Drain Task Force indicates that a large majority of Gen Yers (89%) and baby boomers (87%) say having flexible work options is important.

With women composing nearly one-half the working age population, both men's and women's work and personal lives are becoming increasingly more comingled. In the earlier decades when women were entering the workplace in large numbers, many firms implemented work–family policies to attract and retain working women who needed to balance their work and family responsibilities. Today, these policies are often called *work–life policies* acknowledging that all workers, men and women, married and unmarried, benefit by policies that enable them to juggle both work and personal life commitments.

Today, many men and women have similar career aspirations. A study conducted by the Families and Work Institute revealed that for U.S. workers under age 29, there is no gender difference in their desire for jobs with greater responsibilities. There was also no difference between young women with children and those who had no children in their wanting to have the same responsibilities of young men. In another apparent role reversal, the same study noted that men now report much more work–life conflict than women (Galinsky et al., 2009).

Today, both men and women report a desire for their jobs to provide them with the ability to tend to both their careers and families (Barnett et al., 2012). Significantly, the desire for flexibility is moving up the corporate ladder. A 2005 survey conducted by *Fortune* magazine determined that 84 percent of Fortune 500 male executives would like to have more time for things outside work. These men would like job options that enable them to achieve professional as well as personal goals. Fifty-five percent of these executives say they are willing to sacrifice income for more time outside work, and 50 percent are unsure whether the sacrifices they have made for their professional careers have been worth it. The majority (73 percent) of these executives believe it is plausible to find a better balance between work and home by restructuring senior management jobs. They believe this would simultaneously increase productivity and increase executives' amount of leisure time. An even greater proportion (87 percent) of these male executives believes that companies that make such changes will achieve a competitive advantage through attraction of talent. *Fortune* also found that younger executives are more likely to value more time outside work. Unfortunately, approximately one-half of these male executives believe that bringing up the idea to their boss will ultimately damage their career. Perhaps one of the biggest obstacles to creating more work–life balance is employer perceptions that nonwork aspirations are synonymous with laziness and slackers (Miller, 2005).

Managing a Diverse and Global Workforce

Diversity in the 21st century workplace can take on a multitude of meanings. It can be described in traditional terms of ethnicity, nationality, gender, age, religion, marital status, disability, and sexual orientation. In addition, you see cultural divides along the lines of socio-economic status, political views, and with the obesity epidemic facing the United States, even weight. Given current demographic, immigration, and social trends, diversity will continue to be a salient characteristic of society.

There will also be the potential for more prejudice and bias that can negatively impact employees' perceptions of fairness and hurt morale resulting in lost customers and costly litigation. One growing concern is the attitudes toward and treatment of older workers. With the youngest of the baby boomers already beyond 40 years of age, there is concern that some organizations view older workers with negative stereotypes based on ageism. These stereotypes hold that older workers are less physically and mentally able to perform their jobs as compared to younger workers. Older workers are presumed to be less productive and innovative, more prone to sickness and accidents, and less willing or unable to learn. However, there is substantial empirical research that finds no support for these assumptions (Keene, 2006). In fact, other research has found that older workers have lower rates of absenteeism, tend to be more loyal, and are generally more reliable than younger workers (Peterson and Spiker, 2005).

In addition to being illegal and in violation of the U.S. Age Discrimination in Employment Act (ADEA), organizations that perpetuate these negative attitudes toward older workers will find it difficult to retain experienced workers who possess unique skills that are in high demand. Managing these conflicting agendas will require sophisticated HR practices and effective management coaching. Indeed, older workers who have unique skills and financial resources will want to continue working on their own terms. These older workers will continue to work only if they can assert a degree of control over where they work, how they work, and what they work on (Ulrich, 2006).

The increasingly diverse workplace is also a reflection of the increasingly diverse marketplace. Employees represent the company, especially those who directly interface with customers and the public. Thus, it is a business imperative to have a highly engaged and diverse workplace. Such a strategy can help build customer loyalty and enhance the image of the firm. Clearly, this is a priority for organizations that have operations in different countries. In addition to the added logistical challenges of managing remote businesses, it's equally important to effectively communicate and adapt to culturally diverse customers and employees.

While researching the challenges of managing global operations, Ghemawat (2001) provided a useful framework for thinking about the different types of distances organizations need to transverse. The framework, called CAGE, refers to the cultural, administrative/political, geographical, and economic distances. *Cultural distance* is about the differences in how people around the world communicate, learn, and work, as well as the more subtle differences in social norms, customs, and beliefs. *Administrative/political distance* refers to the different historical and political associations of people that manifest in common currencies, trading blocs, political unions, and other factors that facilitate interactions. *Geographical distance* refers to the different sizes of countries that impact how people interact within and across borders and considers the amount of miles, access to waterways, as well as transportation and communication infrastructure. Lastly, *economic distance* refers to the vast variances in wealth among different trading partners that influence the disparities and intensity of interactions.

Managing a highly ethnically and culturally diverse workforce requires management competencies that were not as important when the workplace was more homogenous. Managers must understand today's workers come to work with different experiences, values, and needs. This reality reinforces one of the continuing themes of this book that there cannot be a one-size-fits-all way of managing. There are obvious challenges such as understanding the different ways people communicate, especially for the growing number of workers whose primary language is not English. Less obvious are the cultural influences that impact how people are motivated.

In his seminal research on culture, Geert Hofstede (2001) defines culture as the "collective programming of the mind," which distinguishes one group of people from another group. It impacts how individuals perceive, process, and react to stimuli from their interactions with others and the environment. Hofstede conducted one of the most comprehensive studies of cross-cultural, work-related values. Based on an analysis of survey data of IBM's employees from around the world, he identified four dimensions of work-related values that provide insight in how culturally diverse employees perceive and respond to different managerial practices, as described in Table 3.4.

Table 3.4 Hofstede's Cross-Cultural Work-Related Values

Value Dimension	Definition
Power distance	The extent to which a society accepts that power in institutions and organizations is distributed unequally. Low power distance cultures have relatively equal power between those with status/wealth and those without status/wealth. High power distance cultures have extremely unequal power distribution between those with status/wealth and those without status/wealth.
Individualism versus collectivism	This dimension reflects the degree to which group members' actions are either independent or dependent on each other, or the degree to which people prefer to act as individuals rather than a member of groups. In collectivist societies, individuals are emotionally attached to members of their organization and expect team members to look after them and protect them.
Uncertainty avoidance	This dimension reflects the extent to which a society feels threatened by uncertain and ambiguous situations and tries to avoid them. High uncertainty avoidance societies do not like ambiguous or risky situations and try to avoid them. Low uncertainty avoidance societies do not mind risky or ambiguous situations and embrace them. Employees in high uncertainty avoidance countries will adhere to rules and be more committed to employers longer than employees in low uncertainty avoidance societies.
Masculinity versus femininity	Societies that adhere to more masculine work roles tend to value achievement, power, and control, as well as assertiveness and materialism. There is also a high differentiation between roles of men and women. Societies that adhere to more feminine work roles tend to value cooperation, collaboration, power sharing, and intrinsic rewards. These societies embrace gender diversity.

A growing challenge facing many organizations is finding global leaders who can effectively manage diverse cultures. To be effective, these leaders need to have cultural agility. *Cultural agility* is a multifaceted competency that enables people to work effectively in diverse settings and with people from multiple cultures (Caligiuri et al., 2010).

Increasing Corporate Social Responsibility

In the highly interconnected world of the 21st century, organizations must manage multiple stakeholders including employees, shareholders, customers, suppliers, and the communities where they conduct their business. With around-the-clock news outlets and multiple sources of media, organizations need to be diligent protecting their image and reputation. How companies respond to management snafus and organizational crises can have a major impact on their well-being.

In the aftermath of the financial crises, many Wall Street firms' reputations were shattered as they collectively lost more than hundreds of billions of dollars and now face more restrictive government regulations. Likewise, the Gulf of Mexico oil spill has cost British Petroleum (BP) tens of billions of dollars settling claims and restoring its reputation. The Occupy Wall Street and environmental movements have mobilized protests against these firms, making them increasingly less attractive to a growing number of workers. These examples highlight the importance of having proper corporate governance and risk management functions as part of a corporate social responsibility (CSR) strategy to proactively prevent disasters like these from occurring.

However, the approach taken at many firms for developing a CSR strategy is nothing more than creating a corporate function that focuses on communicating the activities of philanthropic and public relations programs. However, the public is demanding much higher standards across all organizational activities including marketing and product development, financial reporting, production, and human resource policies. And there are a growing number of organizations that monitor corporate activities that can report suspected wrong-doings at a moment's notice. Thus, it's critical for organizations to engage employees and leaders who act ethically while performing in their jobs. Likewise, organizations need to engage all external stake-holders to ensure they maintain a high standing in society. A success-ful CSR strategy must include developing capabilities to augment and monitor corporate decision-making. Equally important is developing capabilities to help foster and maintain effective relationships with regulators, suppliers, and the public.

Lastly, other competencies are required to promote and protect the image of the company. In addition to having systems in place to monitor internal activities, organizations need to scan and monitor external trends. They need to constantly be in front of any possible problem that can tarnish their reputation. They also need robust com-munication and public relations programs that report meaningful cor-porate initiatives.

Challenges Managing Multiple Sources of Talent

An important talent management challenge facing nearly all organizations is managing nonemployee relationships. Chapter 2 describes this growing and critical component of the workforce as contract human capital. *Contract human capital* includes a wide range of "on demand" talent organizations engaging for multiple business needs including temporary employees, consultants, and independent contractors. It also includes employees of strategic partnerships and outsourced/offshore businesses working with a client company. In all of these situations, managers must manage talent in different work arrangements with very different needs and preferences to accom-plish business objectives.

However, many organizations are ill-equipped at managing contract human capital. Mostly, talent management programs and practices are designed for the traditional employee–employer rela-tionship. The vast majority of organizations specifically avoid any direct strategic efforts for managing this growing and vital segment of their workforce mostly due to a fear of not complying with IRS and Department of Labor regulations. As a result, the department that is most involved in overseeing these work arrangements is purchasing. Indeed, the antiquated regulations governing employers' work relationships with contract human capital are quite restrictive and must be revised to reflect the new realities of the 21st century. However, organizations that manage these workers as commodities whose cost must be minimized are at a strategic disadvantage compared to those organizations that have talent management programs for multiple sources of talent.

The increasing use of contract human capital is a reflection of the new normal and structural shifts occurring in the economy and labor force. In quickly changing work environments, organizations often need talent for short periods of time, such as for project or seasonal work. In such situations, managers must quickly assemble and disassemble teams of workers when needed. At other times, organizations might seek to align fluctuating business needs with their staffing needs. Rather than embarking on a vicious cycle of hiring and firing employees, managers need scalable talent. Lastly, organizations increasingly need access to skills that might not be readily available or are too costly to develop internally. As the demand for workers with unique skills exceeds the supply of these workers, managers need to cast a wide net to capture and engage all workers who have valuable skills. Often, the individuals who have these needed skills are consultants, independent contractors, or employees at strategic partnerships.

Knowledge is also a potential source of competitive advantage at many firms. Not only must firms create knowledge within their boundaries, but they must also expose themselves to an array of new ideas from all available talent outside the organization. Contract human capital can stimulate the accumulation and creation of valuable knowledge. Many of these workers are carriers of best practices that may be unknown to employees who have worked at fewer organizations throughout their careers.

One of the challenges for organizations that manage contract human capital is due to the nature of the employment relationship itself, particularly in how it differs from regular employees.

The employment relationship between employers and employees is based on the assumption that it would continue indefinitely and be at the employer's place of business under the employer's direction. In exchange for a set wage, which helps mitigate the uncertainties of fluctuating markets, employees agree to an incomplete yet implicit contract, which gives the employer tremendous latitude in assigning different tasks as needed. The traditional employment arrangement contains all sorts of implicit (and explicit) provisions that set the boundaries to the range of actions an employee can be directed to perform.

These boundaries define the "zone of acceptance" within which an employee can be expected to follow the directions of management. The expected long-term nature of the employment relationship enables employees to be repeatedly exposed to a range of management practices and get acclimated to an organization's culture, which helps forge a strong identification with the firm. The identification with the firm along with an openness to a range of alternative behaviors create an employment relationship in which there are many ways and ample opportunities for management practices to impact employees' behaviors and performance.

Contract human capital who are employees of other firms have unique employment arrangements. These individuals simultaneously work for an employer while providing a service to a client company. These work arrangements can range from highly skilled workers of strategic partnerships performing critical tasks to low-skilled workers at outsourced businesses performing transactional tasks. In either situation, the manager at the client company is faced with the challenge of how to effectively manage and engage these nonemployee arrangements. Contract human capital who are not employees of a company are typically called temporary employees, consultants, or independent contractors. For simplicity purposes, here these individuals are referred to as *contract workers*. By now, the complexity of managing these multiple sources of talent should be obvious given the difficulty of even labeling the different types of work arrangements.

Managing contract workers poses many challenges. The employment relationship between contract workers and the firm is different than the relationship with employees and strategic partnerships. By its nature, the employment relationship with contract workers is not necessarily expected to be long term, and consequently there is no protection in the form of a guaranteed wage against fluctuating markets. As a result, much of the financial risk is transferred to these individuals, and there is less of an opportunity to develop a strong identification with the firm. These conditions may narrow these workers' "zone of acceptance," limiting the range of possible work behaviors that is acceptable to them.

Contract Human Capital Preferences

Individuals enter into different work arrangements for a variety of reasons, and these preferences differentially influence the type of relationship they seek with the client organization. For example, some individuals voluntarily seek contract work either as a means to achieve flexibility in balancing work and personal objectives, to earn more money, or to develop new skills that will help them to be more marketable. Alternatively, other individuals may be working as a contract worker involuntarily because they are unable to find a traditional job and are hopeful that contract work can be a means to finding a new job.

Individuals who need more control over their time—that is, flexibility—commonly seek contract work. Often the type of flexibility wanted is not the kind offered to employees such as flextime or telecommuting, but flexibility in which days or how long to work. Due to the sporadic nature of these work arrangements, these individuals voluntarily seek contract work. Many of these individuals need to balance personal and nonwork objectives such as pursuing educational goals, managing family and household responsibilities, or just wanting freedom to travel. The individuals who enter into these work arrangements for flexibility bring with them a wide range of skills and experience. Organizations who can manage these relationships effectively while providing the needed flexibility can significantly increase the supply of talent needed to fulfill a variety of business needs.

Other individuals may seek contract work as an opportunity to earn more money. In most cases, these are individuals who have unique skills that can be marketed to the highest bidder. These are the free agents who for various reasons no longer want a traditional work arrangement. They may have gotten tired of the politics, insecurities, and bureaucracy of corporate life. Because organizations compensate contract workers based on their economic value to the firm, they typically pay a large compensating wage differential for these highly skilled workers. You would expect individuals who prefer contract work to primarily earn more money to be highly mobile. Such individuals are likely to jump from assignment to assignment to continually increase their income. Their primary metric for judging whether their employment contracts have been fulfilled is likely to be based on the outcomes they receive in the form of pay, benefits, and the value of learning new skills.

At a time when the half-life of many skills is getting shorter and shorter, some individuals may seek contract work as a way to develop and learn new skills that would make them more employable in the future. Contract work can offer an opportunity for individuals to acquire skills and work experience that may be valuable to potential employers. Organizations that provide the right type of learning opportunities in these work arrangements can attract and engage highly motivated talent.

The dark side of contract work involves individuals who have been forced into these work arrangements involuntarily. Due to the ongoing restructuring and downsizing initiatives at many organizations, large numbers of jobs have been eliminated, leaving many unsuspecting employees in its wake. Many of these employees want traditional jobs that offer a steady income and benefits. However, given the current economic conditions, many laid-off workers cannot find jobs that offer comparable wages and benefits but need to work nonetheless. As a result, a large portion of contract workers in the United States are underemployed people who would prefer regular jobs. In these situations, these individuals are hopeful that contract work can provide them access to permanent positions.

Managing strategic partnerships and outsourced business relationships can be equally as daunting for managers who rely on these other sources of talent. Similarly with contract workers, organizations rely on these external work arrangements for performing both strategic and nonstrategic work. The focus of strategic partnerships is the coordination of knowledge work to achieve strategic objectives. These types of work arrangements require developing collaborative relationships and include processes that encourage cooperation and information sharing. Many nonstrategic outsourced business relationships involve transactional work that is highly standardized. Typically, the work performed by outsourced workers is of low value to the organization and requires general, nonspecialized skills. As such, this work is conducted at "arm's length" and requires minimal interactions with a work group.

All in all, the challenge facing many organizations is how to differentiate managing contract human capital across a range of work arrangements that can positively impact the performance of both contract human capital and the work groups they work with. Furthermore, understanding how to strategically manage this vital and growing segment of the labor force is critical for developing organizational adaptability competencies necessary for navigating the new normal.

Expanding Globally

The 21st century global marketplace provides many opportunities for organizations seeking new customers to grow revenues. However, going global poses a great deal of challenges. The logistics of running operations thousands of miles from headquarters can be daunting. You also need to be knowledgeable of the multitude of different regulations and business customs, as well as the cultural preferences of the marketplace. In particular, the regulatory climate has intensified around the world in response to a public perception that the deregulated business environment in recent decades is partly responsible for the recent global financial collapse. As a result, organizations need to strategically select the appropriate mode of entry when entering into new markets around the world.

For example, although the BRIC (Brazil, Russia, India, and China) countries' expanding markets offer the greatest economic opportunities, there are many obstacles in doing business in these countries. The most common strategy for expanding into the BRICs, as cited by CEOs in PricewaterhouseCoopers (PWC) global survey, is forming strategic alliances (PWC, 2006). The second most common strategy is growing organically by opening new offices, outsourcing, and offshoring ranked third, fourth, and fifth, respectively.

Global expansion is also increasing mergers and acquisitions (M&A) activity. During 2011, the total value of worldwide M&A totaled $2.6 trillion, a 7 percent increase over 2010 levels. Emerging-markets M&A activity accounted for 26 percent of the global total (Mitchell et al., 2012). The strategic rationale for initiating M&A activity as a mode of entry into a region differs between emerging-market acquirers and developed nation buyers. Firms in emerging markets are typically looking to acquire technological know-how and raw materials, whereas firms from developed nations are generally seeking market efficiencies and new customers.

According to a survey of CEOs conducted by The Conference Board, there is clearly not a one-size-fits all set of responses to the driving global forces shaping their organizations. Forming joint ventures in new geographies was cited as a key strategy for global expansion, whereas partnering with local businesses to mitigate risk was another strategy for dealing with global political/economic risk. However, one common theme that emerged was the world is a highly complex place that presents immense challenges but also an abundance of opportunities. According to the respondents, to be successful, organizations must foster an innovative mindset and corporate culture necessary to engage highly diverse and talented people (Mitchell et al., 2012).

The Conference Board study noted that the CEOs of each of the three regions they surveyed (including the United States, Europe, and Asia) had a unique set of challenges. For U.S. CEOs, the top challenge they listed was government regulation, followed by global political/economic risk. The divided Congress and political inertia regarding the national debt and taxation and the overall uncertainty of pending legislation that may significantly impact business were the primary drivers of their concerns. European CEOs noted that global political/economic risk was their top challenge. Their key concerns were attributable to the significant government cutbacks, reduced revenues, growing fears of another recession, and ticking demographic and unfunded pension time bombs the continent is facing.

CEOs in Asia have different concerns that reflect the region's high-growth business environment. Given the emphasis on growth, the top two challenges they listed are innovation and human capital. Their primary concerns are based on the continued large investments this region is making in R&D, the desire to expand beyond regional boundaries, and the realization that existing labor markets will not sustain the future demands for top talent. Talent management is becoming a critical challenge for companies operating in Asia. The continuing war for talent in the region is getting hotter as employment offers from domestic companies and government entities compete with those of multinational companies. As world-class firms in China and India continue to grow, the competition for top talent is significantly closing the wage gap between local firms and multinationals.

Managing International Assignees

Across all regions, there is a growing need for talent mobility to help close skill gaps and talent shortages, as well as facilitating knowledge transfer. To help organizations achieve these goals, there is a growing number of international assignees relocating around the world. At many multinational companies, having experience working in other countries is a requirement for obtaining a leadership position. International assignees, also called expatriates, are sent overseas for both business and development reasons. Organizations that develop global strategies that require standard processes need to send headquarter employees who are familiar with the company's way of doing business overseas to help transfer knowledge and manage their international locations. The 2012 survey of global relocation trends conducted by Brookfield Global Relocation Services reported that 64 percent of responding companies indicated that their international assignee population is increasing (Brookfield, 2012).

In addition to managing a larger number of international assignees, the changing demographics of these workers are creating many new challenges for multinational organizations. For the longest time, the typical international assignee was a middle-aged man. However, an increasing number of female workers are now being sent on global assignments. By 2012, 20 percent of the international assignee populations was female, a 10 percent increase from 2009. In addition to the challenges facing anyone who needs to leave familiar settings and settle in a new country with different norms and culture, there are a number of countries around the world that are not receptive to women managers, making it even more challenging for female expatriates to succeed.

Although the age group most represented continues to be those aged 40–49 (34 percent), there has been a marked increase in the number of younger workers sent on international assignments, from 9 percent to 13 percent. Younger workers may have the technical expertise that make them qualified for an international assignment but may lack the interpersonal or managerial skills required to work with new culturally diverse workers. The Brookfield study also noted that the percent of married assignees has been decreasing from 68 percent to 60 percent, which may be a sign that company policies for managing international assignees are not meeting the needs of employees with working spouses.

Most worrisome, a study conducted by the World Economic Forum in collaboration with Mercer found that fewer than one-half of companies surveyed thought they selected international assignees well, and more than one-half (63 percent) noted that poor candidate selection was the second most important cause of assignment failure. Furthermore, three-quarters of organizations surveyed classified their talent mobility practice as traditional leadership development programs (Schwab, 2012). Moving people for leadership development purposes is important; however, most of the talent needs for globally expanding firms are at all levels.

As organizations' operations become more geographically dispersed, there has also been an increased reliance on virtual teams to accomplish business objectives. Advances in computer and communication technologies have significantly increased both the use and effectiveness of virtual teams. Research reported in *The Wall Street Journal* of companies with more than 5,000 employees noted that more than one-half of these companies use virtual teams (de Lisser, 1999). A Gartner Group study found that more than 60 percent of professional employees surveyed said they have worked on a virtual team (Jones, 2004).

Organizations need to carefully select and train employees who work on virtual teams. Employees working on virtual teams interact less often and with limited forms of communication and thus are less likely to develop relationships or identify with the group. It is also more difficult for virtual team members to form deep bonds necessary for developing trusting relationships due to geographic, cultural, and other differences. Not surprisingly, conflict may be more common on virtual teams due to less collective identity, lack of social cues during communication, and less awareness of mutual context (MacDuffie, 2007).

4

The Imperative of Employee Engagement for Competitive Success in the 21st Century

In the highly complex and competitive world of the 21st century, companies need innovative management systems that engage employees to meet the demands of a highly demanding and customer-driven marketplace. As a result, defining and measuring employee engagement have become a booming business for consulting businesses. However, engagement is an elusive construct, and there seem to be as many different measures of engagement as there are consultants. Given the strategic importance of engagement, it behooves business leaders to get this right.

Many of the current measures of engagement include both the conditions and outcomes of engagement. As a result, organizations that use these types of measures cannot discern how different employees might be engaged due to different drivers and conditions. Only by developing a pure measure of engagement can organizations understand how to engage a highly diverse workforce. Then organizations can strategically identify the true linkages between employee engagement and organizational strategic outcomes.

What Is Engagement?

There is an entire cottage industry of researchers and consultants involved in helping organizations improve employee engagement. However, if you do not know what you are measuring, the action implications will be, at best, vague and, at worst, a leap of faith. Thus, it is critical to understand what exactly engagement is.

Many consider employee engagement to be a dimension of employee satisfaction and loyalty—characteristics that most companies include in their engagement measure for many years. Although correlated with engagement, satisfaction is predominately characterized as a sense of well-being and pleasantness connoting, at most, moderate levels of activation or energy. However, it is the sense of energy and enthusiasm that makes engagement different (Macey and Schneider, 2008). Loyalty or organizational commitment is an important facet of the state of engagement when it is conceptualized as an affective attachment to the organization and measured as a willingness to exert energy in support of the organization, to feel pride as an organizational member, and to have personal identification with the organization.

Indeed, engagement is an elusive construct. It's elusive because some describe it purely as a psychological state, others as a set of behaviors (behavioral engagement), and yet others consider engagement to be more of a trait or disposition (trait engagement). Others try to measure engagement by describing the drivers and outcomes. Common to these multiple definitions is the notion that employee engagement is a desirable condition, has an organizational purpose, and connotes involvement, commitment, passion, enthusiasm, focused effort, and energy, and has both attitudinal and behavioral components.

Engagement has also been defined as a force that motivates employees to higher (or lower) levels of performance, as a high internal motivational state, or in terms of high levels of activity, initiative, and responsibility (Dvir et al., 2002). Yet others define engagement as an expression of a person's preferred self in the work he does characterized as an enhanced personal presence (physical, cognitive, and emotional) and active job performances (Kahn, 1990). In this context, you see engagement defined both attitudinally and behaviorally.

Those who define *engagement* as an internal psychological state suggest that engagement is a motivational construct defined as a "positive, fulfilling, work-related state of mind that is characterized by vigor, dedication, and absorption" (Schaufeli et al., 2002 pg. 72). *Vigor* refers to high levels of energy and resilience, the willingness to invest effort in one's job, the ability to not be easily fatigued, and persistence in the face of difficulties. *Dedication* refers to a strong involvement in one's work, accompanied by feelings of enthusiasm and significance, and by a sense of pride and inspiration. Finally, *absorption* refers to a pleasant state of total immersion in one's work, which is characterized by time passing quickly and being unable to detach oneself from the job. There is considerable agreement that engagement as a psychological state has a strong affective tone connoting, at a minimum, high levels of involvement (passion and absorption) in the work and the organization (pride and identity) as well as affective energy (enthusiasm and alertness) and a sense of self-presence in the work.

Being invigorated and absorbed in one's work comes close to what has been called "flow," a state of optimal experience characterized by focused attention, clear mind, mind and body union, and intrinsic enjoyment (Csikszentmihalyi, 1990). Often you hear the term used in sports as when a basketball player just seems to block out all distractions and make every shot. However, as it relates to engagement, flow is a more complex concept that includes many aspects and often refers to short-term peak experiences, whereas engagement typifies a more pervasive and persistent state of mind. Psychological state engagement can be conceptualized as an antecedent of behavioral engagement, defined in terms of discretionary effort.

Those who define engagement behaviorally consider engagement in terms of "high levels of activity, initiative, and responsibility" (Dvir et al., 2002 pg. 737). Behavioral engagement is also defined in terms of the discretionary effort put forth by individuals. Such behaviors are typically not prescribed and go beyond preserving the status quo and instead focus on initiating and fostering change. This is closely related to another construct labeled organizational citizenship behavior. *Organizational citizenship behavior (OCB)* is defined as behaviors that are discretionary and not explicitly rewarded but can help improve organizational functioning. It's discretionary because the behavior is not an enforceable requirement of the role or the job description; rather, the behavior is a matter of personal choice.

Researchers have identified five dimensions of OCB: altruism, generalized compliance, sportsmanship, courtesy, and civic virtue. This type of behavior is a consequence of other-serving rather than self-serving motivation (Organ, 1997). OCB has also been defined as "contextual performance" or non-task as opposed to task (in-role) performance. Contextual performance includes volunteering for activities beyond one's job responsibilities, persistence of enthusiasm and application when needed to complete important task requirements, providing assistance to others, following rules and procedures even if it's inconvenient, and openly espousing and defending organization objectives.

Those who believe that engagement is a disposition (that is, trait engagement) regard engagement as an inclination or orientation to experience the world from a particular vantage point (for example, positive affectivity characterized by feelings of enthusiasm), and this trait gets reflected in a psychological state called engagement (Macey and Schneider, 2008). Trait engagement is composed of a number of interrelated personality attributes, including trait positive affectivity, conscientiousness, proactive and autotelic personality. All these personality traits suggest an inclination to experience work in a positive, active, and energetic way and to behave adaptively. Trait engagement is also highly related to work centrality, otherwise known as work involvement. Work centrality represents the enduring willingness of an individual to put forth effort toward their career success.

Lastly, other researchers consider engagement to be a multidimensional construct that is composed of all these dimensions. The question remains as to whether engagement is a unique concept or merely a repackaging of other constructs. Many consulting firms focus on the concept of engagement as encompassing, in some combination, affective commitment (for example, pride in the organization and willingness to recommend the organization as an employer), continuance commitment (for example, intentions to remain with the organization), discretionary effort (for example, feeling inspired by the organization, being willing to go above and beyond formal role requirements), and job satisfaction (for example, a sense of contentment and happiness).

Burnout

A good way to understand engagement is to understand what it is not. A lack of engagement can be described as a lack of positive energy toward work and the organization itself, or as a continuum extending from engagement to the absence of engagement to active disengagement, where employees may invest in efforts to undermine the organization. Some consider a lack of engagement to be the result of depleting a limited amount of energy people possess that they can direct toward work activity, suggesting that engagement in some roles comes at the expense of engagement in other roles (Rothbard, 2001).

If engagement requires a degree of energy, it stands to reason that the opposite of engagement can be described as burnout. *Burnout* is a reaction to chronic occupational stress resulting in the draining of physical, cognitive, and emotional resources and characterized by emotional exhaustion and cynicism, that is, a negative, callous, and cynical attitude toward one's job. Occupational stress can be caused by a number of factors including conflicting work roles, poor relationships with management and coworkers, job insecurity, and excessive workload.

In a *USA Today* article, Rebecca Ray, coauthor of a 2012 study on job satisfaction from the Conference Board, based on a survey of 5,000 U.S. households, found only one-third (33 percent) of workers were satisfied with their workload. Other key findings included that 63 percent report they have high levels of stress at work, with extreme fatigue and feeling out of control; 53 percent take frequent "stress breaks" at work; 39 percent cite workload as the top cause of stress; and almost one-half (46 percent) indicate that stress was one of the most common reasons for absence, ahead of medical reasons or caregiving responsibilities. "You can't have massive restructuring and reductions in force without having the workload become a massive issue," Ray says. "Until they're hiring again and bringing some additional capacity into the workplace, we're going to see a continuation of feelings of burnout that we see now" (Jayson, 2012 pg. 1).

Research on the causes of burnout (Maslach et al., 2001) noted that burnout arises from chronic mismatches between people and their work setting in six areas.

1. Workload

Too many demands can exhaust an individual's energy to the extent that recovery becomes difficult. A workload mismatch, as when people lack the skills or inclination for performing certain work, can also wear a person down. Lastly, emotional work can also be especially draining, as when the work requires individuals to display emotions inconsistent with their feelings.

2. Control

Lack of control is related to the inefficacy or reduced personal accomplishment aspect of burnout. For example, individuals who have insufficient control over the resources needed to do their work or have insufficient authority to perform the work in the way they would like to. It can be quite stressful when individuals are overwhelmed by their level of responsibility or when one's responsibility exceeds one's authority. It is also distressing for people to feel responsible for producing results to which they are deeply committed while lacking the capacity to deliver.

3. Reward

A mismatch can occur when there is a lack of an appropriate reward for the work people do. This can be financial, as when people are not receiving the salary or benefits commensurate with their achievements. Or it can be the lack of social rewards, as when one's hard work is ignored and not appreciated. This lack of recognition devalues both the work and the workers. In addition, the lack of intrinsic rewards (such as pride in doing something of importance and doing it well) can also be a critical part of this mismatch.

4. Community

Individuals who lose a sense of positive connection with others in the workplace will begin to feel alienated. People seek an emotional exchange and instrumental assistance from their workgroup, which is a kind of social support that reaffirms a person's membership in a group with a shared sense of values. Jobs that isolate people from each other or make social contact impersonal can sever people's social connections. Chronic and unresolved conflict with others can be destructive to workers' sense of community.

5. Fairness

A serious mismatch between the person and the job can occur when there is a lack of perceived fairness in the workplace. Fairness communicates respect and confirms people's self-worth. Mutual respect between people is central to a shared sense of community. Unfairness can occur when there is inequity of workload or pay, when there is cheating, or when evaluations and promotions are handled inappropriately. If procedures for grievance or dispute resolution do not allow for both parties to have a voice, then those will be judged as unfair. Unfair treatment is emotionally upsetting and exhausting and can fuel a deep sense of cynicism about the workplace.

6. Values

A conflict between the values of the individual and the organization can create disharmony. People can also be caught between conflicting values of the organization, as when there is a discrepancy between the lofty mission statement and actual practice, or when the values are in conflict, such as simultaneously seeking high-quality service and cost containment.

Why Is Engagement So Important?

In a world that is changing both in terms of the complexity of work and diversity of the labor force, having engaged employees is necessary for creating a sustainable competitive advantage. Companies that understand the drivers and conditions that enhance employee engagement will have accomplished something that competitors will find difficult to imitate.

It is difficult to precisely specify workers' roles and responsibilities in a work environment that is constantly changing. To the extent that employees are likely to be faced more frequently with unanticipated and ambiguous decision-making situations, organizations count on them to act in ways consistent with organizational objectives. In an economy dominated by the service and knowledge sectors, it is a strategic imperative to have engaged employees who can excel in fast changing work environments. Nowhere is this more evident than in the United States where more than 79 percent of the economy is classified as services and knowledge work (Central Intelligence Agency, 2008).

In the 21st century workplace, it's also becoming increasingly difficult for organizations to anticipate and respond to unforeseen critical developments that impact customer relationships, product development, and organizational effectiveness. Organizations need engaged workers who can think on their feet when confronted with unexpected challenges and can go above and beyond their explicit job responsibilities when needed. The need to enhance employee engagement has captured the attention of managers insofar as it raises the notion of cooperation to a higher level, made all the more important in the context of growing competitive pressures and more rapid change.

Organizational researchers have long recognized that organizations cannot function through purely transactional relationships with all employees. Organizations require cooperation from employees and other sources of talent rather than mere compliance. In addition, many employees look for work environments in which they can be engaged and feel that they can contribute in a positive way to something larger than themselves. To that end, engagement can be described as the extent to which employees are motivated to perform at a high level and be advocates for the firm's products and services. However, the redefinition of the social contract surrounding the employment relationship makes engagement a more pressing concern. As the old loyalty-for-security bargain has been cast aside, individuals and organizations are more tenuously connected. The challenge then is developing innovative talent management systems that can engage the multiple sources of talent working in an array of employment arrangements.

The benefits of having engaged workers that contribute to organizational success are predicated on managers who can effectively motivate all workers by creating a stimulating and rewarding work environment. As an old saying goes, employees join great companies but leave poor managers. That is, employees are attracted to and join companies for a variety of both idealistic and practical reasons. But, invariably, their working lives revolve around their interactions with their manager and coworkers that can either engage them or demotivate them, causing them ultimately to leave the company or to hang around unproductively.

The realization that the effective management of workers is a necessary component for creating a sustainable competitive advantage has elevated the Human Resource (HR) management function to the strategic apex of the organization. For decades, many organizations achieved a competitive advantage via their financial, operational, and technological resources. However, in today's hypercompetitive markets, it depends less on advantages associated with economies of scale, technology, patents, and access to capital and more on innovation, speed, and adaptability.

More important, it is easy for a competitor to duplicate a competitor's strategy that primarily is based on the deployment of tangible assets. Yet, it is the inability of current and potential competitors to duplicate a firm's strategy that makes competitive advantage sustainable. Organizational strategies based on the deployment of intangible assets including intellectual and social and human capital are much more difficult to duplicate. Complex behavioral systems within organizations are difficult for other firms to observe and even more difficult to replicate, which make HR strategies an important source of a sustained competitive advantage. Sustainable competitive advantage therefore comes from aligning the skills, motives, and opportunities of employees with organizational systems, structures, and processes that achieve capabilities at the organizational level (Hamel and Prahalad, 1994).

If an organization's intangible assets are critical components of competitive advantage, then it's a strategic imperative for organizations to have highly engaged workers. Furthermore, any organizational strategy is worthless if it is not effectively implemented. An organization needs engaged employees to effectively execute its strategy. Strategy implementation is based on a firm's strategic capabilities, which are distinguishable from resources and are embedded in the firm's human capital and organizational processes.

An HR system enables sustainable competitive advantage to the extent that it helps create a workforce whose contributions are valuable, unique, and difficult for competitors to imitate. Because of the social complexity and causal ambiguity inherent in strategic HR management (HRM) practices such as team-based designs, empowerment, and the development of talent, competitors can neither easily copy these practices nor readily replicate the unique pool of human capital that such practices help to create (Huselid et al., 1997).

There is a large body of research linking strategic HR systems and firm performance. The "black box" between the two represents the attitudes and motivations of workers—employee engagement. Thus, this linkage is based on an organization's capability to design and implement HR systems that engage employees to perform. Firm performance is based on the aggregate sum of the employees' performance. Engaged employees have lower turnover and absenteeism and are motivated to behave in ways that are beneficial to the organization. This in turn results in more macro-level outcomes associated with aggregates of individual efforts, such as indicators of productivity, quality of products, and customer satisfaction. These efforts in turn result in financial and accounting outcomes, such as return on equity (ROE), return on assets (ROA), and profitability. Lastly, the most distal outcomes are capital market outcomes, such as stock price and market valuations.

What Is Wrong with Current Measures?

There is still much debate on what exactly engagement is and consequently how to measure it. Many consultants conveniently avoid defining the term and instead refer only to its presumed positive antecedents or consequences, which are much easier to measure. For example, one of the most popular employee engagement measures used by many organizations is the Gallup's Q12 model shown in Table 4.1. The Gallup measure was designed to measure attitudinal outcomes (satisfaction, loyalty, pride, customer service intent, and intent to stay with company) and measure or identify issues within a manager's control that are antecedents to attitudinal outcomes (Harter et al., 2002). The model has 12 measures plus a measure of satisfaction.

Table 4.1 Gallup Workplace Audit (GWA) Items

1.	How satisfied are you with (the company) as a place to work?
2.	I know what is expected of me at work.
3.	I have the material and equipment I need to do my work right.
4.	At work, I have the opportunity to do what I do best every day.
5.	In the last 7 days, I have received recognition or praise for doing good work.
6.	My supervisor, or someone at work, seems to care about me as a person.
7.	There is someone at work who encourages my development.
8.	At work, my opinions seem to count.
9.	The mission/purpose of my company makes me feel my job is important.
10.	My associates (fellow employees) are committed to doing quality work.
11.	I have a best friend at work.
12.	In the last 6 months, someone at work talked to me about my progress.
13.	This last year, I have had opportunities at work to learn and grow.

This model is a good measure of employee satisfaction and important actionable aspects of the work environment that lead to employee engagement. However, surveys that ask employees to describe their work conditions may be relevant for assessing the conditions that provide for engagement but do not directly measure engagement.

A comprehensive review of 12 major studies conducted by top research firms on employee engagement conducted by the Conference Board highlights the inconsistencies among researchers in how engagement is measured (Gibbons, 2006). Each of the studies in this report used different definitions and measures of employee engagement and collectively came up with 26 key drivers of engagement. The study defined employee engagement as a heightened emotional and intellectual connection that an employee has for her job, organization, manager, and coworkers that, in turn, influences her to apply additional discretionary effort to her work.

Across all studies there were eight drivers of engagement that stood out:

1. **Trust and integrity**—Applies to the degree to which employees feel that members of the management team are concerned about their well-being, tell the truth, communicate difficult

messages well, listen to employees and then follow through with action, and demonstrate the company's expressed goals and values through their own personal behavior.

2. **Nature of the job**—Refers to the day-to-day content and routine of the employee's job and the degree to which he derives emotional and mental stimulation from it. This includes opportunities to participate in decision-making and autonomy.

3. **Line-of-sight between individual performance and company performance**—Refers to how well the employee understands the company's goals, is aware of its overall performance, and, most important, knows how her individual contribution impacts this performance.

4. **Career growth opportunities**—The degree to which an employee feels that there are future opportunities for career growth and promotion within the company and, to a lesser degree, is aware of a clearly defined career path.

5. **Pride about the company**—Refers to the amount of self-esteem an employee derives from being associated with her company. This driver has been linked to behaviors such as recommending the company to prospective customers and employees.

6. **Coworkers/team members**—Recognizes the significance of the influence that an employee's colleagues have on his level of employee engagement.

7. **Employee development**—As opposed to career growth opportunities, this driver refers to the degree to which employees feel that specific efforts are being made by their company or manager to develop the employees' skills.

8. **Personal relationship with one's manager**—The degree to which an employee values the relationship that she has with her direct manager. This does not refer to professional or job-related aspects of her relationship.

This is an excellent study that clearly separates the measure of employee engagement and the antecedents (drivers) of engagement. However, countless organizational measures of engagement often include both the drivers and outcomes of engagement. It's important to separate these measures to discern which drivers have the greatest impact on engagement for different employees and organizational outcomes. Another problem is how many direct measures of engagement include the wrong attitudinal measures. For example, two attitudinal measures of employee engagement found in many organizations' employee engagement surveys include measures of employee job satisfaction and continuance commitment, which focus on employees' intention to remain with the company. Yet, the research correlating job satisfaction and job performance has mixed results, and a number of studies found a negative relationship between continuance commitment and job performance.

The Hawthorne studies in the 1930s are commonly credited with emphasizing the linkage between employee attitudes and performance. However, subsequent research over the years has not provided conclusive confirmation or disconfirmation of the job satisfaction–job performance relationship. Some studies have shown that job satisfaction and job performance are reciprocally related. Perhaps employees who perform well are satisfied and those who are not performing well are less satisfied. Other studies indicate that the relationship between job satisfaction and job performance is moderated by other variables. Lastly, a number of studies have shown there is no relationship between job satisfaction and job performance (Judge et al., 2001). As any manager knows, it is quite possible to have content employees who perform poorly, which is why satisfaction does not capture the essence of engagement, which has a high correlation with job performance.

Continuous commitment by definition is negatively related to turnover. However, it is also highly likely that some employees who have no intention of leaving are poor performers who do not have any other choice but to stay. Rather than use continuance commitment in an engagement measure, a better measure would include affective commitment. Employees who want to belong to the organization (affective commitment) rather than those who need to belong (continuance commitment) are more likely to perform well.

Another concern regarding how to measure engagement is to ensure the focus is on the right level of analysis. Many organizational surveys measure employee engagement at the individual level of analysis but make references and conclusions at the organizational level. The organizational level applies to any meaningful unit above the individual, for example, work group, department, division, and so on. If you analyze the antecedents (for example, work conditions and leadership) and consequences (organizational effectiveness) of engagement at the organizational level of analysis, it is logical to also conceptualize and measure engagement at the organizational level (Pugh and Dietz, 2008).

Using poor measures also jeopardizes organizations' abilities for assessing how employee engagement levels impact the attainment of strategic objectives. As director for Rutgers University Center for HR Strategy, I convened an employee engagement working group consisting of a number of large global firms. One firm in particular was interested in understanding a number of inconsistencies when analyzing their engagement survey results. The division with the highest aggregate engagement score had lower customer satisfaction ratings than the division with the lowest aggregate engagement score. These findings contradict everything we know about the relationship between engaged employees and customer satisfaction.

There were two problems with their analysis. One was they were aggregating individual engagement measures rather than measuring the engagement climate for the division. This is not an uncommon problem. Many organizations aggregate all individual survey responses as a proxy for measuring engagement at the work group or organizational level. However, the average of all individual responses at a particular organizational level may differ from a true organizational level of analysis. The organizational level includes different aspects such as social norms and team dynamics that are not included when measuring individual levels.

If each individual response in a work group were measured as having a high level of engagement, then you cannot aggregate these responses to assume a high level of engagement for the work group. If the focus is at the work group level, then each individual should be asked to assess the level of engagement for the work group, and the aggregate of these responses may be quite different than the aggregate of individual measures. For example, ask respondents to describe what they see in the behavior of others within their work unit (helping others, persistence, and taking initiative). The aggregate of these responses is a better measure of the organizational climate for engagement. For example, you and many of your team members may feel individually engaged, but you may not rate the level of engagement of the team as equally high. This may look like splitting hairs, but it is an important factor to consider when using engagement results to assess organizational strategic outcomes.

The second problem with the working group firm's analysis was making an organizational generalization with not enough data. Like many other organizations, this organization was interested in the relationship between employee engagement and customer satisfaction. However, the customer satisfaction ratings were only available at the divisional level. This organization had four divisions. Thus, the organizational analysis was based on a sample of four. Without getting too geeky here, you cannot draw any reasonable statistical conclusions with only a sample of four. The common thinking is you should have at least 30 samples to have confidence that the relationships you assess are valid.

In a subsequent engagement survey, after rewording their employee survey questions (at the group level) and aggregating customer satisfaction ratings at the departmental level (there were 55 departments), the analysis made business sense. They demonstrated that those departments that had the highest engagement scores also had the highest customer satisfaction ratings. Also, because their employee engagement measure did not include the drivers of engagement, they could analyze which drivers had the greatest impact in each department.

Indeed, there were different drivers that enhanced engagement within different departments. In some departments, it was rewards and benefits; in other departments, it was developmental opportunities. By separating the true measure of engagement and the many different drivers of engagement, they surgically analyzed the specific management practices and programs that had the greatest impact on employees' engagement working in different parts of the organization.

Most important, because they could now show executive management that there is a strong relationship between employee engagement and strategic outcomes, they could make the necessary investments and changes to management practices for the benefit of both employees and the business.

Employee Engagement Measure

Before organizations can understand how to enhance employee engagement to achieve strategic outcomes, they need a pure measure of engagement. However, as previously stated, there are a multitude of different measures of engagement that commonly include both the drivers and outcomes. Engagement is a psychological state, separate from its drivers and outcomes. It is what many researchers have called the "black box" (see Figure 4.1).

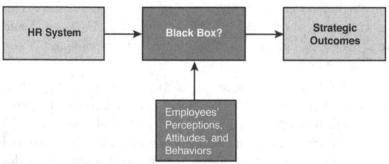

Figure 4.1 What is employee engagement?

There is a large body of research linking various management practices and programs (drivers) and various organizational outcomes such as customer satisfaction and financial performance. However, much of this research failed to address how this occurs. At a micro level, it seems there is a black box that consists of employees' perceptions, attitudes, and behaviors that is the key link between these drivers and outcomes. You can take this one step further and separate employees' perceptions and attitudes, which are a psychological state, and employee behaviors that result in achieving strategic outcomes.

Psychological State Engagement

Engagement as a psychological state has embraced several related ideas representing some form of job involvement (passion and absorption), affective commitment (pride and identity), and positive affectivity (enthusiasm and alertness). These collective measures provide an excellent measure of employee engagement.

Job Involvement

Job involvement refers to identification with and interest in one's work and is an important facet of the psychological state of engagement (Macey and Schneider, 2008). Job involvement has been considered the key to activating employee motivation. From an individual perspective, it has also been considered a key to personal growth and satisfaction within the workplace, as well as with motivation and goal-directed behavior (Hackman and Lawler, 1971, Kahn, 1990). A state of involvement implies a positive and relatively complete state of engagement of core aspects of the self in the job (Kanungo, 1982).

Individuals who have high job involvement may also experience a sense of "flow" defined as a holistic sensation that people feel when they are immersed in what they are doing and act with total involvement (Csikszentmihalyi, 1990). When individuals are in a flow state, little conscious control is necessary for their actions and time seems to fly by. As a result, they are able to narrow their attention to specific stimuli and be totally engaged in the activity they are focusing on. Individuals in a flow experience do not need external rewards to motivate them as the activity itself presents constant challenges.

Job involvement is closely related to job absorption. Absorption is an active cognitive state that reflects intensity and attention. Absorption means being engrossed in a role and refers to the intensity of one's focus on a role (Kahn, 1990). Clearly this is one of the reasons why there is a high correlation between engagement and job performance. Attention refers to cognitive availability and the amount of time one spends thinking about a role. Attention and absorption components of engagement are closely related because they both represent motivational constructs, specifically, the motivation to act.

Affective Commitment

Organizational commitment can be conceptualized three different ways including as affective commitment, continuance commitment, and normative commitment (Meyer and Allen, 1991). Employees with a strong affective commitment remain with the organization because they *want* to, those with a strong continuance commitment remain because they *need* to, and those with a strong normative commitment remain because they *ought* to.

The bases for the development of affective commitment are personal involvement, identification with the relevant target, and value congruence (Becker, 1960). In contrast, normative commitment develops as a function of cultural and organizational socialization, and the receipt of benefits that activate a need to reciprocate (Wiener, 1982). Continuance commitment develops as the result of accumulated investments, or side bets that would be lost if the individual discontinued a course of action, and as a result of alternatives to the present course (Becker, 1960).

Research shows that affective commitment has the strongest and most favorable correlations with aspects of engagement and consequently with job performance, OCBs, attendance, and intentions to stay. Normative commitment had moderate correlations. Most interesting, continuance commitment tends to be unrelated, or negatively related, to these behaviors (Meyer et al., 1989).

Thus, only affective commitment is a component of the measure of psychological state engagement. Affective commitment is an important facet of the state of engagement when it is conceptualized as a positive attachment to the larger organizational entity and measured as a willingness to exert energy in support of the organization to feel pride as an organizational member and to have personal identification with the organization. The concept of reciprocity has been postulated as a mechanism by which affective commitment is translated into behavior. The motive arising from affective commitment might best be described as a desire to contribute to the well-being of the organization to maintain equity in a mutually beneficial association.

Affective commitment is also highly correlated with organizational identification. Identification occurs when people adopt attitudes and behaviors to be associated with a satisfying, self-defining relationship with another person or group. Employees who understand and believe in the organization's strategy and values take pride in being a part of the organization. As a result, employees would want to remain with the organization and exert effort on behalf of the organization because of the benefits they derive from the relationship. When employees identify with the organizations because of congruence of interests and values, they become more engaged and committed to helping the organization achieve its goals.

Positive Affectivity

Positive affectivity is another important component of psychological state engagement. It reflects a more positive and energetic state of mind as compared to satisfaction. The descriptors used to characterize positive affectivity include among others attentive, alert, enthusiastic, inspired, proud, determined, strong, and active (Watson et al., 1980). This is also reflected in the definition of engagement posited by Schaufeli, Bakker, and Salanova (2006) as a persistent, positive affective–motivational state of fulfillment in employees that is characterized by vigor, dedication, and absorption. Other researchers have shown that employees who are personally engaged in their work use varying degrees of their selves, physically, cognitively, and emotionally, in the roles they perform, and the more they draw on their selves to perform their roles, the more stirring are their performances (Kahn, 1990).

Collectively, these three dimensions (job involvement, affective commitment, and positive affectivity) capture the essence of psychological state engagement. Furthermore, there are elements of each dimension that can be combined to develop a pure measure of engagement including organizational identification (OI), vigor (VI), dedication (DE), absorbed (AB), and affective commitment (AC). Working with professors Stan Gully and Jean Philips at Rutgers University Center for HR Strategy, we developed a parsimonious 15-item measure of engagement that incorporates these dimensions. Two variations of the measure were developed: one measuring individual engagement, which should be used when assessing individual outcomes, for example, turnover, employee productivity, and so on (see Table 4.2) and another measuring collective engagement, which should be used when assessing group or organizational outcomes, for example, production, revenues, and so on (see Table 4.3).

Table 4.2 Individual Engagement (Used for Individual Outcomes)

1.	When I talk about this company, I usually say "we" rather than "they." (OI)
2.	I believe this company's successes are my successes. (OI)
3.	When someone praises this company, it feels like a personal compliment. (OI)
4.	At my work, I feel energetic. (VI)
5.	At my work, I always persevere, even when things do not go well. (VI)
6.	I am enthusiastic about my job. (DE)
7.	My job inspires me. (DE)
8.	When I get up in the morning, I feel like going to work. (VI)
9.	I feel happy when I am working intensely. (AB)
10.	I am proud of the work that I do. (DE)
11.	I am immersed in my work. (AB)
12.	I get carried away when I am working. (AB)
13.	I really feel as if this organization's problems are my own. (AC)
14.	This organization has a great deal of personal meaning for me. (AC)
15.	I would be very happy to spend the rest of my career with this organization. (AC)

Table 4.3 Collective Engagement (Used for Group/Organizational Outcomes)

1.	When talking about this company, members of my work group usually say "we" rather than "they." (OI)
2.	Members of my work group believe this company's successes are their successes. (OI)
3.	When someone praises this company, members of my work group take it as a personal compliment. (OI)
4.	Members of my work group feel energetic. (VI)
5.	Members of my work group always persevere even when things do not go well. (VI)
6.	Members of my work group feel enthusiastic about their jobs. (DE)
7.	Members of my work group are inspired by their jobs. (DE)
8.	When we get up in the morning, members of my work group feel like going to work. (VI)
9.	Members of my work group feel happy when they are working intensely. (AB)
10.	Members of my work group are proud of the work that they do. (DE)
11.	Members of my work group are immersed in their work. (AB)
12.	Members of my work group get carried away when they are working. (AB)
13.	Members of my work group really feel as if this organization's problems are their own. (AC)
14.	This organization has a great deal of meaning to everyone in my work group. (AC)
15.	Members of my work group would be very happy to spend the rest of their careers with this organization. (AC)

5

Leveraging What We Know: An Employee Engagement Framework

Armed with a true measure of engagement, you can now describe the drivers, conditions, and outcomes of engagement. By separating these components of engagement, organizations can assess how different management practices and programs, and different work environments, impact employee engagement and important organizational outcomes. This chapter integrates a large body of cutting-edge research on engagement into a strategic framework. This framework demonstrates the entire engagement process: Human Resource (HR) systems—drivers of engagement—conditions of engagement—employee engagement—behavioral outcomes—strategic outcomes—financial outcomes, and the moderating effect of trait engagement, as shown in Figure 5.1. Such a framework can help organizations understand the dynamic processes of employee engagement necessary for effectively engaging a highly diverse workforce.

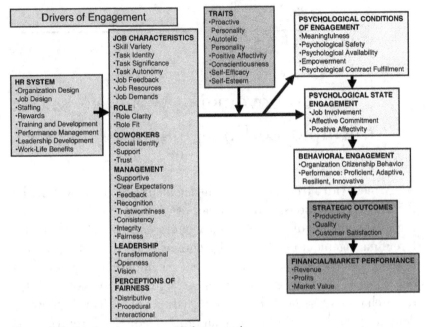

Figure 5.1 Employee engagement framework

HR Systems

The organization's HR system is the primary driver of employee engagement. An HR system consists of internally and externally aligned HR practices. Internally aligned practices complement one another producing synergistic results. Externally aligned practices are designed to help the organization respond to various business and environmental challenges. As shown in Figure 5.2, an HR system refers to how different HR practices are used in combination to address three primary issues: employee competencies, employee attitudes and behaviors, and the work environment. For example, an organization's staffing, training, and development practices contribute to the development of employee competencies that enhance competitive advantage and help to ensure a good organization and employee fit. Rewards, benefits, and performance management practices help motivate employees to behave in ways that benefit the organization. Organizational and job designs help create the proper work environment conducive to employees' development and organizational effectiveness.

An **HR system** refers to how different HR practices are used in combination to address three primary issues:

Recruitment, Selection, Training, and Development

Work Environment

Job Design
Organizational Structure
Participation/Empowerment

Employee Competencies

Employee Attitudes and Behaviors

Incentives and Rewards
Performance Evaluation and Appraisal
Compensation

Figure 5.2 What is an HR system?

There has been a debate in management research regarding whether there is a universal or best practice approach for developing HR systems or whether HR systems should be customized for specific organizational contingencies. Proponents of a *universal perspective* of HR argue that certain HR practices tend to achieve competitive advantages across all organizations. In other words, these HR practices are considered the "best practices" that will work in most organizations.

The *contingency perspective,* on the other hand, holds that the effects of HR practices vary depending on the context, which is also referred to as *external fit.* The context can be internal organizational context such as company strategy, life-cycle stage, culture, technology, structure, and so on or external environmental context such as industry, economy, national culture, and such. In general, fit is defined as the degree to which the needs, demands, goals, objectives, and structure of one component of an organization are congruent with the needs, demands, goals, objectives, and structure of another component of the organization.

The strategic HR management (HRM) research highlights a number of HR systems consisting of different HR practices that are argued to achieve a range of business objectives. For example, the goal of control HR systems (Arthur, 1994) is to reduce costs or improve operational efficiency and consist of narrowly defined jobs, lower skill demands, and minimal training that result in a transactional employment relationship. Alternatively, the goal of high-commitment HR systems is to motivate employees to identify with organizational goals and consists of HR practices such as highly selective staffing, intensive training, and high level of compensation that result in a relational employment relationship. High performance work systems (Huselid, 1995) strive to improve the knowledge, skills, and abilities of a firm's employees and contain elements of both high-commitment and high-involvement HR systems and consist of such practices as selective staffing, intensive training, performance appraisal, information sharing, and so on.

Somewhat integrating both views, the *configurational perspective* is concerned with how the pattern of multiple HR practices is related to performance. The configurational perspective differs from the universalistic and contingency perspectives in that it is guided by a holistic approach in which there can be specific configurations or "bundles" of HR practices that enhance firm performance. The *architectural perspective* extends this view and suggests that not all employees within a single organization are managed by the same HRM practices (Lepak and Snell, 1999). In other words, there is not a one-size-fits-all way for managing workers.

The HR Architecture

Lepak and Snell (1999) developed a contingency framework called the HR architecture that is particularly relevant for managing the 21st century workforce as shown in Figure 5.3. The framework consists of a portfolio of different HR configurations for managing human capital (HC) based on their value and uniqueness in relation to achieving the firm's strategy. The resulting four HR configurations are differentiated in terms of employment modes (externalized versus internalized) and employment relationship (relational versus transactional). In this model, work that is of low strategic value to the organization is externalized, whereas, work that is of high strategic value is internalized. The organization does not need to control all the work activities of individuals performing work that is not adding strategic value. This type of work can be externalized and performed by strategic partners or contract workers.

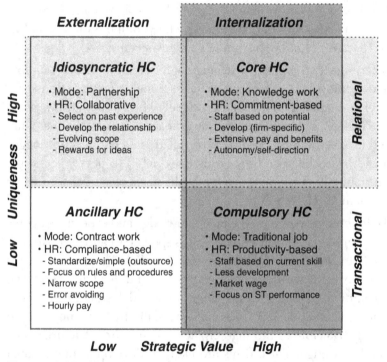

Figure 5.3 The HR architecture

Data Source: Lepak, D.P., & Snell, S.A. 1999. "The human resource architect: Toward a theory of human capital allocation and development." *Academy of Management Review*, 24: 31–48.

Externalization of work can enable the firm to decrease overhead and administrative costs, enhance organizational flexibility, and provide access to competencies and capabilities when needed that are not critical to the success of the organization. Alternatively, work that contributes to the competitive advantage of the firm must be internalized and controlled. The benefits of internal employment include greater stability and utilization of a firm's stock of skills and capabilities, better coordination and control of work processes necessary to execute the business strategy, and enhanced socialization of team members. This type of work should be performed by employees.

The type of employment relationship between workers and the firm is based on the level of uniqueness of workers' human capital. An employment relationship is based on the "psychological contract" of individual beliefs, shaped by the organization, regarding terms of an exchange agreement between individuals and their organizations (Rousseau, 1995). Work status (regular employee versus contract worker) is a major determinant of this exchange agreement because it influences perceptions of obligations such as compensation, benefits, access to training, and opportunities for advancement.

There are two types of exchange agreements between employers and employees: transactional and relational contracts (Rousseau, 1995). Transactional contracts are typically, though not always, short term (ST), have a primarily economic or materialistic focus, and entail limited involvement by both parties. Relational contracts are longer term and broad because they are not restricted to purely economic exchange but also include terms for loyalty in exchange for security or growth in an organization.

Uniqueness is based on the tacit knowledge and expertise or complex and ambiguous social capital that is specific to a firm. Firms are not likely to find these skills in the open market. Thus, firms should develop a relational employment contract with individuals who bring unique human capital to the organization and foster a committed and engaged relationship. Alternatively, skills that are not unique are widely available in the marketplace and require standardized or general knowledge. Thus, firms are likely to develop a transactional employment contract with individuals whose skills are not unique, and the relationship is based on a "quid pro quo" economic exchange.

Within this framework, human capital that is highly valuable and highly unique is considered *core human capital* engaged to perform knowledge work. Organizations manage these workers with commitment-based HR systems. The organization should invest in the development of these employees, particularly in areas related to firm-specific skills. As the focus is on the development and utilization of proprietary knowledge, managers are likely to structure knowledge work to allow for flexibility, change, and adaptation. To maximize their contributions, firms are likely to empower these workers, encouraging participation in decision-making and discretion on the job. Staffing decisions focus on aptitude rather than achievement. Given the importance of learning, performance appraisals focus on development and feedback. Compensation will be heavily based on knowledge-based pay that rewards employees for accumulating multiple skills, as well as equity-based pay to reinforce long-term commitment.

On the opposite end of this framework, human capital that has low value and uniqueness is considered *ancillary human capital* hired to perform contract work. Organizations manage these workers with compliance-based HR systems. Organizations typically contract out this work and manage these standardized transactions to ensure contract compliance. Here, firms simply focus on the economic aspects of the employment contract and strive to ensure worker compliance with present rules, regulations, and procedures. Performance is based on measurable results of specific tasks, and compensation is based on the going market rate.

For human capital that is unique, yet not critical, to the firm's strategy, this framework specifies establishing alliances with external partners. Firms manage these relationships with collaborative HR systems. Firms need to invest heavily in developing effective collaborative relationships with these partners, oriented toward sharing information and developing trust between partners. Given the need for joint production (a characteristic that distinguishes alliance partners from contract work), managers would likely recruit/select partners who can integrate their knowledge and experience into the firm. Firms will invest heavily in the relationship itself rather than developing the alliance partner's human capital. Evaluations would emphasize developmental issues such as the extent of knowledge-sharing and the evolution of the relationship. Compensation would be based on established collective incentives that encourage both parties to share and transfer information.

Lastly, human capital that possess skills and knowledge that are of high value to the organization yet are general and abundant in the marketplace are considered *compulsory human capital* engaged to work in traditional jobs. Because their skills are transferable, firms are unlikely to make the same level of investments in these workers as with knowledge workers. These employees are managed with productivity-based HR systems in which the employment relationship is designed to last as long as it serves the needs of both parties. Given the focus on productivity, these employees are paid market-based wages, and appraisals are based primarily on job performance. Here, you have a buy versus a make decision for human capital. Rather than developing generic skills, firms will opt to acquire individuals who already possess the needed skills. Given that these individuals may leave, many of these jobs are likely to be standardized to facilitate more rapid replacement.

The architectural framework offers a unique perspective on the HRM systems: performance relationship. First, though employees vary in their strategic value to a firm, all employees have the potential to impact a firm's bottom line. This is particularly relevant for firms that use multiple employment modes consisting of employees and contract human capital. Second, it may be that the configuration of HRM systems used for different employee groups, rather than a single HRM system, impacts performance.

The bottom line is all roads to employee engagement begin with the thoughtful development of strategic HR systems. Over these last few decades, more and more organizations compete with their human and intellectual capital. Thus to a large extent, what often differentiates the top performing organizations from less successful organizations is how they manage talent. To drive business results and achieve sustainable competitive advantage in the 21st century, organizations need human capital management capabilities that produce talented and engaged workers and leaders. The goal is to develop the right combination of internally and externally aligned HR practices and programs that result in balanced HR systems that make economic sense and meet the needs and goals of a highly diverse workforce.

Drivers of Engagement

In addition to understanding how different HR systems support different external and internal organizational strategic objectives, it's equally important for organizations to understand which HR practices have the greatest impact on employee engagement. There is a rich body of research identifying the key drivers of employee engagement that are the result of proper alignment of HR practices including job characteristics, role clarity/fit, coworker and management relations, leadership, developmental opportunities, and perceptions of fairness.

You must understand that there can be significant variance within each of these drivers. For example, the type of developmental opportunities provided employees in traditional positions might be different than the opportunities provided employees in strategic positions. Likewise, different employees may value one of these drivers significantly more than the others. However, just as you need to have a true measure of engagement, organizations need to understand what to measure to assess what is driving engagement for different employees.

Job Characteristics

Job design has a significant impact on employee engagement. It impacts the level of skill, autonomy, and decision-making required to do the work and the degree of flexibility as to when and where the work is to be done. For example, organizations can design jobs to be highly standardized requiring a few simple tasks to be performed, which require little decision-making and autonomy. Alternatively, jobs can be designed broadly requiring a range of tasks to be performed and empowering employees to have decision-making authority. There is strong evidence that certain job characteristics can directly affect employee attitudes and behaviors at work (Hackman and Lawler, 1971). The following job dimensions have been shown to have a positive impact on employee engagement: skill variety, task identity, task significance, autonomy, and feedback. Employees whose jobs are high on these core dimensions show high work motivation, satisfaction, performance, and attendance.

Skill variety is the degree to which a job requires a variety of different activities in carrying out the work, which involve the use of a number of different skills. *Task identity* is the degree to which the job requires completion of a "whole" and identifiable piece of work, that is, doing a job from beginning to end with a visible outcome. *Task significance* is the degree to which the job has a substantial impact on the lives of other people, whether in the immediate organization or in the external environment. *Autonomy* is the degree to which the job provides substantial freedom, independence, and discretion to the individual in scheduling the work and in determining the procedures to be used in carrying it out. *Feedback* is the degree to which carrying out the work activities required by the job results in individuals obtaining direct and clear information about the effectiveness of their performance.

Another approach for understanding how job design impacts employee engagement is the job demands–resources (JD-R) model, as shown in Figure 5.4 (Demerouti et al., 2001). *Job demands* refer to the physical, psychological, and social features of a job (in addition to organizational features) that are related to physiological and psychological costs (for example, work overload, job insecurity, role ambiguity, and role conflict). *Job resources* refer to physical, psychological, social, or organizational features of a job that help achieve work goals, reduce job demands, and stimulate personal growth, learning, and development (job control, access to information, performance feedback, and social support). Thus, high job resources relative to job demands promote engagement, whereas low job resources relative to job demands contribute to burnout and reduced engagement.

Job Resources	**Job Demands**
- *Job Control*	- *Work Overload*
- *Access to Information*	- *Role Ambiguity*
- *Performance Feedback*	- *Role Conflict*
- *Social Support*	- *Job Insecurity*

Job Resources > Job Demands = Engagement

Figure 5.4 Job demands–resources (JD-R) model

Data source: Demerouti, E., Bakker, A.B., Nachreiner, F., and Schaufeli, W.B. 2001. "The job demands–resources model of burnout." *Journal of Applied Psychology*, 86, 499–512.

An interesting study of women physicians found that when they can control the number of hours they work, they experienced higher levels of work engagement as compared to their colleagues who had less work control. Significantly, they also reported having a higher quality of life at home (Barnett et al., 2005). These physicians were more productive and had lower rates of turnover. The research demonstrating the relationship between job characteristics and employee engagement has supported the growth of many work–life programs including flextime that enables workers to alter their beginning and ending work schedules, job sharing when two part-time employees combine their schedules to equal one full-time worker, and many types of telecommuting arrangements that permit workers who work at home to also set their own work schedules.

A noted workplace flexibility study found that employees whose flexibility at work matched their needs were significantly more engaged than those who did not have a good fit between their needs and their companies' flexibility policies. One of the more interesting findings of this study was that older employees (45+ years of age) who had the flexibility they needed were significantly more engaged than younger employees who had the flexibility they needed (Pitt-Catsouphes and Matz-Costa, 2008).

All in all, job design impacts engagement levels by impacting the amount of developmental opportunities provided employees and the amount of freedom they have when performing in their jobs. Closely related to job design is *organizational design*. Highly standardized positions that require less skills, autonomy, and decision-making and offer few developmental opportunities are commonly organized in hierarchical organizational structures; whereas, broadly defined jobs that require higher skills and greater autonomy and decision-making are more likely organized in flatter or networked structures.

Clearly, the hierarchical model has many limitations for enhancing engagement levels. *Hierarchical structures* typically organize work in functional units that reinforce silo thinking. Such structures result in narrowly defined jobs and vertical career paths that overemphasize company experience. Top-down structures also limit decision-making to those at the top, which reduces the amount of autonomy and empowerment given to employees. The only way to advance is up, by climbing the proverbial corporate ladder. The result is a highly competitive organizational culture that discourages collaboration and knowledge sharing.

Flat and networked organizational structures are conducive for enhancing employee engagement. In such structures, jobs are broadly defined and work is organized within cross-functional teams. Career paths often include lateral moves that provide developmental opportunities for employees. Employees advance by increasing their skills and contributing to the success of their teams. These organizational structures are designed to encourage collaboration and knowledge sharing. Broadly designed jobs and nonhierarchical structures create highly engaged organizational cultures that promote employee development, empowerment, and flexibility.

Role

In today's ever-changing work environment, people often must engage in multiple roles to fulfill job expectations (Rothbard, 2001). Thus, it is meaningless to refer to engagement without being specific about the role in question. The different roles occupied by organizational members include one's job, group membership, and organization role. Employee engagement is likely to vary from role to role, and engagement in one role has implications for engagement in other roles.

In particular, role clarity helps to relieve tensions between individual and organizational needs, whereas role ambiguity involving the absence of clear information about one's job responsibilities creates stress. Role conflict involving mutually incompatible job responsibilities are also known as role stressors that diminish individuals' coping mechanisms and performance.

Employees willingly contribute their time when their roles are consistent with their personal goals and when they see themselves invested in their role performance (Sheldon and Elliot, 1999). Work role fit is the relation of the individual employee to the role that she assumes in an organization. A number of authors argue that a perceived fit between an individual's self-concept and her role will lead to an experienced sense of meaning due to the ability of the individual to express her values and beliefs (Shamir, 1991). This stream of research also maintains that human beings are self-expressive and creative, not just goal-oriented. That is, people seek out work roles that enable them to behave in a way that expresses their authentic self-concept. Other research suggests that employees who see their work as consistent with their personal values will be more engaged (Bono and Judge, 2003).

Coworkers

Individuals who have rewarding interpersonal interactions with their coworkers also experience greater meaning in their work. When individuals are treated with dignity, respect, and value for their contributions, and not simply as occupants of a role, they are likely to obtain a sense of meaningfulness from their interactions. To the extent that coworker interactions foster a sense of belonging, a stronger sense of social identity and meaning should emerge.

Interpersonal relations among employees that are supportive and trusting should also foster psychological safety whereby employees are comfortable being themselves and expressing their concerns (Kahn, 1990). The bases for interpersonal trust can be either cognitive or affective. Cognitive-based trust concerns the reliability and dependability of others. Affective-based trust is rooted in the emotional relationships between individuals. People who trust each other emotionally generally express concern for the welfare of each other, believe in the intrinsic virtue of such relationships, and are willing to make future emotional investments in the relationship.

People working in the same group have more chances to interact with each other and so have more possibilities to be involved in negative as well as positive psychological contagion processes. Psychological research in organizations has shown that when employees have positive coworker relationships, common motivational and behavioral patterns emerge resulting in collective emotions, shared perceived collective efficacy, and high group potency. Thus, engagement as a motivational construct can also be shared by employees in the workplace (Bakker and Schaufeli, 2008). Such affective relations among group members are also referred to as morale, cohesion, and rapport.

Management

Effective managers are those who get the work done with the people they have, do not try to change them, and attempt to capitalize on the competencies their people have, not what they, the manager, wished they had (Buckingham and Coffman, 1999). The relation with one's immediate manager can have a dramatic impact on an individual's perceptions of the work environment. A Conference Board report of 12 major employee engagement studies found that across different locations and cohorts, an employee's direct relationship with his manager is the strongest of all drivers of engagement (Gibbons, 2006). A supportive, and not controlling, relationship is known to foster perceptions of safety (Edmondson, 1999) and enhance employee creativity (Deci et al., 1989). Supervisors who foster a supportive work environment typically display concern for employees' needs and feelings, provide positive feedback, and encourage them to voice their concerns, develop new skills, and solve work-related problems. Such supportive actions enhance employees' self-determination and interest in their work.

Employees who are self-determined experience a sense of choice in initiating and regulating their own actions (Deci et al., 1989 pg. 580). Individuals in such supportive environments are likely to feel safer to engage themselves more fully, try out novel ways of doing things, discuss mistakes, and learn from these behaviors (Edmondson, 1999). Supervisory supportiveness of employees' self-determination has also been linked with enhancing trust, an important condition of engagement (Deci et al., 1989).

Five categories of behavior that have been linked with employees' perceptions of managerial trustworthiness include behavioral consistency, behavioral integrity, sharing and delegation of control, communication (accuracy, explanations, and openness), and demonstration of concern (Whitener et al., 1998). Behavioral consistency, or predictability, involves behaving in the same manner across time and contexts. Behavioral integrity entails consistency between words and deeds. Sharing of control involves employee participation in decision-making. Open communication fosters accurate explanations for managerial actions. Finally, benevolence involves consideration, protecting employees' interests, and refraining from exploitation.

Research on employees' perceptions of organizational support found employees who work for managers that make expectations clear, are fair, and recognize superior behavior feel more engaged and behave in adaptive and constructive ways (Rhoades and Eisenberger, 2002).

Leadership

There is a great deal of research indicating that leaders who engage in "transformational/charismatic" behaviors produce transformational/charismatic effects (Shamir et al., 1993). Transformational leaders enhance employee engagement by fostering a sense of passion for work as well as employees' capacity to think independently, develop new ideas, and challenge convention when no longer relevant (Dvir et al., 2002). While teaching an executive education class on leadership, I was asked to explain the difference between a traditional situational leader and a transformational leader. I remembered reading an inspirational quote by an anonymous author that perfectly explained the differences between good (traditional) and great (transformational) leaders. "Good leaders get people to believe in them; great leaders get people to believe in themselves." The characteristics of a transformational leader are shown in Table 5.1.

Table 5.1 Characteristics of Transformational Leadership

Idealized influence	Admired, respected, and trusted; consider followers' needs; consistent conduct
Inspirational motivation	Provide meaning and challenge
Intellectual stimulation	Stimulate followers' efforts to be creative and innovative
Individualized consideration	Pay attention to each individual's need for achievement

Data Source: Avolio, B. J., & Bass, B. M. (1988). Transformational leadership, charisma, and beyond. In J. G. Hunt, B. R. Baliga, H. P. Dachler, & C. A. Schriesheim (Eds.), *Emerging Leadership Vitas* (pp. 29–49). Lexington, MA: Lexington Books.

Leaders also play an important role by defining and communicating the organization's vision, purpose, and goals. Engaged employees understand and identify with their leader's vision and strategy. Top management openness, defined as the degree to which top management is believed to encourage and support suggestions and change initiatives from below, has also been shown to enhance employee engagement (Ashford et al., 1998).

Perceptions of Fairness

Employees' perception of fairness is a significant driver of engagement. Fairness consists of three types of subjective perceptions: (a) the fairness of outcome distributions, (b) the fairness of the procedure used to determine outcome distributions, and (c) the fairness and quality of the interpersonal treatment employees experience in the workplace. These forms of equity are typically referred to as distributive justice (Leventhal, 1980), procedural justice (Leventhal, 1980), and interactional justice (Bies and Moag, 1986).

Distributive justice is derived from equity theory research (Adams, 1965), which used a social exchange theory framework to evaluate fairness. According to this theory, what people are concerned about is not the absolute level of outcomes per se but whether those outcomes were fair. Employees determine whether an outcome is fair by calculating their ratio of outcomes (for example, compensation, promotions, and development) to their contributions or inputs (for example, effort, time, education, intelligence, and experience) and then compare that ratio with that of a comparison to others who have similar inputs. For example, I would expect someone in my organization who is performing similar work and has the same amount of education and experience (inputs) as I have to also have the same amount of compensation and benefits (outcomes) as I do. If their outputs are higher than mine, I would perceive that as unfair and will be disengaged. Alternatively, if someone's inputs were clearly higher than mine, I would understand why her outcome would be higher and would perceive that comparison as fair.

The notion of *procedural justice* was first established in legal contexts. Extending this notion into organizational settings, procedural justice judgments focus on six criteria that a procedure should meet if it is to be perceived as fair. Procedures should

- Be applied consistently across people and across time
- Be free from bias—for example, ensuring that a third party has no vested interest in a particular settlement
- Ensure that accurate information is collected and used in making decisions

- Have some mechanism to correct flawed or inaccurate decisions
- Conform to personal or prevailing standards of ethics or morality
- Ensure that the opinions of various groups affected by the decision have been taken into account

If employees do not understand and agree how important decisions are made that impact their performance, compensation, and opportunities, then they will question the fairness of those decisions, diminishing their commitment to the organization and engagement.

The most recent advance in the justice literature focuses on the importance of the quality of the interpersonal treatment people receive when procedures are implemented. *Interactional justice* (Bies and Moag, 1986) is fostered when decision-makers treat people with respect and sensitivity and explain the rationale for decisions. Interactional justice has come to be seen as consisting of two specific types of interpersonal treatment (Greenberg, 1990). The first, labeled interpersonal justice, reflects the degree to which people are treated with politeness, dignity, and respect by authorities or third parties involved in executing procedures or determining outcomes. The second, labeled informational justice, focuses on the explanations provided to people that convey information about why procedures were used in a certain way or why outcomes were distributed in a certain fashion.

It's critical for employees to feel that they are given truthful and accurate information from their managers and organizational leaders. Equally important is to ensure that there is no tolerance for abusive and unethical people in authority. Employees' trust and positive day-to-day interactions with management are important drivers of engagement. All in all, fairness has long been considered one of the key predictors of employees' affective state including engagement. And when employees feel that they are being treated fairly, they reciprocate through higher performance, including engaging in organizational citizenship behaviors (OCBs) (Organ, 1988).

Psychological Conditions of Engagement

This framework makes a distinction between the drivers and conditions of engagement. One of the goals is to demonstrate the flow and interconnectedness of each step in the engagement process. Up to this point, you have reviewed how HR systems create the drivers of engagement, which in turn create the conditions of engagement. Both the conditions of engagement and engagement itself reflect a psychological state, which is quite distinct from the drivers and outcomes of engagement.

Early research specifying the psychological conditions of engagement identified three conditions: meaningfulness, psychological safety, and psychological availability that were shown to influence the degree to which people engage in their roles at work. Employees seem to ask themselves three questions in each situation: (1) How meaningful is it for me to bring myself into this performance? (2) How safe is it to do so? (3) How available am I to do so? (Kahn, 1990). Other studies have shown two additional conditions that are related to psychological state engagement: employees' sense of empowerment and psychological contract fulfillment (see Table 5.2). Thus, to understand the dynamics of employee engagement, you need to understand not only the drivers, but also the conditions that enhance employee engagement.

Table 5.2 Psychological Conditions of Engagement

Meaningfulness
Psychological safety
Psychological availability
Psychological empowerment
Psychological contract fulfillment

Meaningfulness

There is a large body of research demonstrating the meaningfulness of work as a condition of engagement. Employees who see the impact of their work and believe in the organization's mission invest more of themselves when performing work. Within this research, job enrichment and work role fit were positively linked to meaning-fulness. One experiences meaningfulness as a feeling of receiving a return on investments of one's self in a currency of physical, cognitive, or emotional energy (Kahn, 1990). People also experience their work as meaningful when they perceive it to be challenging, worthwhile, and rewarding.

Dimensions of meaningfulness include the extent to which employees feel that (a) they make a significant contribution toward achievement of organizational goals; (b) the organization adequately recognizes their contributions; and (c) their work is challenging and conducive to personal growth. Meaningfulness has also been defined as the value of a work goal or purpose, judged in relation to an individual's own ideals or standards (Hackman and Oldham, 1980).

Psychological Safety

In the highly diverse world of the 21st century, employees come to the workplace with a different set of values and have different ways of expressing themselves. To feel engaged, employees need to be who they are at work. Psychological safety is defined as an employee's sense of being able to show and be one's self without fear of negative consequences to self-image, status, or career (Kahn, 1990). Supervisory and coworker behaviors that are supportive and trustworthy in nature are likely to produce feelings of safety at work. Other factors that are indicative of psychological safety include the extent to which (a) management is perceived as flexible and supportive and employees feel they have control over their work and the methods they use to accomplish it; (b) organizational roles and norms are perceived as clear; and (c) employees feel free to express their true feelings in their work roles.

Psychological Availability

Given that engagement requires a high degree of energy and involvement, employees need to come to work feeling rested, stress-free, and sharp. Psychological availability is defined as an individual's belief that she has the physical, emotional, or cognitive resources that are necessary to be engaged at work (Kahn, 1990). In essence, it reflects the readiness, or confidence, of a person to engage in her work role given that individuals are engaged in many other life activities. Most jobs require some level of physical exertion, and some demand intense physical challenges that may result in injuries. Emotional demands of jobs also vary in type and scope. Some jobs, particularly service sector ones, require much emotional labor. Theoretical work on the dimensions of emotional labor postulates that not only does emotional dissonance lead to depletion of emotional resources (that is, exhaustion), but the frequency of the emotional display, duration, and intensity of such displays and variety of expressed emotions also decrease these resources (Morris and Feldman, 1996).

Cognitive demands and resources also vary by job and person, respectively. Some roles require more information processing than individuals can handle. They become overwhelmed at the amount of information or "balls in the air" and lack of ability to think clearly. This is reflected as "role overload" in the stress literature. Finally, activities outside the workplace have the potential to draw away individuals' energies from their work and make them less psychologically available for their work roles. In other words, managing multiple roles can drain resources, prohibiting a person from performing at their highest level (Edwards and Rothbard, 2000).

Clearly, this is reflected in the JD-R model, where employees need to have all the necessary resources to fully invest themselves in their work. Employees who have a clear understanding about their role, have flexibility regarding how to accomplish their objectives, and have the support of managers and coworkers will be more psychologically available and engaged.

Psychological Empowerment

To feel engaged, employees need to experience a sense of authority and responsibility at work. As a psychological state, empowerment has been broadly defined as an increase in intrinsic work motivation manifested in a set of four cognitions reflecting an individual's orientation to his work role: meaning, competence, self-determination, and impact (Thomas and Velthouse, 1990).

Meaning in this context refers to the value of a work goal or purpose, judged in relation to an individual's own ideals or standards, and results in high commitment and concentration of energy. *Competence* or self-efficacy is an individual's belief in her ability to perform activities with skill, and results in effort and persistence in challenging situations, high goal expectations, and high performance.

Where competence is a mastery of behavior, *self-determination* is an individual's sense of having choice in initiating and regulating actions (Deci et al., 1989). Self-determination reflects autonomy in the initiation and continuation of work behaviors and processes; examples are making decisions about work methods, pace, and effort. Self-determination results in learning, interest in activity, and resilience in the face of adversity (Deci and Ryan, 1987). *Impact* is the degree to which an individual can influence strategic, administrative, or operating outcomes at work. Impact is highly associated with employee engagement and high performance.

If organizations are going to empower employees, they must make as much information available to as many employees, at all levels, through multiple devices (Kanter, 1989). Two specific types of information are critical for empowerment (Lawler, 1992): (1) information about an organization's mission and (2) information about performance. With regard to an organizational mission, until people feel informed about where an organization is headed overall, they won't feel capable of taking initiative (Kanter, 1989). Information about the mission is an important antecedent of empowerment because it helps to create a sense of meaning and purpose (Conger and Kanungo, 1988) and it enhances an individual's ability to make and influence decisions that are appropriately aligned with the organization's goals and mission (Lawler, 1992). With regard to information about performance, people need to understand how well they and their work units are performing to make and influence decisions to maintain and improve performance in the future.

Psychological Contract Fulfillment

The psychological contract has been defined as an individual's beliefs, shaped by the organization, regarding terms of an exchange agreement between individuals and their organizations (Rousseau, 1995). These beliefs refer to employee perceptions of the explicit and implicit promises regarding the exchange of employee contributions (for example, effort, ability, and loyalty) for organizational inducements (for example, pay, promotion, and security). There are two types of psychological contracts that describe two ends of the employee–employer relationship: transactional and relational. *Transactional contracts* are typically short term, have a purely economic or materialistic focus, and entail limited involvement by both parties. *Relational contracts* are long term and broad, as they are not restricted to purely economic exchange but also include terms for loyalty in exchange for security or growth in an organization (Morrison and Robinson, 1997).

A perceived breach of contract occurs when one's organization has failed to meet one or more obligations in a manner commensurate with one's contributions (Morrison and Robinson, 1997). Perceived breach signals an imbalance in the social exchange process in which an employee does not receive expected outcomes from an organization for fulfilling his obligations (Morrison and Robinson, 1997). Research has shown a negative relationship between perceived breach and desirable outcomes such as job satisfaction, organizational commitment, and performance (Robinson and Morrison, 2000); whereas psychological contract fulfillment has been found to associate positively with job satisfaction, organizational commitment, organizational citizenship behaviors, and performance (Robinson and Morrison, 2000).

Trait Engagement

Clearly, there are people who have different personality traits that can either positively or negatively impact their perceptions at work and their levels of engagement. In this framework, employees' traits are presented as a modifier of the relationship between drivers of engagement and both psychological conditions and state of engagement. Although it is easy to state that people who have passion for their work are more likely to feel engaged and demonstrate engagement behaviors, it is more difficult to state why some people have passion for their work and others do not. Those more likely to experience feelings of engagement and who demonstrate engagement behavior are also more likely to choose the environment that provides the opportunity to do so (Macey and Schneider, 2008).

The personality traits that are positively linked to engagement include autotelic personality, positive affectivity, proactive personality, conscientiousness, self-efficacy, and self-esteem. Employees with *autotelic personality* traits have a general propensity to mentally transform potential threats into enjoyable challenges (Csikszentmihalyi, 1990). These are great coworkers when there is a crisis or pressure to perform. Those who have *positive affectivity* traits have a proclivity for active interaction with their work environment. These are fun people who have a positive impact on morale. Individuals who have *proactive personality* traits consistently take action to change things for the better and persist to overcome opposition. These are employees who have the ability to foresee and respond to possible threats that may negatively impact the group. *Conscientiousness* is one of the "big five" personality traits that is known to strongly correlate with work engagement and performance. It's defined as a combination of dependability, carefulness, thoroughness, responsibility, and perseverance (Costa and McCrae, 1985).

Self-efficacy, defined as having confidence in one's ability to perform, has been shown to increase personal initiative at work. Employees with high self-confidence feel comfortable righting a wrong and bringing about positive change. Closely related to self-efficacy is a personality trait called *locus of control*, which explains the degree to which people believe they, rather than external forces, determine what happens in their lives (Rotter, 1966). Locus of control is another key dimension of empowerment, a psychological condition of engagement (Thomas and Velthouse, 1990). *Self-esteem* is a personality trait defined as a general feeling of self-worth and is also related to empowerment. Individuals who hold themselves in high esteem are likely to extend their feelings of self-worth to a work-specific sense of competence (Bandura, 1977). Conversely, individuals with little self-esteem are not likely to see themselves as able to make a difference or influence their work and organizations.

All in all, different people with different personality traits react differently to different organizational environments. Some employees have personality traits that are more conducive to engagement where others do not. This is one reason why employees who work in the same group and are exposed to similar management practices can have different levels of engagement. You must also realize that organizations have "personalities" referred to as *organizational culture*. Just as some personality traits may not positively relate to engagement, some employee traits may not fit in with a specific organizational culture. For example, a highly passive, cooperative employee may not fit in at an organization that has an aggressive and competitive culture. Poor person–organization fit is negatively related to engagement and is known to be highly related to turnover.

Behavioral Engagement

In a world of continual rapid change, companies need workers who question the status quo, who are experimental, and who actively search for new ways of doing things. Unlike most engagement models, in this framework, behavioral engagement is an outcome (not a measure of engagement). In differentiating engagement from the entire scope of behavioral work performance, engagement implies something special, extra, or at least atypical. Thus, it is common to define behavioral engagement as putting forth "discretionary effort" defined as extra time, brainpower, and energy. Others refer to it as "giving it their all."

Some argue that it is limiting to define engagement solely as a matter of doing something extra, for example, those who are psychologically present bring more of themselves to their work and thereby may do something different and not just something more (Kahn, 1990). Engagement behaviors typically extend beyond expected job performance. The label that is probably most common in human resource management research is contextual performance (Borman and Motowildo, 1997). Contextual activities include volunteering for work activities that are not formally part of the job and helping and cooperating with others in the organization to get work done.

As noted in Chapter 4, "The Imperative of Employee Engagement for Competitive Success in the 21st Century," there is also a large body of research that defines behavioral engagement as *organizational citizenship behaviors (OCBs)*. Early research described five dimensions of OCBs (Organ, 1988):

1. **Altruism** (for example, helping others with their work, orienting new people)

2. **Conscientiousness** (for example, being on time, having good work attendance, making proper use of work time)

3. **Courtesy** (for example, notifying others before acting in a way that will affect them)

4. **Sportsmanship** (for example, maintaining a positive attitude, not complaining)

5. **Civic duty** (for example, attending meetings and reading organizational communications)

Subsequent research (Organ, 1997) pared back the number of dimensions and emphasized only three forms of OCBs: helping (which was earlier called altruism), courtesy, and conscientiousness.

Others have considered behavioral engagement as active engagement in terms of taking personal initiative as well as responsibility (Dvir et al., 2002). Personal initiative can be thought of as composed of three facets: self-starting, proactivity, and persistence (Frese and Fay, 2001)—all of which can be described as adaptation in response to organizational challenges. For many organizations, the interest in creating an engaged workforce stems from a desire to increase innovation. Innovative behaviors reflect the creation of something new or different. Innovative behaviors are by definition change-oriented because they involve the creation of a new product, service, idea, procedure, or process.

Empowered employees who are intrinsically task motivated are known to engage in innovative behaviors. Because empowered individuals believe they are autonomous and have an impact, they are also likely to be creative (Amabile, 1988). Along these lines, a more modern-day concept of behavioral engagement has emerged focusing on employee performance and includes *proficiency* (fulfills the prescribed or predictable requirements of the role), *adaptivity* (copes with, responds to, and supports change), and *proactivity* (initiates change, is self-starting, and future-directed) (Griffin et al., 2007).

Strategic Outcomes

Employee engagement fosters and drives discretionary behavior, eliciting employees' highest productivity, their best ideas, and their genuine commitment to the success of the organization. Engaged employees behave in ways that contribute significantly to an organization's performance, leading to improvements in the following:

- Productivity
- Service quality
- Innovation
- Customer satisfaction

Strategic outcomes in turn lead to long-term financial results.

The linkages shown in the employee engagement framework (refer to Figure 5.1) leading to organizational strategic outcomes and financial results are the reasons why there is so much interest in understanding the mechanisms for creating an engaged workforce. As a result, at most companies, the intended focus of employee engagement outcomes can be summarized as organizational effectiveness. Thus, the primary unit of analysis for employee engagement is the organization. However, when assessing the linkages between employee engagement and strategic outcomes, employee survey data can be aggregated by any meaningful unit above the individual level, for example, work group, business unit, division, and so on. In doing so, the focus is on assessing the "engagement climate." The question is how individual engagement feelings and behaviors emerge to create organizational success.

For example, if you treat your employees well, they will treat your customers well and that will enhance organizational performance. Treating your employees well is not about making them feel happy or satisfied in their jobs. The key factors that trigger the value creation chain are the HR systems that create the conditions and psychological state of engagement of employees. Employees contribute to organizational effectiveness when they are involved and see the intrinsic value in the work they do, are empowered to make decisions, understand the organization's strategy and see a clear line of sight between their job and the organization's goals, and feel they are treated with dignity by those who they work with and lead them.

A noteworthy study published in the *Harvard Business Review* demonstrated a significant relationship between employee engagement (defined using a Gallup measure) and customer engagement. The researchers found that employee attitudes affect customer attitudes, and customer attitudes affect financial performance. They found that work groups whose members are positively engaged have high levels of productivity and profitability, better safety and attendance records, and higher levels of retention. Most important, they were also more effective at engaging the customers they serve. They also found that disengaged employees can have a profound negative impact. They estimate that they cost companies $300 billion per year in lost productivity in the United States alone. They also destroy customer relationships with remarkable facility, day in and day out (Fleming et al., 2005).

Financial Outcomes

An engaged workforce, demonstrating engaged behaviors, helps organizations achieve strategic outcomes leading to long-term financial success including an increase in

- Revenues
- Profits
- Market value

There is evidence that both state and behavioral engagement at the organizational level of analysis are positively related to (a) organization-level customer satisfaction (indicators of cash flow and brand equity), (b) return on assets, (c) profits, and (d) shareholder value, which in turn are all significantly related to competitive advantage (Schneider et al., 2009).

Research conducted by Hewitt Associates (2005) indicates that they "have established a conclusive, compelling relationship between engagement and profitability through higher productivity, sales, customer satisfaction, and employee retention."

A meta-analysis of the financial performance of 1,979 business units in 10 companies found that business units that score above the database median on both employee and customer engagement metrics were on average 3.4 times more effective financially (in terms of total sales and revenue, performance to target, and year-over-year gain in sales and revenues) than units that rank in the bottom half on both measures (Fleming et al., 2005).

A study conducted by Watson Wyatt (2009) showed a relationship between employee engagement and improved shareholder value. Firms with engagement scores in the upper quartile had earnings-per-share growth rates that were 2.6 times higher than firms in the bottom quartile. Over a 5-year period, companies with highly engaged employees had total shareholder returns that were 13 percent greater than companies with less-engaged employees.

Aon Hewitt's 2012 Engagement 2.0 Employee Study compared key business drivers (innovation, quality of products, customer satisfaction, cost/efficiency, and revenue growth) across employee groups segmented by their engagement levels. Their analysis, representing more than 9 million employees in 758 companies around the world, showed that companies in the top quartile of engagement scores had 50 percent higher total shareholder return than companies with average engagement scores (Aon Hewitt, 2012). The research is compelling; organizations need engaged employees if they are to achieve sustainable competitive advantage in the highly competitive marketplace of the 21st century.

6

The Increasing Need for Organizational Adaptability

In an ever-changing unpredictable world, organizational adaptability is critical for a sustainable competitive advantage. Indeed, many successful organizations are responding to the new normal by developing organizational adaptability competencies. Some of the most well-thought-out strategic plans become obsolete when organizations are confronted with unexpected shocks called *black swans*. Some economists are now describing the global economy as complex adaptive systems. As such, the traditional, rational way of looking at how decisions are made is replaced with more realistic assumptions about inductive, nonoptimal decision-making. The new economics looks beyond organizational behavior to how agents interact with one another in a dynamic web of relationships (Beinhocker, 1997).

Complex adaptive systems are known to have periods of punctuated equilibrium, which is a natural feature of the evolutionary process. This occurs when periods of relative calm and stability are interrupted by chaotic periods, or *punctuation points*. Punctuated equilibrium creates difficulties for organizations' long-term survivability because many of their strategies and competencies are finely tuned for stable periods of growth. When organizations are faced with market upheavals and disruptive technologies, strategies quickly become obsolete. To succeed, they must either adapt to the market or innovate and move ahead of the market. More specifically, they need to be both a strong competitor in today's market and be able to evolve.

The key to sustainable competitive advantage is to continuously adapt to changing market conditions by developing new sources of temporary advantage that change over time. To continue to grow, complex adaptive systems at any given point in time must remain at the edge of chaos. Here lies the point between rigidity and resistance to change, and oversensitivity and chaos. In practical terms, organizations need to achieve both numerical and functional flexibility. *Numerical flexibility* requires organizations to create multiple structures that enable them to effectively align their workforce needs with fluctuating business needs. *Functional flexibility* requires organizations to have access to multiple sources of talent that enable them to integrate and deploy new resources when needed.

In PricewaterhouseCoopers' (PWC) 9th annual global CEO survey, 41 percent of CEOs agree strongly that complexity is an inevitable byproduct of doing business today. The overall theme of the survey is companies need to be adaptable and flexible to survive (PWC, 2006). CEOs surveyed by the Conference Board cited global political/economic risk as their third most-critical challenge. These major external risks disrupt strategic plans and require immediate action by executive management. If these risks emerge slowly over time, firms might adapt their business models. However, when they are sudden and unpredictable, it is difficult to effectively respond to these black-swan events and mitigate those risks (Mitchell, 2011). Not surprisingly, European CEOs facing the current sovereign debt and banking crisis, a high risk of recession, and the possible breakup of the European Union rate this challenge as their most pressing one.

Problems with Black Swans

The future often resembles the past but is never exactly the same, which is why extrapolating past data to predict the future is not effective. Yet, there are countless computer models used to predict the future that have this fatal flaw. As a result, bubbles develop and people are surprised when they burst. Whether it was the Amsterdam tulip mania of the 17th century, the South Sea Bubble of the 18th century, the railroad boom of the 19th century, the dot-com boom of the 20th century, or the financial collapse of the 21st century, few saw the bubbles forming and most people were surprised when they burst.

On May 6, 2010, the financial markets experienced a "flash crash" that sent the Dow Jones Industrial average down nearly 1,000 points in a mere 300 seconds, making it the largest single-day drop in history.

In total, nearly $1 trillion of wealth vanished in an electronic black hole. The culprit was a multitude of electronic trading systems driven by complex algorithms that trade millions of trades per second going awry. Indeed, rare disasters do happen, and the problem is we typically underestimate the occurrence and size of these events. The problem is many statistical models are based on the assumption of a normal distribution of data (or events) that all fall within three standard deviations above and below the mean. Such models give increasingly low probabilities for outcomes that exceed three standard deviations.

As a result, none of the "experts" saw these black swans. And it is not just business catastrophes that experts fail to predict. Before Google went public in the 1990s, the founders tried to sell the company with its patented search engine technology for $1.6 million. A number of noted venture capitalists and Yahoo Inc. didn't even make an offer. The Google founders were lucky that there were so few people who could predict the value of their company because in less than 10 years (by 2008), the market value of the firm was $230 billion (Makridakis et al., 2010)!

In today's highly interdependent and complex world, the workforce trends we would like to predict are also beyond many of our current forecasting models. The mathematician Andrei Andreyevich Markov pioneered many of the forecasting models used in workforce planning. These models calculated the rates of movement of multiple variables, such as company growth rates, individual attributes, average tenure, and so on. However, as these models had to accommodate movements of employees working in flexible hierarchies and across functional silos, their complexity and the amount of mathematics required to describe them expanded exponentially (see, for example, Dill et al., 1966). As a result, the confidence in these models diminished as the probability of forecasting error increased.

Organizational Adaptability

The traditional response to the increasing complexities and uncertainties of the marketplace has been an elevation of the corporate strategy function. The goals of corporate strategists are to leverage organizational capabilities and exploit market opportunities to create a competitive advantage. However, this approach is most successful in a relatively stable and predictable world. The rate of change among the top firms in market leadership is evidence of the pitfalls of strictly relying on strategy making to ensure their long-term viability. From 1960 to 2008, the percentage of companies dropping out of the top three rankings in their industry increased from 2 percent to 14 percent (Reeves and Deimler, 2011). Given all the advances in organizations' capability to gather and analyze information and formulate strategy, the problem may not be flawed strategies but an inability to adapt.

What good is a strategy if organizations are too rigid to make the necessary changes needed to execute the strategy? To succeed in a rapidly changing and competitive world, organizations need to effectively execute their current strategy while simultaneously adapting the strategy to meet future challenges. In the classic book *In Search of Excellence*, authors Thomas Peters and Bob Waterman argued that organizations must simultaneously be "tight" in executing and "loose" in adapting (Peters and Waterman, 2004). In *Winning Through Innovations*, authors Michael Tushman and Charles O'Reilly talk about the "ambidextrous" organization that can operate as well as innovate (Tushman and O'Reilly, 2002). New organizational structures that reflect the complexities of doing business today have the characteristics of open, flat, and networked structures. The boundaries that typically define a firm are becoming blurry, as the relationships among people within and outside the company are comingled.

The traditional benefits of a vertically integrated organization are rapidly diminishing as advances in communication and information technologies reduce the costs of controlling and coordinating work across various entities that previously were bureaucratically integrated in one organization. These technologies enable organizations to effectively manage internal employee networks and various sources of contract human capital including outsourced vendors, independent contractors, and strategic partnerships. As sophisticated electronic networks reduce the costs of acquiring and managing information, more decentralized, market-based mechanisms are replacing centralized bureaucracies. These new flexible work systems are more efficient and adaptable to changing local or global markets. For example, although there is a hierarchy at Google, given the size and scope of its business, the company strives to operate as "flat" as possible by creating only as much structure as necessary and hiring people who are good at many things to give them the ability to respond to opportunities (Society for Human Resource Management Foundation [SHRM], 2010).

Clearly, organizations that have organizational adaptability competencies will have a competitive advantage navigating the 21st century marketplace. Organizational adaptability requires engaging and managing multiple sources of talent including employees and contract human capital for a variety of strategic reasons in response to both internal organizational and external environmental forces. Contract human capital are all "nonemployee" workers including temporary employees, consultants, independent contractors, and individuals who may be employees of other firms, for example, strategic partnerships and outsourced providers, who provide services to the organization. The strategic reasons for engaging contract human capital typically reflect various business-unit needs. At the business-unit level, organizations are much more dynamic and not so easily categorized. Important strategic decisions at this level determine how resources are deployed to satisfy business unit and organizational goals.

Indeed, contract human capital can help individual business groups achieve multiple strategic objectives including the need to reduce human capital cost, gain access to specialized skills and expertise, and respond to fluctuations in operational demands. Given the continuing pressures of global competition and the efficiencies achieved with technology, employing contract human capital to reduce labor costs is a common strategy. Contract human capital are often not provided the same benefits given to regular employees, such as healthcare, paid time off, and pension plans. Firms that have generous benefits are more likely to use contract human capital particularly in a dynamic competitive environment in which employment levels fluctuate.

Also, recruitment costs are minimal because many of these workers are directly sourced or are employed through intermediary firms. Training costs are insignificant because many of these individuals have the prerequisite skills to do the work or are specialists in their field. In situations in which firms must pay wage premiums to attract high-skilled contract human capital, labor costs are controlled by paying these workers only for time worked. Lastly, there are substantial savings related to the firm's capability to manage its capacity more efficiently. For example, when a firm has to reduce its employment levels, it can reduce contract staffing levels without having to pay severance benefits or hurting its reputation by laying off core employees.

Outsourcing components of their operations has been another method for organizations to reduce labor costs. Firms pursuing this strategy typically seek to outsource nonstrategic work that can be provided by other organizations either more efficiently or at a reduced cost. Outsourcing basic administrative or general services to outsource providers that have access to lower-cost labor willing to provide these services can result in significant savings. However, the quality of the services provided must meet agreed upon standards for any cost-savings to be fully realized. Also, outsourcing certain professional services to outsourced providers that have a greater expertise or access to advanced technological capabilities in providing these needed services can improve operational efficiencies resulting in significant cost-savings.

Another strategic reason for engaging contract human capital is to gain access to knowledge that does not exist internally, or gain access to highly specialized skills that are needed for a limited period of time. Knowledge is a potential source of competitive advantage at many firms. Not only must firms create knowledge within their boundaries, but they must also expose themselves to an array of new ideas from all available talent outside the organization. Contract human capital can stimulate the accumulation and creation of valuable knowledge. Many contract human capital are carriers of best practices that may be unknown to core employees who have worked at fewer organizations throughout their careers. They can also help firms fill in knowledge gaps when important expertise is unavailable or inadequate internally.

Numerical Flexibility

For the longest time, many strategic managers associated organizational adaptability with organizational scalability. This was during a time when organizations had ample access to needed talent but still had to navigate economic and business cycles. The focus was primarily aligning staffing needs with fluctuating business needs. Costs were controlled by the ability to quickly adjust staffing levels in response to market demands. A common strategy was to create a workforce consisting of core and noncore employees. By creating a competent and committed core group of employees buffered by an array of external employment relationships, organizations had access to on-demand and specialized resources that can be quickly expanded or contracted as dictated by the needs of the business.

This is the classic core-periphery model (Osterman, 1987) or doughnut model, as shown in Figure 6.1, in which part of the labor force is made peripheral by the use of contract human capital. The relationship with contract human capital under this strategy is likely to be short term and involve a pure economic exchange.

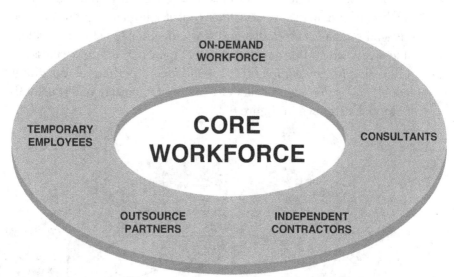

Figure 6.1 Core-periphery/doughnut model of organizational scalability

However, in today's hypercompetitive marketplace in which finding high-skilled talent is becoming increasingly difficult, organizations need both numerical and functional flexibility, which together create the organizational adaptability competencies that are so critical for organizations' success in the 21st century.

Functional Flexibility

To create functional flexibility, organizations must strategically engage contract human capital to help them to respond to fluctuations in operational demands. Rather than scalability, here the need is to gain access to and redeploy resources to achieve changing strategic objectives. Often this requires organizations to integrate contract human capital, who have the skills required to meet operational demands, with core employees. Perhaps the organization is changing strategies in response to competitors' actions or needs to quickly respond to changes in product demand or customer needs. Other researchers have labeled this resource flexibility as the extent to which a resource can be applied to a large range of alternative uses (Lepak et al., 2003).

As firms engage multiple sources of talent to achieve functional flexibility, it is vital for them to foster a collaborative mindset. Thus, both regular employees as well as contract human capital must be engaged to share knowledge and work together to achieve business objectives. Integrating contract human capital in the core business is a different approach compared to the older core-peripheral (doughnut model) and reflects a new model I call the Organizational Adaptability Model, as shown in Figure 6.2.

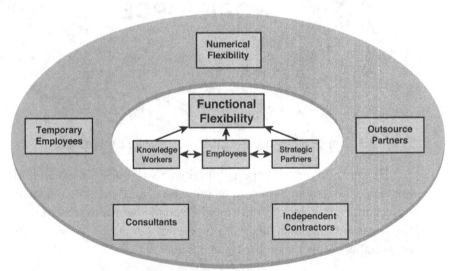

Figure 6.2 Organizational Adaptability Model

In this model, highly skilled contract human capital, referred to as knowledge workers, and strategic partners work together with core employees. In other words, nonemployee workers are not relegated to perform only nonstrategic work because many of them are employed because of their in-demand unique skills. When contract human capital are integrated in the core business, firms can alter the mix of all human capital in response to economic, strategic, and technological developments. However, creating and managing a blended workforce of employees and nonemployees to create organizational adaptability can pose many challenges.

It's critical to ensure all workers, both regular employees and contract human capital, are fully engaged. Much of the engagement research presented in Chapter 5, "Leveraging What We Know: An Employee Engagement Framework," does not distinguish whether one is an employee or nonemployee. Thus, applying these methods can positively impact the level of engagement across all workers. However, organizations face unique challenges managing and engaging workers who are not regular employees that must be considered. To that end, a new framework called the contract human capital human resources (HR) architecture is presented that demonstrates how organizations can manage and engage contract human capital.

Contract Human Capital HR Architecture

In a highly unpredictable and constantly changing world, organizations need to have both scalability and functional flexibility, that is, organizational adaptability, to succeed. Organizational adaptability requires not only innovative structures, but also a totally new way of managing contract human capital. Although much of the management research has focused on the traditional workforce, it fails to address how a diversified pool of human capital consisting of employees and contract human capital work together. Yet, it's not uncommon to find an array of different workers at many organizations consisting of traditional full-time employees, part-time and temporary workers, consultants, and remote workers all working together. Organizations that effectively manage and engage all their talent can enhance both operational efficiencies and their strategic capabilities.

In a knowledge economy, intellectual and social capital are sources of competitive advantage. In particular, networks of relationships can have a big impact on an organization's competitiveness. Organizations that engage contract human capital can develop effective networks of social and intellectual capital, which are vital for sustaining competitive advantage of the firm. Thus, just as with regular employees, it is critical for organizations to understand how to strategically manage and engage contract human capital.

Extending the high-performance HR systems and HR architecture research, I developed the contract human capital HR architecture that demonstrates how organizations can manage and enhance the engagement of contract human capital. Before thinking about how organizations may differentiate how they manage contract human capital, it's helpful to understand the different ways organizations might hire these workers.

Contract Human Capital Engagement Modes

The term *engagement* here means the different ways organizations engage or hire contract human capital. Two dimensions are identified that nicely describe four different ways organizations hire contract human capital (see Figure 6.3). The first dimension that has important implications for how firms manage contract human capital is *work interdependency*. This characterizes the degree that contract human capital must work closely with regular employees or are jointly responsible for performing tasks. The range of work interdependency influences the extent to which the work performed by contract human capital needs to be coordinated versus integrated with work performed by employee coworkers.

The second dimension of work that impacts how firms might engage contract human capital is the *criticality* of the work. Organizations are expected to strategically manage contract human capital who perform work that is valuable or requires unique skills not readily available in the labor market. Alternatively, work that is of low criticality would be managed in a more transactional way. The intersections of the levels of work interdependency and criticality form a matrix of four different types of work contract human capital can be hired to perform, or engagement modes, labeled project work, knowledge work, contract work, and partnerships. The levels of work interdependency and criticality indeed impact how organizations manage contract human capital.

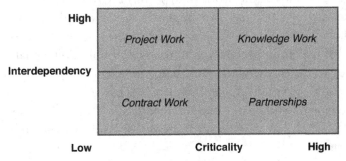

Figure 6.3 Contract human capital engagement modes

Interdependency

Variation in the nature of interdependency is related to the degree contract human capital must depend on the work group to perform their work based on how workflow is organized—that is, pooled, sequential, reciprocal, or integrated; the amount of information that has to be exchanged with the work group to accomplish work goals; and the amount of time required working directly with the work group and in face-to-face communications.

Contract work that is designed to be performed in a pooled or sequential way that requires a minimal amount of face-to-face communications and information to be exchanged with employees is performed independently by contract human capital. Alternatively, contract work that is designed to be performed in a reciprocal or integrated way that requires face-to-face communications or information to be exchanged with employees is performed by working interdependently with employees.

Another factor to consider is how easy or difficult it is to monitor contract human capital behavior and work product. If it is difficult for managers to monitor the behavior and output of contract human capital, it may be beneficial to have them work interdependently with the work group. Conversely, if there is no need to monitor behaviors and if the work product is easily observable, all else being equal, this type of work can be done independently.

Criticality

Beyond interdependency, contract human capital can vary in terms of the criticality of the work they perform. Criticality of contract human capital work has two dimensions: value and uniqueness (Lepak and Snell, 1999). *Value* is based on the degree the work directly contributes to important work group or organizational goals, or the degree to which the work contributes to a firm's core competencies and competitive advantage. *Uniqueness* is based on the degree to which the type of work is rare and not readily available in the labor market, or the degree to which it is specialized or is idiosyncratic to a particular firm.

Organizations view work performed by contract human capital that requires unique skills not readily available internally as also being valuable. A unique characteristic of contract human capital work, that is, of high criticality, is the emphasis on knowledge development and sharing. Such relationships are also characterized by a high degree of collaboration. Collaboration refers to a method by which competing interests reach win-win outcomes. High-collaborative work groups are uniquely identifiable by high levels of transparency, mindfulness, and the synergy they display.

Conversely, contract work that is of low criticality is characterized by the tasks that are required to be performed and requires skills that are widely available in the labor market. The key objectives of this type of engagement are to ensure a productive and compliant relationship and proper coordination of all tasks.

Managing Contract Human Capital

In my research of a large sample of firms, a common refrain I heard from many companies' HR managers was they are only responsible for overseeing the management of their employees. The most common explanation was fear of violating the joint employer doctrine or IRS regulations governing the employment status of workers. Indeed, these are legitimate concerns and I am a strong proponent for modifying these regulations to reflect the new realities of today's workplace. However, it should not result in the total abandonment of effective talent management practices. In many of these organizations, the purchasing department was the primary function overseeing the management of contract human capital. As a result, the focus for managing these relationships was primarily on cost control. The everyday management of contract human capital was thought to be the responsibility of intermediary firms that either directly employed or represented these workers who worked on assignments for their clients.

However, when I had an opportunity to meet with hiring managers, the feedback was different. Many of these managers were on the front lines already managing multiple sources of talent on their own. It was common to find work groups consisting of employees, independent contractors, consultants, temporary employees, and representatives from outsourced relationships and strategic partners. These multiple sources of talent were in an array of different work groups involved in a multitude of projects across a variety of business functions. Everyday managers interacted with each of these workers to accomplish critical business objectives. These managers instinctively knew that if they were going to be successful, the entire work group had to be successful. However, many of the managers I interviewed lamented about the lack of support they received for managing all these relationships.

The goal of my research was to help managers understand how to effectively manage multiple sources of talent working side-by-side with regular employees in a work group. Drawing from research on the human resource architecture (Lepak and Snell, 1999), I expected that organizations that effectively differentiate how they managed contract human capital would have a strategic advantage over those who do not. An important first step in understanding how to manage and engage multiple sources of talent is assessing how these workers view the different types of employment arrangements they may experience.

Psychological Contract Breach

A growing area of interest pertaining to the study of contract human capital work relates to the nature of the psychological contract held by those workers—that is, the beliefs that workers have concerning the reciprocal obligations between themselves and their employing organization. Thus, it is critical to develop the right combination of HR practices that properly align with the four contract human capital engagement modes to ensure there are balanced and reciprocal relationships. The level of investment of each HR configuration may vary but must be designed to achieve the appropriate level of equity based on the expected contributions of contract human capital. A lack of alignment between engagement modes and HR configurations might be viewed as a psychological contract breach. If contract human capital perceive the employer has failed to meet one or more of their obligations in return for the contributions they make, then they will reciprocate by not fulfilling all the employer objectives.

A lack of alignment can result when organizations manage individuals employed to perform work high in criticality (for example, knowledge work and partnership) with transactional HR configurations. Considering the unique and valuable contributions made by contract human capital performing work of high criticality, they are likely to expect a relational rather than an economic exchange with the organizations. Transactional HR configurations are based on establishing an economic exchange, whereby the employer offers short-term, purely economic inducements in exchange for well-specified contributions by the worker. Alternatively, relational HR configurations are based on establishing a social exchange that focuses on unspecified, broad, and open-ended obligations on the part of both parties (Blau, 1964). The goal then is to have aligned HR configurations and engagement modes that are balanced and provide the right level of investment to ensure contract human capital are engaged and perform well.

Contract Human Capital HR Configurations

The HR configurations most effective for managing contract human capital are composed of four HR practices: selection, appraisal, compensation, and communication. Not surprisingly, training was not a commonly used practice. At many companies, training is considered a benefit primarily for employees, often given for developmental purposes. However, including contract human capital in internal communications and information sharing meetings can be viewed as an alternative to training depending on the level and depth of the communication. There are significant differences in how contract human capital are managed, based on the interdependency and criticality of the work. More important, there were distinct HR configurations that positively impacted these workers' perceptions of fairness and job performance, defined as task performance (adequately completing all assigned and essential duties) and organizational citizenship behaviors (OCBs) (defined as offering ideas to improve the functioning of the work group; volunteering for things that were not required; performing work conscientiously; helping others; and always completing work on time)—measures closely related to employee engagement.

The aligned HR configurations that positively impact contract human capital engagement and performance compose the Contract Human Capital HR Architecture (see Figure 6.4). There are three HR configurations—High Commitment, High Involvement, and Transactional—aligned with each engagement mode.

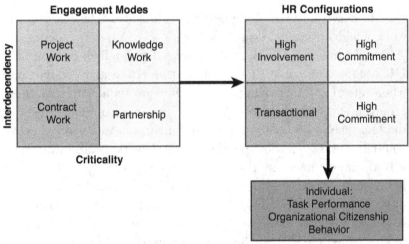

Figure 6.4 Contract Human Capital HR Architecture

It is worth noting that the original model proposed four HR configurations. However, when contract human capital performs work of high criticality, regardless of the level of work interdependency, the same set of HR practices enhanced their performance and engagement. It is interesting that it made no difference whether it was a knowledge worker working interdependently with a workgroup or a strategic partner working independently. Individuals involved in both types of work had the highest level of performance when managed with a high-commitment HR configuration. Organizations were willing to heavily invest in these relationships due to the strategic importance of the work being performed.

Another interesting finding was how best to manage project workers. The original model expected organizations to manage these individuals in a transactional way due to the low criticality of the work performed. However, managing project workers with a purely transactional HR configuration resulted in a negative impact on their performance. Due to the high interdependency of the work they perform, these workers sought a different type of work relationship. A modified relational HR configuration, labeled High Involvement, resulted in a positive impact on their perceptions of fairness and performance.

High-Commitment HR System

The best results for managing contract human capital who perform work of high criticality, regardless of the level of interdependency, are achieved when these workers are managed with a high-commitment HR system. The name "high-commitment HR system" sounds odd when referring to managing contract human capital. After all, these arrangements typically do not last for long periods of time. However, the focus is not on continuous commitment, but rather on affective commitment. Given the type of work these workers are involved in, it is a strategic necessity that these workers are engaged. Perhaps a better name would be "high investment" rather than "high commitment." The goal is to manage these workers in a highly relational way. It's imperative that these workers are appropriately selected and are motivated to help achieve the business objectives at hand.

These individuals are selected by the organization or an intermediary staffing firm using a comprehensive selection process including multiple interviews and tests. Selection is based on a thorough evaluation of industry knowledge and expertise, ability to contribute to strategic goals, and work in a collaborative environment, as well as an assessment of their reputation.

Performance appraisal is based on contribution to strategic objectives, willingness to share knowledge, and effective collaboration with a work group. Given the strategic importance of their work and because of the bargaining power they have to negotiate a wage premium, compensation must be competitive and ensure equity with both work group and industry peers.

Finally, it is important to create an environment that encourages an open exchange of information that fosters knowledge development and sharing. What is needed is an atmosphere in which there is an acceptance of others' opinions and a willingness to incorporate all perspectives into decision-making processes.

Transactional HR Configuration

Organizations that engage contract human capital that work independently and perform work of low criticality typically use a compliance-based HR configuration for managing this type of work relationship. The selection of these workers is based on assessing their abilities to perform the required tasks, as well as their reputation and reliability to perform quality work.

Because these relationships are based on purely economic exchanges, the appraisal process for these workers focuses on the wanted end product or on specific and measurable results. Equally important is to ensure compliance with preset standards and procedures. Due to the general and independent nature of this work, compensation is based on the standard market (going) rate, and only a minimal amount of communications is expected to effectively coordinate the work product with the work group.

Not surprisingly, it is hard to measure the engagement level of these workers. All these workers demonstrated high task performance but no OCBs. Given their independence, there was little opportunity for them to engage in these behaviors. Also, differences existed in their perceptions of fairness (POF). Those individuals who voluntarily sought this type of work because of their need for flexibility had high levels of POF. Conversely, those individuals who preferred a traditional job and entered into this work involuntarily had low levels of POF.

High-Involvement HR Configuration

There is a large body of research that demonstrates the benefits of using high-involvement HR systems for managing employees. However, because we are referring to contract human capital, this term has a slightly different connotation. In this context, a high-involvement HR configuration is designed to engage project workers who are involved in work that is not critical to the organization, yet work interdependently with a work group. As a result, this HR configuration is a hybrid of transactional and relational practices.

Because project workers have skills that are easily replaced in the labor market, organizations do not invest heavily in these employment relationships. However, due to the high interdependency of the work they perform, these workers value being treated as part of the team. Including project workers in work group activities and encouraging more social interactions between them and regular employees has a positive impact on their morale. It is also important to create an environment that encourages an open exchange of information. These workers excel in an atmosphere in which there is an acceptance of their opinions and a willingness to incorporate their perspectives into decision-making processes. These practices enhance project workers' identification with the work group and often with the organization.

Organizations select project workers based on their abilities to perform required tasks and work in a team-based environment. The appraisal process for project workers focuses on adequately performing general tasks and observable team-based behaviors. Due to the general nature of this work, compensation is based on the standard market (going) rate. However, because these workers work interdependently with a work group, often organizations provide subsidies to cover basic benefit costs. It is important to ensure this type of equity if it is a long-term assignment to maintain group cohesiveness and avoid possible regulatory violations.

7

Practices to Create Employee Engagement in the New Normal

It should be clear by now that the technological, global, economic, and demographic trends impacting organizations today require them to develop new strategic management competencies. The old one-size-fits-all methods for managing and engaging employees need to be revised. Throughout this book, a great deal of the research presented focuses on various strategic management models and frameworks for effectively managing and engaging workers in the 21st century. What you see developing are a number of management themes that perhaps apply to one or more segments of the workplace. For example, there are proven strategies deployed by various companies that respond to the multiple challenges they face including managing multigenerational workers, creating organizational adaptability competencies, and managing a highly diverse and global workforce. To bring much of this research to light, throughout this chapter, evidence-based research is presented highlighting the specific practices many of these organizations have successfully deployed.

Strategic Mindset

Thinking about what management practices might or might not motivate and engage a highly diverse workforce requires managers to acquire a strategic mindset. All too often, executives respond to short-term financial losses by cutting funding of Human Resource (HR) management programs at the detriment of their long-term competitiveness. This mentality was common during my many years working at a Wall Street company. As soon as the markets fell, HR budgets and programs were slashed and burned. As markets moved upward, budgets and hiring followed. The result was a constant cycle of hiring and firing tens of thousands of workers. Clearly, expenses have to be managed during downturns, but investments made to sustain competitive advantage should remain intact. This lack of management sophistication led to the downfall of this company and many others that operated the same way.

Companies, particularly those that rely on their human and intellectual capital, must strategically manage HR. As discussed throughout this book, companies need to be adaptable to navigate unforeseen market and economic swings and have engaged workers who can perform in both good and bad times. One of the biggest myths I have encountered while conducting research and consulting with companies is the belief that it's impossible or not worthwhile to increase employee engagement during an economic downturn. In fact, I have identified three myths listed in Table 7.1.

Table 7.1 Three Myths of Employee Engagement in an Economic Downturn

Myth 1	Improving employee engagement costs money—and the expense can't be justified.
Myth 2	Employee engagement will decrease in an economic downturn, regardless of what we do.
Myth 3	Employee engagement does not influence organizational effectiveness enough to make it a priority.

Myth 1: Improving Employee Engagement Costs Money— and the Expense Can't Be Justified

This belief stems from thinking that innovative HR practices and programs designed to motivate and engage employees are expensive and must be cost-justified before implementing. In fact, the key drivers of employee engagement have no direct costs associated with them. A review of the key drivers of engagement proves this point:

- **Job characteristics**—Employees whose jobs are designed to increase skill variety, task identity, task significance, autonomy, and feedback have more developmental opportunities and are more engaged.

- **Role clarity and fit**—Ensuring role clarity and role fit dramatically increases employee engagement, whereas role ambiguity and role conflict diminish individual's coping mechanisms and performance.

- **Coworkers**—Positive interactions among coworkers foster a sense of belonging that builds the morale, cohesion, and rapport associated with engaged employees.

- **Management**—A supportive, trustworthy management style that emphasizes clear expectations, feedback, and recognition increases employee engagement.

- **Leadership**—Transformational leadership that clearly communicates the company vision and is open to suggestions encourages engagement by fostering passion and independent thinking.

- **Perceptions of fairness (POF)**—When employees feel they are treated fairly, they reciprocate by performing the organizational citizenship behaviors (OCBs) that indicate engagement.

Myth 2: Employee Engagement Will Decrease in an Economic Downturn, Regardless of What We Do

This belief stems from thinking that money is the sole driver of engagement and the stress of working during economic downturns demotivates employees and reduces engagement levels. A look at Myth 1 highlights that there are many nonmonetary drivers of engagement that can be implemented during any economic cycle. Furthermore, when it comes to money, though employees like to be paid more, they are most concerned about equity. Many employees can accept lower raises and bonuses as long as they are fairly distributed.

Most important, many employees thrive in challenging environments in which they can be engaged and feel they contribute in a positive way. Organizations that understand the conditions that enhance employee engagement and select employees who portray engaging personality traits can accomplish something that competitors find difficult to imitate. In fact, an economic downturn may provide the opportunities that challenge these individuals to an even higher level of engagement. These personality traits include the following:

- **Autotelic personality**—A general propensity to mentally transform potential threats into enjoyable challenges
- **Trait positive affectivity**—A proclivity for active interaction with one's environment
- **Proactive personality**—Taking action, overcoming opposition, and changing things for the better
- **Conscientiousness**—Dependability, carefulness, thoroughness, responsibility, and perseverance

Myth 3: Employee Engagement Does Not Influence Organizational Effectiveness Enough to Make It a Priority

This myth is based on the misconception that drivers of engagement influence only individual outcomes. There is a large body of research that organizational outcomes are the sum of all employee outcomes. For example, if you treat your employees well, they will treat your customers well, and that will enhance organizational performance. Employee engagement dramatically influences a number of organizational effectiveness measures. It has been conclusively linked to positive

- **Employee outcomes**—Job performance, low absenteeism and lateness, and low turnover
- **Strategic outcomes**—Customer satisfaction and retention, productivity, and quality
- **Financial outcomes**—Revenue, profits, and shareholder value

Differentiated Engagement Strategy

Determining what motivates workers is as complex and diverse as today's workplace. Even determining what success means differs from one individual to another and changes as people go through different life cycles. Cutting-edge management researchers have long known the benefits of differentiated workforce strategies. Work and life are too complex to think there is only one set of practices for achieving a given business strategy or for motivating a unique individual with their own set of circumstances and preferences. After all, the entire economy is moving in the direction of customization. Marketing companies customize messages for the different likes of consumers; products are customized to meet the different needs of buyers; and services are personalized to enhance the experience of recipients.

Clearly, it makes strategic sense to customize workplace practices to meet the different needs and preferences of employees and enhance their levels of engagement. Customized practices provide a more personalized work experience for employees. Some workers value flexibility because they are in a unique time in their lives when they need to balance work and personal needs such as taking care of family responsibilities or going back to school. Other workers place a high premium on development to help them gain marketable skills to launch their careers. There are as many possible different ways to customize practices as there are workers' needs and preferences. However, one thing that is constant is meeting the needs of workers and providing them an experience that will enhance their engagement.

Current research demonstrates that many organizations respond to the different needs of employees, particularly high-performing employees they desperately want to retain, by offering them special work arrangements referred to as idiosyncratic employment arrangements, or *i-deals* (Rousseau et al., 2006). I-deals are traditionally thought of as special-case scenarios in which employees in unique situations negotiate mutually beneficial work arrangements with their employers. These custom arrangements are becoming more common in response to the changing needs of workers and the growing complexity of the workplace.

I-deals have the following characteristics: individually negotiated, heterogeneous, benefiting both employer and employee, and varied in scope. I-deals are not as strategic as differentiated HR systems that result in different types of practices and programs for different groups of employees based primarily on the economic impact of these individuals. I-deals are individually negotiated, custom work arrangements that can motivate employees to help the organization achieve its strategic objectives. These special work arrangements can include giving an employee greater voice in how work is done, providing flexibility regarding when and where to perform work, or creating a special developmental assignment to increase an employee's skills.

As with the differentiated HR systems approach, i-deals by design create situations in which different employees experience different work arrangements. As a result, i-deals impact the perception of equity in the workplace. However, bargaining for special assignments or work arrangements does not have as strong of an impact on equity perceptions as bargaining for increases in pay. Differences in compensation, particularly among employees performing similar work, tends to be viewed more negatively because employees are generally more sensitive to monetary differences in compensation (Rousseau et al., 2006). Clearly, some employees may perceive these special arrangements as unfair, believing the employer favors some employees over others. However, i-deals are not the same as favoritism because favoritism is based on relationships and political ties and does not benefit the company, and thus is not mutually beneficial. I-deals are more likely to be perceived as fair when they are openly communicated and when they conform to organizational values.

The best approach is for organizations to have a variety of policies, practices, and programs that can engage all employees. This requires having an understanding of the preferences and needs of employees and having the ability to customize work arrangements. What makes i-deals effective is that they send a signal to employees that they are valued. Coworkers are more likely to feel an i-deal is fair if they believe they can also receive similar work arrangements. The Holy Grail of talent management is creating a work environment in which all employees feel valued.

Employee Engagement Toolkit

It is common to see specific drivers of engagement targeted to specific cohorts, for example, older workers, working parents, Gen Y, and so on. As previously discussed, employees come to the workplace with their own set of values, needs, and preferences. Although there are common themes that reoccur for different cohorts, it's not wise to generalize. After an organization evaluates which drivers of engagement have the greatest impact on motivating different workers, it needs to have a toolkit (Table 7.2) at its disposal of different practices, programs, and benefits that can be strategically implemented when needed. What follows is a description of successful initiatives that organizations have developed to engage all the talent they need to be successful in the 21st century workplace.

Table 7.2 Employee Engagement Toolkit

Person–organization fit
Performance management and reward systems
Employee involvement program
Training and development programs
Mentoring program
Career management program
Flexible work arrangements
Work–life programs
Innovative time-off policies
Phased retirement programs
Wellness programs
Financial wellness
Diversity programs
Corporate social responsibility (CSR) programs

Person–Organization Fit

Organizations that develop effective HR systems know that increasing employee retention is necessary to get a return on these investments. To ensure the greatest return on investment (ROI), employees must not only have the required job competencies but also fit the organizational culture. Research has shown such employees perform at higher levels and are much less likely to quit (Saks and Ashforth, 1997). As a result, organizations must invest in sophisticated recruitment and selection capabilities that ensure all new employees have a good person–organization fit. For example, Hewlett-Packard developed an innovative approach that allowed applicants to test themselves online to see how they might qualify on multiple dimensions for open positions. Such an advanced job-posting system can improve not only person–job fit, but also help improve person–organization fit by putting the onus on candidates to assess the fit of their own attributes (Fulmer et al., 2000).

One of the most effective ways to ensure a good person–organization fit when hiring for critical positions is to rehire outstanding former employees who left under good terms. Firms such as McKinsey & Company maintain a famously loyal group of alumni. Such groups attract former employees who want to get in touch with people they used to work with. To help organizations manage these relationships, firms like Selectminds.com provide a platform that helps their client companies develop and stay in touch with their employee alumni. Companies can then track what their former employees are doing by looking at their profiles and can target the most attractive candidates and recruit them back into the organization.

Performance Management and Reward Systems

Although a great deal of industrial organizational (IO) psychology research highlights the importance of intrinsic versus extrinsic rewards for enhancing employee engagement, money is still a big motivator for many individuals. This is not surprising in such unstable economic times in which there are millions of workers who are either unemployed or are in fear of losing their job and who have far too little savings for retirement. In a survey conducted by Ernst & Young of Fortune 1000 companies, 61 percent said that reward systems was the talent management program most utilized to motivate and engage employees (Ernst & Young, 2010). Differentiated reward systems are most effective for retaining and engaging high performers. When tied to effective performance management systems, rewards are effective for shaping employee behavior to achieve business goals.

Rewards for performance are an important part of employees' perceptions of fairness, which is strongly linked to engagement. The inability to be recognized and rewarded for discretionary effort and high performance is often a factor in top performers' decisions to exit the firm. Only when performance levels against clear objectives are accurately measured and rewarded can workforce planning effectively prepare for deployment; can learning and development initiatives be

designed to address critical skills gaps; can strategic plans be implemented and effectively executed; and can succession management
processes develop and determine the readiness of the leadership
pipeline (Mitchell, 2011).

Employee Involvement Program

Organizations that design jobs that encourage employees to be
involved in decisions that impact their work increase their sense of
empowerment and level of engagement. A large body of research has
shown a strong relationship between employee involvement programs
and both employee and organizational performance. A number of
well-known employee involvement management systems have been
successfully used by organizations to enhance employee engagement
and organizational performance. One of the best-known examples of
this strategy is General Electrics' Work-Out program. Though popu-
larized in the 1990s, this method of engaging employees is as equally
if not more applicable today. The cornerstone of this strategy was to
involve employees to eliminate inefficiencies and create a boundary-
less organization.

Jack Welch, who was CEO at the time, broke through the top-
down approach to management and recognized that some of the best
ideas come from those closest to the work itself. Welch's leadership
principles enforced a team-based approach to improvement, motivating employees through action-oriented learning, recognizing their
achievements, and clearly stating the company's mission. His primary
focus was to get everybody in the organization involved.

GE work-out sessions would typically involve people from different ranks of the organization in groups of 40–100 employees and a
facilitator. Employees were informed at the beginning of the session
that management would commit to two things: to give an on-the-spot
"yes" or "no" to 75 percent of the recommendations from the session and resolve the remaining 25 percent within 30 days. Employees
worked in self-directed teams throughout the day and communicated
their recommendations to management at the end of the day (Welch,
2001).

Training and Development Programs

Providing training and development opportunities to enhance employees' knowledge and skills have all been shown to be strong drivers of engagement for many different employees. In a study conducted by Towers Perrin, the lack of development and advancement opportunities was the biggest factor explaining why workers were not engaged in their jobs (Towers Perrin, 2006). In a work environment in which specific skills can become obsolete overnight, employees value the opportunity to develop new and marketable skills. Whether it's a young worker seeking to gain marketable skills, an older worker wanting to be retrained, or a highly skilled professional looking to upgrade skills, providing developmental opportunities for these workers can positively impact their level of engagement.

In the not-too-distant past, companies exchanged job security for employees' loyalty and job performance. Today, both employers and employees realize this older social contract no longer holds weight in the new normal environment. Instead, companies that invest in employees' training offer employability in exchange for performance. Furthermore, as corporate hierarchies continue to shrink, the developmental opportunities in climbing the corporate ladder also are shrinking. In flatter organizational structures associated with broadband grades, there are fewer vertical development moves for employees but more lateral developmental moves. In such an environment in which skills are the basis for advancement, many individuals place a high value on learning new marketable skills.

Despite massive reductions in force and restructurings in the United States and Europe, a survey of CEOs conducted by the Conference Board indicated that the development of internal talent is a critical challenge they all face. They noted that human capital is a crucial enabler of business growth. The top three strategies identified to meet their human capital challenge was to grow talent internally, improve leadership development programs, and provide employee training and development (Mitchell, 2011). In a recent survey conducted by the Society for Human Resource Management (SHRM) and WSJ.com, 44 percent of HR professionals reported that their organizations provided or paid for skills training and professional development for their U.S. workforce. The top three training methods provided to employees were instructor-led workshops or courses (83 percent), on-the-job training (82 percent), and continuing education courses (80 percent) (SHRM and WSJ.com, 2008).

However, training effectiveness depends on several factors, including the career stage of employees. For example, 73 percent of early-career employees rate coaching or mentoring as an effective training method, compared to only 45 percent of mid-career employees (SHRM and WSJ.com, 2008). Not surprising, early-career employees also highly rated online tutorials and guided programs. Younger workers seem to prefer informal, less structured training formats than traditional classroom style skill training. An interesting finding in this study was late-career employees also highly rated both mentoring and online training methods. Older workers value one-on-one relationships as well as learning at a self-directed pace.

Employee development programs are critical at organizations that are worried about the impending loss of knowledge as more and more experienced workers retire. These companies are worried about the systematic loss of organizational knowledge that can extend learning curves and cause inefficient duplication of efforts. The strategic imperative at these companies is the transfer of knowledge from one generation of workers to a younger generation. In a survey of organizations dealing with these issues, the most common practices used to facilitate the transfer of knowledge across generations were succession planning, the creation of knowledge networks, and mentoring programs (Ernst & Young, 2006).

Given the chaotic world we live and work in and the increasing emphasis on organizational adaptability, a number of organizations are also developing innovative training programs that simulate chaotic conditions to enhance employees' comfort with uncertainty and performance. The benefits of this type of training became known worldwide during the 2008 Olympics in Beijing, when U.S. swimmer Michael Phelps won the gold medal in the 200 individual medley after his goggles filled with water blinding him for most of the race. After the race, his coach Bob Bowman talked about how Phelps was trained to be familiar with chaos by mimicking these types of conditions during his training routines. Before meets, Bowman routinely hid goggles so that Phelps had to swim without them, or cracked the goggles so that they would fill up with water obstructing his vision. By creating uncertainties in these low-risk situations, Phelps was prepared to deal with the unexpected and had the mental adaptability to perform under these less than ideal conditions (Allen, 2012).

Training individuals to develop mental adaptability and have the capacity to perform in chaotic situations is not only used in sports, but is also commonly used in the military and in business. In an interview with Sanyin Siang at the Coach K Center on Leadership and Ethics, at Duke's Fuqua School of Business, General Martin Dempsey shared his thoughts on training the U.S. military for a 21st century world. An important part of the training is simulating chaos in the developmental experience to enhance operational adaptability and the ability to deal with the unexpected (Allen, 2012). In a *Forbes* article, Leadership Editor Frederick Allen talks about the importance of organizations training employees to be ready for chaos. By simulating chaos in which there is a high chance of failure in low-risk situations, employees can have the opportunity for the greatest growth by learning how to adapt and succeed in uncertain situations (Allen, 2012).

At organizations that pursue a business strategy based on innovation, offering creative developmental opportunities for employees is a strategic imperative. Developmental programs are important to creative employees looking to further develop their skills and vital to companies seeking to be at the bleeding edge of innovation. No other company is more aware of this than Google. Speaking at the 12th Annual Society for Human Resource Management Foundation Thought Leaders Retreat, Shannon Deegan, Director of People Operations, told the audience that Google is institutionalizing the practice of innovation. According to Shannon, Google employees can dedicate 20 percent of their time working on anything they want. Significantly, employees are not evaluated on what they accomplish during their free time, but if they do something great, they will be recognized. At Genentech, the IT organization used the concepts of mindfulness and self-motivation to design an innovative program to develop top talent. Employees receive peer coaching and guidance to improve a skill and goal of their own choosing (McKinsey, 2012a).

Nestlé, the world's leading food company operating in nearly every country, believes that it is important to provide employees the opportunities for life-long learning. The company also considers training to be a critical part of its business sustainability strategy. In their communications to employees, all are called upon to upgrade their skills in a fast-changing world. The company's commitment to employee development has greatly enhanced its ability to set up operations around the world and attract and retain talent needed for all levels of their operation.

To remain a premier leader in food production, Nestlé continues to introduce increasingly sophisticated production techniques at its facilities around the world. However, as the level of technology in its factories continues to rise, the need for training has significantly increased at all levels. At many locations, the focus of training is upgrading employees' essential literacy skills. At a plant in South Africa, the company developed an Adult Based Education Training (ABET) program that provides training in four levels of math, reading, and writing. Employees attend 2-hour sessions twice a week, with 1 hour donated by Nestlé; the other is on the employee's time. Employees who complete the program are recognized with a National Diploma (Nestlé, 2003).

Nestlé's apprenticeship program is another example of what smart companies are doing to address the growing labor force skills gap throughout the world. The success of these types of programs is based on a company's ability to collaborate with a viable local vocational education system. This is one area in which the United States is sorely lacking. Unfortunately, in the United States, there are few options for high school graduates to develop marketable skills who do not go to college. However, in many parts of the world, Nestlé collaborates with local vocational schools whereby students gain valuable on-the-job training during designated work periods while attending classes and completing their education (Nestlé, 2003).

Complementing these training programs are a series of professional and management training programs customized to meet the different needs of employees around the world. These programs cover a wide range of topics such as leadership and strategy, sales and marketing, and a range of offerings focused on developing employees' competencies in such areas as communication, management, and finance for nonspecialists. Computer-based distance learning platforms have also enabled Nestlé to expand its training offerings. Many Nestlé companies have dedicated corporate training assistances that facilitate distance learning programs. Employees can select from a wide range of courses that meet their individual needs and complete them at their own pace at convenient times.

Nestlé also partners with external training sources to augment its executive education offerings. Its primary partner is the International Institute for Management Development (IMD), an institute that Nestlé was instrumental in creating. IMD delivers Nestlé's Program for Executive Development (PED). The PED offering is divided into two 5-week sessions attended 12–18 months apart. The program is designed to help high-potential, mid-managers develop skills needed to advance in their careers. They also have relationships with other universities such as the Institut Européen d'Administration des Affaires (INSEAD) in France, and Harvard and Wharton in the United States.

Given that both the employer and employee benefit from training, the former as a result of increased productivity and the latter due to an increase in marketable skills, a smart strategy is for both to share the costs. This can be achieved in a number of ways. Notwithstanding the Fair Labor Standards Act (FLSA) regulations in the United States that require employers to pay all the costs of training required by the employer, employers can ask employees to contribute to the costs of training that is developmental and not required for their current jobs. Another common approach in a diversity of occupations is to offer a training wage. Organizations that provide extensive training can reduce the wage of employees until the end of the training period. Many apprentice positions are paid this way as well as junior consultants and lawyers.

Like any other investment, organizations must assess the costs of training and development programs relative to their impact on strategic objectives. However, despite how much companies spend on these programs, most measure their impact by measuring the number of training hours and employee satisfaction of the training. In one study of organizational training programs, 90 percent of surveyed companies indicated that building employee capabilities is a strategic priority, yet only 8 percent said they measure the ROI of their training programs. Not surprising, only one quarter of these firms believed their training programs improved firm performance (Cermak and McGurk, 2010).

One of the best ways of measuring training ROI is by analyzing employee engagement drivers and outcomes. If as suggested throughout this book, employee engagement surveys include separate measures for HR practices and programs (drivers), psychological state engagement, behavioral outcomes, and strategic outcomes, then calculating training ROI is easy. By including all HR practices and programs, you can specifically assess how much of a driver training is on employee engagement and outcomes. The costs of training can then be compared to the benefits derived by achieving strategic and financial outcomes.

Mentoring Program

One of the most effective ways for developing employees is through mentoring programs. Learning directly from a seasoned leader about what it takes to be successful at an organization is a valuable learning experience. Through mentoring relationships, the mentee has the unique opportunity to interact with company leaders and observe how they behave and dress, to get insights on company politics, and to better understand the organization's culture and strategy. Mentoring is vital at organizations that experience a "changing of the guards" as their experienced and knowledgeable employees begin to retire in large numbers. This is particularly the case at companies that have job-specific competencies, such as many utility and engineering firms.

Mentoring programs in the 21st century are not the informal relationships of yesteryear but are viewed as strategic investments that help develop talent, build knowledge networks, and improve cross-functional learning. At a world-class multinational company like Boeing, mentoring programs are an important part of leadership development that support one of the organization's core principles to have a "fervent desire to become the best at what they do; learning from one another" (Sterling, 2007 pg. 31). Mentoring within Boeing takes place through dialogue and discussions about the differences and communication styles between mentor and mentee that strengthen Boeing people across the enterprise. Boeing has built its mentoring program to incorporate tools that enhance cross-cultural dialogue with the goal to retain and develop global talent.

Key components of the program include selecting mentors and mentees who have different backgrounds and focusing on teaching people to work across different cultures and working together. Both mentor and mentee are given clear objectives. The program includes an orientation, a training, and a mentoring agreement that identifies goals, objectives, and role definitions. It also has regular evaluations to track progress toward objectives along with input from the mentee's manager. These comprehensive tools and metrics help ensure a value-added experience. Participants meet monthly (in person and/or by phone) for 1 year with the mentee's manager actively contributing to some of the mentoring discussions.

The value for Boeing in company-wide mentoring programs lies in the underlying reality that within the next 5 years, tens of thousands of Boeing employees will be eligible for retirement. Thus, the competition to identify, attract, retain, and develop top talent from within Gen Y will be fierce, particularly in an industry like aerospace where there's a significant demand for scientific and technical expertise. Thus, Boeing is leveraging mentoring as a way to impart knowledge to and develop potential future leaders. Equally important is the need to develop diverse leaders as Boeing's customer base becomes increasingly global. In the end, that means building a pipeline of leaders at Boeing who more closely mirror the demographics of Boeing's workforce, customers, and communities (Sterling, 2007).

Career Management Program

Another great strategy to increase engagement for employees is creating effective career management programs that complement training and development initiatives. There are a wide variety of different practices and programs that support a career management strategy including performance management, job postings, orientation and socialization, lateral job rotation, and tuition reimbursement programs. Realizing that employees need to manage their own careers today, a number of companies help employees develop career plans by offering career-planning workshops that provide self-assessment exercises, information on organizational career paths, and resources for identifying and applying to open positions.

At Duke Power, employees can actually post their job, with their supervisor's permission, to see whether someone in the company at an equivalent job level and pay grade would be interested in swapping. At the retailer Gap, employees with at least 2 years of experience have access to an internal headhunting function that helps them look for other positions throughout the company (Cappelli, 1999). Another great example of a cutting-edge career management strategy is the Deloitte Career Connections (DCC) program, established in 2002. Employees have access to an array of services through the DCC website including detailed information on job openings, self-assessment and feedback tools, and information on building career plans. Employees also have resources designed to enhance their advancement-related skills (such as networking and interviewing) and have access to career coaches (Cappelli, 2008). To help retain older workers who have unique skills, Deloitte Consulting offers tailored comprehensive career management programs for its older workers including career assessments and redesigned career tracks (Callanan and Greenhaus, 2008).

An important component of any career management program is having effective performance management programs that evaluate employees' job performance and developmental potential. Advances in technology along with changes in how work gets done are altering how firms are evaluating employees. Rather than a single boss or management team evaluating the performance of employees, alternative ways of appraising performance are emerging. According to Michael Chui, Senior Fellow at McKinsey Global Institute, cutting edge firms today are migrating to "720-degree evaluation" systems—a twist on the older "360-degree evaluation" system, in which an employee is evaluated by everyone within the company and by those they interact with outside the company. In essence, one's degree of connectedness and influence in the network is a key part of the evaluation and consequently their career success (Bollier, 2011).

Flexible Work Arrangements

Flexible work schedules including flextime, job sharing, and tele-commuting have been in vogue since the 1990s. In the early days, many organizations implemented flexible work schedules as a way to recruit and retain working mothers. Fast forward to today, and these work arrangements are attractive to a vast array of workers including Gen Y and Gen X, transitioning retirees, and dual-income couples. A survey of HR professionals cited in the 2011 SHRM Workplace Forecast noted that companies are becoming more sensitive to the needs of caregivers. Forty-six percent said they have policies aimed at encouraging workplace flexibility, and another 24 percent said they plan to implement such policies in the near future.

The report also noted that workers are increasingly asking for flexibility to manage their work and outside commitments; whether due to caregiving responsibilities, parenting, or balancing work and personal needs, many employees seek benefits such as telecommut-ing and flexible work schedules (SHRM Workplace Forecast, 2011). In a survey of Fortune 1000 companies conducted by Ernst & Young, 31 percent said they have implemented flexible work strategies to engage employees including job sharing, telecommuting, phased-retirement, and flex hours (Ernst & Young, 2010).

Creating a flexible workplace can also provide a strategic edge for many firms. At JetBlue Airways in Salt Lake City, the company's 1,500 agents work from home where they collectively handle more than 30,000 calls a day. JetBlue's flexible work arrangement of part-time workers working from home eliminates the need to create an expensive centralized call center. To enhance employees' productiv-ity and commitment, managers focus on effective communication and conduct monthly in-person training sessions and staff meetings. Other innovative policies include offering voluntary time off when call volume is down and having annual family days when all employ-ees and their families get together (Benko and Anderson, 2010e).

IBM has known the benefits of telecommuting for some time as a result of its successful workforce on demand strategy. Roughly 40 percent of IBM's staff are mobile and telecommute from home or at a client location (Meister and Willyerd, 2010). Research conducted by IBM noted employees who telecommute increased their productivity by up to 50 percent. Similar results were found at Compaq Computer Corporation where employees who telecommute saw an increase in productivity ranging from 15 to 45 percent (Harnish and Lister, 2010).

Offering innovative flexible work schedules has also helped companies reduce their staffing costs without having to lay off employees. For example, in January 2009, KPMG unveiled its new Flexible Futures program for its United Kingdom employees. The program was a creative way to reduce costs in a difficult economic environment without negatively impacting employee morale. The company offered employees the options to either work a 4-day work schedule with a 20 percent reduction in base pay, take a 4- to 12-week sabbatical at 30 percent pay, combine these options, or stick with the status quo. The company estimated a potential savings of up to 15 percent of payroll costs (Hewlett, 2009).

Best Buy incorporated flextime in 2006 as part of its new strategy to create a "results only work environment" referred to as ROWE. Like many companies, Best Buy struggled with changing a culture that strictly valued "face time." Management reasoned that given the challenges of managing multiple generations, it's a perfect time to initiate a different approach to how work is performed. Given that it has the technology (teleconferencing, emailing, text messaging, and cell phone calling) to extend where and when the work gets done, now it's just a matter of will to implement the strategy (Conlin, 2006).

The essence of a flexible work culture is acknowledging that employees can achieve their work objectives without having to be physically in one place. The key is to have measurable objectives that employees can achieve while working their own hours. The goals of ROWE were to give employees flexibility by judging performance on output rather than on hours spent at the office or in meetings (Conlin, 2006). Under ROWE, Best Buy employees have the flexibility to leave in the middle of the workday to attend to personal needs. Workers pulling into the company's headquarters at 2 p.m. aren't considered late, nor are those pulling out at 2 p.m. seen as leaving early. There are no set schedules as long as the work gets done. There are also no mandatory meetings; however, employees typically call in to conference calls while out of the office or log in to get updates anytime, day or evening.

After ROWE, Best Buy reported that voluntary turnover significantly dropped, while involuntary turnover increased. Having measurable performance objectives enabled management to more accurately assess which employees were performing well and which ones were not. After implementing ROWE, employee productivity increased by 35 percent. A study of the effectiveness of the Best Buy's ROWE strategy conducted by the Flexible-Work and Wellbeing Center at the University of Minnesota found that employees reported higher organizational commitment, job satisfaction, and job security as compared to other comparable employees surveyed in their study (Bond et al., 2002).

Time and time again, the evidence is clear that flexible work programs can be highly motivating for many employees, which results in tangible benefits for the organization. In a 2007 *CNN Money* article, the Bailey Law Group, a 16-member company in Washington, DC, was noted for having a cross-country telecommuting program that had spectacular results. Rather than lose two high-performing employees who were moving to another part of the country, the firm's founder, Kathy Bailey, agreed to let them work remotely from their new homes. Bailey noted that the firm's flexibility helped them triple the company's revenues primarily as a result of a whole roster of new clients brought into the firm by the employees retained by this policy (Sahadi, 2007).

Sadly, there is a view at many organizations that flexibility is not something that high-performing employees should seek. In the mid-1990s, as VP of HR Policy and Planning for a top Wall Street firm, I helped implement alternative work arrangement policies that included flextime, telecommuting, compressed workweek, and job sharing. The day we communicated these new policies, I looked at my boss and said (tongue-in-cheek) what type of flexible work schedule can I work. Without missing a beat, she said, no problem, you can work 7:00 a.m. to 7:00 p.m. or 8:00 a.m. to 8:00 p.m. The message was clear: If you want to advance, you should forget about flexibility. I am happy to say that a lot has changed since that time, but unfortunately this mentality still exists among many executives who manage large organizations.

Most surprising has been the well-publicized communication to Yahoo's employees by their new female CEO Marissa Mayer ending the company's longstanding work-from-home policy. One week after the announcement, Best Buy stated it will end its flexible work policy as well (Tkaczyk, 2013). Both companies are reacting to the severe economic challenges they are facing. When companies are under severe pressure, particularly from the investment community, they resort to Draconian, short-term, cost-saving strategies. Yet, eliminating their flexible work programs flies in the face of all the research that demonstrates the significant impact such programs have on attracting, retaining, and engaging employees. Echoing these sentiments, a survey by *Fortune* of young executives found that approximately one-half of these executives believe that expressing an interest in flexibility to their boss will ultimately damage their career. It seems that with all the progress in changing corporate cultures to embrace flexibility, there is still a lingering perception at some firms that non-work aspirations are frowned upon for those climbing the corporate ladder (Miller, 2005).

Work–Life Programs

Due to the increasing numbers of dual-income couples, single parents, and people going back to school, the number of workers who seek alternative work arrangements or have to temporarily leave the workplace is also increasing. Acknowledging these trends, Deloitte and Touché designed the Personal Pursuits Program to help employees who must leave the firm due to family issues. Employees who leave the firm in good standing can remain plugged in to the company for as long as 5 years. The company continues to pay employees' certification requirements and provides access to company career and work–life programs. Not only are employees' skills kept up to date, but they also remain committed to the company. When they can go back to work, they are ready and likely to return to Deloitte (Deloitte, 2012).

After analyzing their employee engagement survey results, Hewlett Packard found many other factors besides salary influenced employee engagement. Collectively, these other drivers of engagement became part of a series of work–life programs. A key driver was flexibility, so the company implemented a policy whereby employees have the option of taking one Friday afternoon off every month and making up the hours at other times. Employees also are permitted to design their daily work schedules regarding starting and ending work hours and lunchtimes. In addition, the company expanded part-time opportunities for employees who temporarily want to work fewer hours. Other initiatives included offering a time management course to help employees effectively manage many of their work and life activities, a telecommuting program that permitted employees to work a portion of their time offsite, and a health management program (Poelmans and Chinchilla, 2001).

Procter & Gamble (P&G), one of the largest consumer goods companies in the world, found that offering work–life programs that enable employees to balance their professional and family needs significantly enhanced their image as an employer of choice while positively impacting productivity. These programs enabled P&G to expand its pool of qualified workers who value these types of programs including working mothers, dual-income couples, and Gen Y workers. Internally, a series of work–life policies and programs were introduced as part of a broader corporate principle that employees are P&G's most important asset, which included maternity and adoption leave, career breaks, sabbaticals, flexible work arrangements, family advisory services, childcare vouchers, eldercare, active parenting, and career networks. In no small part, these policies and programs have contributed to P&G's standing as one of the world's most-admired companies. After launching these programs, results of employee engagement surveys indicated a vast improvement in employee satisfaction and motivation metrics (My Family Care, 2011).

Innovative Time-Off Policies

Organizations competing in the technology sector have long known the importance of having innovative time-off programs for attracting and retaining employees. One example is the Cisco voluntary sabbatical program, which helped them retain valuable talent during the 2000 Internet bubble burst and severe market downturn in 2001. The program paid employees one-third of their salaries for a period if they went to work for a nonprofit organization. As a result, the company reduced costs while improving their corporate image. Most important, employees had an opportunity to be productive during this downturn and were readily available when business picked up (Cappelli, 2008).

The global consulting firm Booz & Company's Partial-Pay Sabbatical program was introduced as part of an innovative strategy to increase employee engagement and cut expenses. The program, which was first offered to consultants, was made available to all employees in 2009. Eligible employees can request a sabbatical ranging from a minimum of 1 month to a maximum of 12. Employees on company-approved sabbaticals receive 20 percent of their base pay and full healthcare benefits. To make the program more economically attractive, Booz offers "salary smoothing," so that employees planning a sabbatical can start deducting 20 percent of their pay beforehand to help subsidize their time-off pay (Hewlett, 2009).

An innovation program at Semco, a Brazilian industrial company, permits employees to use 1 day a week for personal aspirations. For instance, some employees use the time to pursue their outside interests such as art and athletic endeavors or perform volunteer work at organizations they support (McKinsey, 2012a). Some organizations that hire highly specialized talent mirror what major research universities provide tenured professors. For example, in 2007, employees who worked at Intel's Chandler, Arizona office were eligible for 2 paid, consecutive months off every 7 years (Sahadi, 2007).

Phased Retirement Programs

Attracting, engaging, and retaining older workers is a strategy necessary for many organizations facing talent shortages. Also, given the "barbell" nature of the labor force with large numbers of younger and older workers, there is a growing need for experienced managers who can mentor and lead the younger workers entering the workplace. A study conducted by the Urban Institute for the Alfred P. Sloan Foundation found that today's 50 and older workers are healthier and more educated than previous generations and plan to work well beyond traditional retirement ages. Furthermore, the 21st century workplace consists of fewer strenuous jobs than in the past, making it more likely that older workers will remain in the workforce for a longer period of time. To accommodate older workers who, in their later years of employment, do not want traditional full-time jobs, many organizations are experimenting with flexible work arrangements including part-time employment, flexible work schedules, job sharing, telecommuting, and contract work. A number of organizations formalize these arrangements into phased retirement programs (Johnson, 2010).

According to a study conducted by the American Association of Retired Persons (AARP), 38 percent of workers 50 years of age and older indicated that they would be interested in a phased retirement program, and 78 percent said that such a program would motivate them to remain in the labor force for a longer period of time (Brown, 2005). Phased retirement programs permit older workers to gradually transition into retirement by slowly reducing their work hours and job responsibilities. Such programs enable workers to pursue their outside interests while continuing to be productive and maintaining important social relationships. The organization benefits by having access to the skills and knowledge of employees who otherwise would be gone. As these employees slowly transition into retirement, they can mentor younger workers who are inline to succeed them.

Developing programs to engage older workers who otherwise would leave the workplace not only makes good strategic sense for organizations, but is also quickly becoming an economic necessity for the United States. The rapid growth of older Americans who qualify for Social Security and Medicare is threatening the nation's economic security. Between 2000 and 2020, the number of workers for every nonworking individual age 65 and older will fall from 4.5 to 3.3, based on current employment patterns (Johnson and Steuerle, 2004). If this trend persists, publicly funded benefit programs will likely be cut, workers will have to pay higher taxes, and growth in per capita economic output will likely slow.

Permitting older workers to stay in the workplace longer not only makes good economic sense, but can also enhance their well-being. Workers who delay their retirement can increase their retirement incomes by accumulating more Social Security, pension credits, and other savings, and reducing the number of retirement years they must fund. For example, a typical worker who delays retirement until age

67 instead of retiring at age 62 would gain about $10,000 in annual net income at age 75 (Butrica et al., 2004). Most important, delaying retirement has been shown to enhance physical and emotional health by keeping older adults active and engaged and providing more meaning in their lives (Calvo, 2006).

In 2006, executives at American Express questioned whether the next generation of workers will be equipped to run the show as baby boomers begin to retire. A taskforce that was commissioned to investigate these concerns concluded that not only will a large number of employees become eligible for retirement in the next 5 to 10 years, but also the company has done little to retain the invaluable institutional knowledge they would be taking with them. The knowledge these workers possessed regarding the intricacies of client relationships, legacy computer systems, and the like would be difficult and costly to replace if lost (MacMillan, 2008).

The solution was a phased retirement program that gives soon-to-be retirees less work and more time to pass along their expertise to younger workers. The goal is to permit employees to gradually reduce their hours, give up normal work activities, and provide more time for mentoring and teaching master classes to their successors. The reduced work schedule also enables workers to pursue other life activities of their choosing such as spending time on a hobby, doing charity work, and planning for the next phase of their life in retirement. The phased retiree continues to receive a portion of their salary and continues to receive benefits. In turn, the company gets to retain valuable and engaged workers who willingly transfer their knowledge to the next generation of workers.

Firms like American Express acknowledge the importance of retaining valuable institutional knowledge at a time when many organizations are finding it difficult to attract and retain enough highly skilled talent to run their businesses. One of the unique features of its phased retirement program is the strong emphasis on mentoring and knowledge sharing. Phased retirees in the program are trained to learn teaching tools such as learning maps, interactive media such as wikis, and social media.

Other things worth noting that American Express is doing well can make for a successful phased retirement program:

- Having effective workforce planning programs that capture critical information of the workforce, age profiles, and worker competencies that facilitate succession planning at all levels within the organization
- Extending the careers of valuable employees through smart career management planning
- Developing a culture of open communication in which there is an active exchange of information that acknowledges the value of knowledge held by workers and making knowledge transfer a part of everyone's job
- Establishing mentoring programs throughout the organization so there is a natural progression for those valuable employees phasing into retirement
- Demonstrating that the program supports the business strategy, such as controlling costs, improving innovation, and supporting the growth of the business

Some organizations have faced challenges when developing phased retirement programs. For example, organizations that have defined benefit (DB) programs that calculate retirement benefits based on employees' earnings during their last years of employment are problematic. Working a reduced part-time schedule at lower pay will negatively impact these employees' retirement income. Another problem is the loss of other benefits such as health insurance. At many organizations, health insurance is not offered to employees working reduced schedules. One solution is a retire-rehire program that permits employees to retire and receive their full benefits and then rehires them as part-time employees.

Monsanto Corporation has a program called Resource Reentry, in which retired workers can come back to work on projects that can last from 1 week to 1 year (Callanan and Greenhaus, 2008). However, a number of organizations have policies that prevent retired employees from being on the firm's payroll. One common solution to this problem is to use a workforce management company to manage these relationships by either directly hiring these workers or engaging them as independent contractors while they work as a contractor at their previous company. This is not a problem at many government and educational institutions that have phased retirement programs, because many of these public employers have Deferred Retirement Option Plans (DROPs) that permit workers to accrue benefits they would have received under a DB program in a separate account that is paid out to the employee when they stop working.

However, the limitations of DB programs are becoming less of an issue for phased retirement programs as a result of most private employers offering defined contribution (DC) programs (Bureau of Labor Statistics, 2009b). Unlike a DB program, which is an annuity plan based on the number of years an employee works, in a DC program, both employers and employees typically make direct contributions to an employee's retirement account, such as a 401(k) plan that they have access to when they retire. Because contributions continue as long as employees remain employed, there is no significant penalty for individuals transitioning to a part-time schedule. Their annual retirement contributions will be reduced as they begin working fewer hours, but their overall retirement savings account balance will continue to grow. Indeed, research has shown that employees in DC plans tend to work on average 2 years longer than employees in DB programs (Friedberg and Webb, 2005).

As an increasing larger segment of the labor force consists of retired workers who still would like to work, many companies are developing creative work arrangements to accommodate these workers. Two companies known for their innovative programs for hiring retirees are CVS and Home Depot. Both of these large retail companies target older workers to fill both part-time and full-time positions at tens of thousands of stores throughout the country. To help accommodate these workers, they created "snowbird" programs that enable their retiree workers to temporarily move to warm climates during the winter and work at stores in those areas and then come back to work at their original stores for the remainder of the year (Bisson et al., 2010). CVS deliberately recruits and trains older workers to mirror the aging customer base of the company. CVS has also partnered with the U.S. Department of Labor, which provides government funding, to create seven regional training centers to assist older workers looking for work (Farrell et al., 2005).

Wellness Programs

Given the correlation between age and risk of illness, wellness and disease prevention programs are particularly attractive to older health-conscious workers. However, as a result of the current obesity epidemic facing the United States, wellness programs are becoming increasingly appealing to employees of all ages. Also, a growing number of active younger workers are attracted to companies that offer such benefits as onsite workout facilities and programs promoting healthy lifestyles. According to a survey conducted by the SHRM, 54 percent of companies are currently implementing wellness programs and another 26 percent plan to (SHRM Workplace Forecast, 2011).

IBM is well known for investing in prevention and well-being programs for its employees. It does so because it makes sense for employees as well as its business. A study the company sponsored in 2008 showed some alarming rates of increased obesity, high blood pressure, and sugar among the 18,000 individuals surveyed, prompting IBM to expand their employee wellness strategy to prevent its employees from falling prey to these diseases. The IBM Wellness for Life program was established with the intention to create a global wellness strategy that cultivates a "culture of health" that fosters long-term healthy lifestyles and the reduction of health-related risks among employees and their families.

IBM's comprehensive approach to employee wellness includes interventions for reducing major risk factors such as weight management, physical activities, nutrition, stress management, and tobacco cessation programs. There is also a dedicated budget that supports a staff that includes preventive medicine doctors, certified fitness and public health professionals, and program managers who design and implement IBM's wellness strategy. Outside health experts are also hired to enhance program offerings (Goodspeed, 2011). Not surprising, IBM developed an innovative web-based system to deliver and communicate programs to employees worldwide that provides access to flexible, behavior-based programming designed to enhance employees' engagement in their health improvement. In 2008, IBM's efforts to enhance employee wellness were recognized when it received the C. Everett Koop National Health Award (The Health Project, 2010).

To increase participation, IBM offers employees incentives for participating in one of four wellness programs that include physical fitness and activity, diet and nutrition, children and family health, and personal vitality programs. Employees can earn up to $150 for each program they complete up to $300 per year. The programs are voluntary and are offered online for 12 weeks. Each program is designed to engage employees through a welcoming check in to help employees determine their readiness for specific lifestyle changes, offering resources to help employees set realistic goals, suggesting resources and activities to help achieve their goals, providing access to online communities that provide social support, logging and monitoring progress, and a final check out. IBM's long history of creating healthier and engaged employees has resulted in significant cost-savings. For example, between 2005 and 2007, these programs have saved IBM an estimated $190 million, and overall healthcare costs are rising at a slower rate (Goodspeed, 2011).

The benefits of effective corporate wellness programs go beyond increasing employees' perceptions of organizational support and levels of engagement, or reducing companies' increasing healthcare costs. Increasing the health of all workers complements national initiatives to curtail out-of-control health care expenditures. A 2007 study conducted by the Milken Institute concluded that reorienting the U.S. health system toward prevention rather than disease management can reduce by 40 million the number of cases of cancer, heart disease, and other chronic illnesses over the ensuing 15 years. By doing so, the estimated cost of medical care and lost productivity would be reduced by $1.1 trillion (Andrews, 2007).

Financial Wellness

One of the benefits of employee wellness programs is the positive effects it can have on reducing employees' stress. Given the need for engaged employees to have enough physical, cognitive, and emotional resources to fully invest themselves in their work, reducing stress levels can have a positive impact on engagement and performance. A major stress factor affecting many workers is money management. After experiencing one financial disaster after another and seeing their investments diminish, many workers' financial conditions are in dire straits. This is a major concern for baby boomers who are financially ill-prepared for retirement. Aetna, a U.S.-managed care company, decided to take action to help relieve the financial stress of its employees. In 2007, Aetna's head of retirement and financial benefits, Carol Klusek, and her team became aware of a distressing trend while monitoring employee calls to the 401(k) Retirement Plan Call Center. Many individuals calling the center were under pressure to quickly make withdrawals from their retirement accounts. The level of distress in their voices was palpable, as many knew the pitfalls of drawing down retirement savings (Davis, 2012).

It quickly became apparent to Aetna's management team that providing financial planning resources to relieve employees' stress should be part of its overall wellness strategy. In 2008, Aetna rolled out an innovative financial wellness program to approximately 32,000 employees as part of a comprehensive wellness initiative that centered on employees' physical, emotional, and financial well-being. The program provided an array of resources to help employees navigate the uncertain financial landscape and develop financial savings and investment plans to secure their future financial and retirement needs.

Aetna used a multichannel approach to deliver financial education and services to employees including interactive webcasts, videos, workshops, and one-on-one planning sessions. Employees also have access to an online financial wellness center and personalized retirement counseling. Through the "grow your money" campaign, employees receive timely information each month to help them manage their finances including reducing debt, improving credit, saving for retirement, and estate planning.

Another innovation was partnering with external financial experts to offer a robust program of personalized financial services. Financial Finesse-certified financial planners were engaged to offer employees one-on-one financial planning sessions. ING and Aon Hewitt offered specific retirement planning advice for employees participating in Aetna's retirement program. UBS provided employees a range of asset and wealth management services.

The overwhelming positive response from employees confirmed how important it is to help employees manage an important aspect of their well-being. A 2010 survey revealed that nearly 90 percent of Aetna employees have used some aspect of the program and nearly all (99 percent) reported feeling better prepared to make financial decisions and would recommend the program to a coworker. The same percentage considered the financial wellness program an important employee benefit (Field, 2012). In 2012, Carol Klusek's efforts in launching the program was acknowledged when she earned the Employee Benefit News (EBN's) Benny award for benefits leadership in retirement (Davis, 2012).

The success of Aetna's financial wellness program is proof that helping employees manage their financial needs makes good business sense. Demonstrating to employees that the organization cares about their well-being and helping them to reduce a major contributing stress factor in their lives has been shown to positively impact their engagement and job performance.

Diversity Programs

The rise of the global workforce and U.S. population trends are leading to increased diversity within companies. It behooves organizations interested in creating a highly engaged workforce to ensure diverse employees identify with the organization and feel a sense of inclusion. According to a study conducted by the Economist Intelligence Unit on behalf of the SHRM, more than one-half (55 percent) of the senior executives surveyed said they have policies that promote diversity and inclusion (SHRM Workplace Forecast, 2011).

Diversity in the 21st century workplace is not just about race, gender, and ethnicity or sexual orientation and marriage status. Today, there are generational differences regarding how people should look and dress in the workplace. For example, Gen Y is more acceptable of tattoos, piercings, and colorful hair than baby boomers. In a survey of Fortune 1000 companies conducted by Ernst & Young, 56 percent said that they plan to launch internal inclusiveness and diversity initiatives focused on different generations including baby boomers, Gen X, and Gen Y (Ernst & Young, 2010). In a Conference Board study, surveyed CEOs indicated that developing diversity and cross-cultural competencies was one of their top human capital management challenges. Developing employee capability in diversity and cross-cultural competencies is critical to global expansion plans, as well as customer service skills, given the growing number of diverse customers and clients (Mitchell, 2011).

In a highly diverse world, it is a strategic imperative for organizations to have effective diversity programs to ensure all employees, both minorities and nonminorities, feel they are part of an inclusive and supportive workplace. Well-managed diversity programs also enhance increasingly diverse clients' identification with the organization. An effective diversity strategy must respond to diverse employees' needs for inclusion as well as the organization's need to stay competitive in a diverse marketplace. In a review of the diversity research and of effective diversity programs at noted organizations, there were six initiatives that formed the foundation of all successful programs that are worth mentioning for any organization implementing a diversity strategy:

1. **Executive management support**—Top management must "walk the talk." It is not enough to just communicate policies and support various programs that target minorities, leaders must play an active role in shaping the organizational culture to embrace diversity. This is accomplished by holding other managers and themselves accountable for achieving specific and measurable goals. At one company, each executive set specific diversity goals including recruiting, development, and retention objectives for each of their business managers, which accounted for 30 percent of their variable compensation. Executive management must also play an active role in elevating the importance of all the firm's diversity initiatives. This can include kicking off various events and highlighting the importance of these events for achieving important strategic goals, celebrating the firm's diversity gains, and being a good ambassador of the firm when dealing with outside diversity organizations.

2. **Diversity mentorships**—An effective mentorship program requires having the resources and commitment for identifying, supporting, and involving senior minority managers to mentor high-potential minority employees. Identifying with someone who has been successful is invaluable for someone trying to understand the corporate culture and what it takes to be successful. Diversity mentorship programs are one of the most effective ways for developing, promoting, and retaining minority talent.

3. **Strategic talent management**—Those organizations that are most successful at creating a diverse and inclusive work environment recognize that strategic talent management is an essential component of their success. These organizations invest in integrating workforce and succession-planning processes, and have robust recruiting and selection capabilities. They have a detailed understanding of the competencies needed for all positions and have proven recruiting and selection systems. As a result, these organizations have the capabilities to target and develop qualified diverse employees and have valid recruitment and selection systems that reduce potential biases that negatively impact minority candidates.

4. **Affinity groups/employee resource groups**—Though these terms are often interchangeable, *affinity groups* are communities within an organization that are organized around employees who have similar needs and goals. These groups typically have a more social and mentoring focus. Although *employee resource groups (ERG)* provide similar benefits, the focus of these groups is utilizing diverse employees as a business resource (Harvey and Allard, 2011). For example, to help Eli Lilly pharmaceuticals increase the proportion of Hispanics in its clinical trials to gain more data on medicine safety and effectiveness within this population, its Latino ERG worked closely with the medical staff and the Latino community to develop

effective recruitment techniques for this population. At the Ford Motor Company, its Employees Dealing with Disabilities Group provided input to help design vehicles for people with physical challenges, and the Parenting Network helped with its minivan designs (Hartley, 2010).

Creating opportunities for diverse employees to network with other employees who have access to information also facilitates knowledge sharing throughout the organization. At Chevron, diversity networks sprung from the huge success of its knowledge networks and communities of practice. Likeminded employees have access to both systems and employee networks that facilitate knowledge sharing. For example, there is an employee network devoted to age-related issues and another one that brings together Hispanic employees. Jim O'Brient, manager of Chevron's Leadership Development, regarding the success of these networks, noted that each network must have a business sponsor and charter and is responsible for setting its metrics tied to helping employees as well as helping the business as a whole (*Training Magazine*, 2001).

5. **Supplier diversity program**—Organizations that truly embrace diversity also consider the impact their business decisions have on the many organizations they conduct business with. Just as the minority representation at many organizations in professional and managerial jobs is lagging, so it is with the proportion of business given to minority-owned businesses. Developing supplier diversity programs as part of an overall corporate philosophy that embraces diversity can have a positive impact on employees, potential employees, customers, and suppliers who value and seek to have relationships with organizations that espouse these enlightened principles.

AT&T began a supplier diversity program beginning in 1968, when it set aside $175,000 to purchase goods and services from women and minority-owned businesses. Today, the company considers supplier diversity to be an integral part of its business strategy and has spent more than $43 billion doing business with women, minority, disabled, and veteran-owned business-es. AT&T has a staff of 16 employees supporting its supplier diversity program. The company also partners with universities to provide graduate-level training and offers an array of web-based workshops to participating suppliers to help them grow their businesses (Harvey and Allard, 2011).

6. **Philanthropic diversity program**—Corporate foundations donate billions of dollars each year to support a multitude of causes. Channeling some of those dollars to support various diversity initiatives can have a powerful impact on those individuals and organizations that need such funding. Although both internal and external stakeholders benefit, corporate philanthropy provides many advantages to the organization. For example, organizations receive tax breaks on these contributions while enhancing their reputations within increasingly diverse markets. Consumers and potential employees are attracted to companies that are viewed as good corporate citizens.

In addition, company contributions to diversity universities and organizations greatly benefit diversity-recruiting initiatives. Providing scholarships to diverse students who otherwise could not afford to go to college enhances the image of the organization and makes it attractive to talented diversity graduates. Such programs can have a significant impact on these individuals' commitment to the firm and engagement levels.

One example is the Aetna Inc. Foundation college scholarship program that helps educate future Hispanic leaders, as part of a $24.5 million campaign to also help the Habitat for Humanity build homes for the disabled, and provide a grant for the construction of the Martin Luther King memorial in Washington, DC. Another example is the more than $100 million that Cox Communications, one of the largest U.S. cable companies, gives annually to a number of diversity causes such as the National Urban League and the United Negro College Fund (Harvey and Allard, 2011).

Corporate Social Responsibility Programs

There is a growing interest in social conscientiousness among the young and old that has been a driving force behind many organizations' corporate social responsibility (CSR) programs. Socially responsible organizations are attractive to socially conscientious employees. Employees who identify with the organization's values are likely to be more engaged and willingly help the organization achieve its goals and to do well.

Although the research is clear that many Gen Yers identify with social conscientious organizations, there are also large numbers of baby boomers who have postponed the idealistic views of their youth to climb the corporate ladder and who are increasingly concerned about the society. A study conducted by the Center of Talent Innovation (CTI) found that 91 percent of Gen X women, 76 percent of Gen X men, and 79 percent of baby boomers feel it is vital to contribute back to the community or wider world through work (Hewlett, 2012).

Given the income disparities around the world, which is a major concern for rich organizations' images, a number of multinationals have developed innovative CSR programs aimed at helping the working poor. For example, the Coca-Cola Company has created more than 6,000 new jobs in 15 countries across Africa through a program that aims to significantly expand its network of locally owned, low-cost, micro-distribution outlets.

In partnership with Central America's Indigenous Product Commercialization Program, Walmart Mexico offers producers living in poverty the opportunity to sell its products in Walmart stores and provides transportation, distribution, and logistical support. PepsiCo partners with the United Nations World Food Programme to help deliver food aid to poor people around the world. PepsiCo provides its expertise in logistics to accelerate the delivery of aid to more than 100 million people. SABMiller plc helps thousands of subsistence cassava farmers to become income-generating commercial farmers by producing and marketing a cassava-based beer in Angola. The main objective of these programs is to help these poor regions develop a self-sustainable "virtuous cycle" of wealth creation (Mitchell, 2011).

Among companies operating in Asia, there is a growing recognition of the importance of sustainability, an issue that is growing more popular with employees and consumers across the region. Companies in that region engage with stakeholders and local communities as a way to connect their corporate brand with their sustainability initiatives. CEOs operating in this region recognize that sustainability needs to be incorporated into company values and cascaded down to all employees. Their strategies for accomplishing this are incorporating social and sustainability goals into strategic performance objectives and improving sustainability measurement and reporting (Mitchell et al., 2012).

Corporate volunteer programs are also part of many organizations' CSR programs that help enhance the organizations' socially conscientious image. Corporate volunteer programs are offered at many organizations as part of broader engagement initiatives designed to attract, develop, and retain talent. These programs are also an important component of strategic business initiatives. Ernst & Young, one of the largest financial services firms in the world, is an example of an organization that promotes volunteerism through its Social Responsibility program. Employees participating as CSR fellows are sent to help companies in Central and South America for a period of 3 months to do the same line of work they perform in their home offices. The goal of the program is to help local entrepreneurs who have limited resources with pressing business problems. The range of services offered include developing an HR strategy for a Uruguay-based business that provides road accident prevention and risk management services, and organizing financial records for a Chilean company that makes reusable shopping bags (Hewlett, 2012).

Ernst & Young considers volunteering a core part of its corporate culture and partners with the World Bank, the World Economic Forum, and Transparency International to help find ways to address the social and economic challenges of today. The success of the program has helped Ernst & Young gain a foothold in developing markets while winning the loyalties of its own employees by creating a socially responsible workplace. The program also provides great developmental experiences for participating employees. Community engagement is an important component of Ernst & Young's learning and development programs. These skills-based volunteering assignments enable employees to gain new experience in project management, teamwork, and leadership while giving back in a way that brings real value to their communities.

A significant number of companies target their philanthropic social causes that align with their core values, missions, and stakeholders. Such a strategy further enhances the organization's image and reputation for being a socially-conscious organization. For example, Tyco, a manufacturer of safety and security products, gives financial support to programs that help reduce home-based injuries. The Walmart Foundation targets its financial support to charitable causes that are important to the customers and associates who live in the neighborhoods where they do business (Harvey and Allard, 2011).

Managing Contract Human Capital

As shown in Chapter 6, "The Increasing Need for Organizational Adaptability," managing contract human capital is a challenge for many organizations. Unfortunately, the adaptation of sophisticated HR practices for managing contract human capital has been evolving slowly. Firms that strategically manage this important segment of their workforce have a distinct competitive advantage over their competitors who continue to outsource or worse ignore how contract human capital are managed. The research presented on the contract human capital HR architecture demonstrates the advantages of effectively managing these unique employment arrangements.

Toyota has long known the benefits of strategically managing both its employees and contract human capital. Nearly 35 percent of Toyota's workforce consists of contract workers who work side-by-side with core employees on its assembly lines. Toyota's blended workforce enables them to preserve their well-known employment security for their core employees while responding to unpredictable swings in market demand (MacDuffie, 2007). However, Toyota also employs high-involvement HR systems for managing these workers. Toyota includes contract workers in all work-related communications and mixes regular and contract workers in all training activities. Worker uniforms also are not differentiated based on employment status. Toyota attributes its continuous improvement and problem-solving capabilities that have enabled them to increase productivity while producing high-quality products to its philosophy of effectively managing and treating all workers with respect.

Strategic Flexible Staffing Model

The complexity of managing multiple sources of talent is a daunting task for many organizations. However, those organizations that have the competencies and resources to effectively recruit and engage all needed talent, including employees and contract human capital, will have a distinct competitive edge in the 21st century. These capabilities are needed to create organizational adaptability competencies that are vital for achieving a sustainable competitive advantage. Organizations that do this well employ a strategic flexible staffing model, as shown in Figure 7.1, which integrates workforce management and recruiting software, along with effective external and internal recruiting and talent management capabilities.

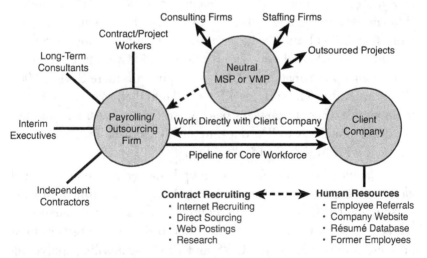

Figure 7.1 Strategic flexible staffing model

Technological advances in workforce-managed services, as well as advances in workforce analytics, are fundamentally changing how contract human capital are managed. The Managed Service Providers (MSPs) play an important role in helping organizations effectively manage all their talent management needs. MSPs sometimes are contracted to manage multiple staffing vendors and to measure their effectiveness in filling positions according to a customer's standards and requirements. In effect, the MSP serves as a "neutral" party that offers the customer a complete workforce solution while ensuring efficient operation and leveraging multiple staffing companies to obtain competitive rates. MSPs typically use a Vendor Management System (VMS) as a software tool to provide transparency and efficiency—along with detailed metrics to the user—related to every aspect of the contingent and contract workforce. The model has proven its usefulness in the private sector, notably among Fortune 500 companies, and is poised to become more common in the government arena. MSPs often use specialized software to control and deploy managed services to their customers known as Remote Monitoring and Management (RMM) software.

Key players in this space now integrate their technological, staffing, and workforce management capabilities enabling them to become true strategic partners with organizations that require multiple sources of talent. One such company is the Adecco Group, based in Zurich, Switzerland, a world leading provider of HR solutions. With more than 33,000 full-time equivalent (FTE) employees and more than 5,500 branches in more than 60 countries and territories around the world, Adecco Group offers a wide variety of services, connecting approximately 700,000 associates with more than 100,000 clients every day. The services offered fall into the broad categories of temporary staffing, permanent placement, career transition, and talent development, as well as outsourcing and consulting. The Adecco Group is a Fortune Global 500 company.

In January 2013, the Adecco Group launched Pontoon, a unified global contingent workforce solution (CWS) and recruitment process outsourcing (RPO) organization. Pontoon is the 2012 combination of Adecco Group's Beeline MSP and Adecco Solutions business lines into an independent global CWS and RPO organization, providing true workforce acquisition and management solutions through both contingent and permanent industry expertise. Recognizing the trend of increasing demand for workforce planning and talent management across the globe, Adecco strategically combined forces of these two companies to compete in the HR space.

Firms like Adecco's Pontoon are one part of a strategic flexible staffing model. The other component is having an effective internal talent management function that focuses on the recruitment and management of multiple sources of talent. An effective strategic staffing function consists of both internal and contract recruiters that source both regular and contract talent. Internal talent management functions have an array of capabilities that complement good strategic staffing partners. An effective strategic staffing function employs the direct sourcing model shown in Figure 7.2, which consists of both internal and contract recruiters utilizing robust recruiting and applicant tracking systems.

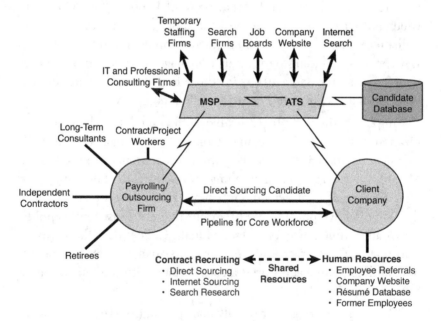

Figure 7.2 Direct sourcing model

In addition to staffing regular full-time positions, internal recruiters can utilize the same recruiting sources to identify individuals interested in working in part-time, temporary, and independent contractor positions. These recruiting sources include employee referrals, former employees, company websites, social media, and job postings. Contract recruiters can also be used to direct source individuals using search research techniques. The real power comes from leveraging technology that links multiple recruiting channels with an applicant tracking system and candidate database.

The last component of the strategic flexible staffing model is partnering with a payrolling firm to manage contract human capital who are directly recruited through internal recruiting sources. These firms vet individuals to determine who meets the criteria to be an independent contractor and who should become a regular employee of the payrolling firm. A real benefit is having one firm deal with all the "req. to check" issues including position approvals, timekeeping, payrolling, and recordkeeping. It is not uncommon for the MSP to also provide these services. If not, the MSP would manage the payrolling firm like any other vendor. This strategy protects the organization from possible IRS and Department of Labor (DOL) violations, which are major concerns in the United States when hiring contract human capital. A good payrolling partner should also offer a range of HR services including performance management, a comprehensive benefits program, and a 401(k) for those individuals who are hired as employees and contracted out to the client company.

Implementing a strategic flexible staffing model can help an organization enhance the engagement of contract human capital while significantly reducing costs. The three professional groups (Talent Management, MSP, and Payrolling) involved with the staffing and management of contract human capital enable the organization to develop effective policies and programs that are consistently applied across all staffing partners and individuals. Collectively, these groups can create effective recruiting, performance management, compensation, and communication programs that align with the type of talent being engaged.

Organizations that strategically manage multiple sources of talent benefit by having an engaged and productive workforce and achieving significant costs-savings. Based on research I have conducted at Fortune 500 companies and the U.S. government, the amount of money spent on their temporary, consultant, and independent contractor workforce is in the hundreds of millions of dollars. At the largest organizations, the costs can exceed a billion dollars. By strategically managing this workforce, organizations select and vet the best staffing partners and have effective service-level agreements (SLAs) that are managed by a sophisticated talent management function.

In the strategic flexible staffing model, the role of the MSP is to manage all staffing partners to ensure they meet the talent needs of the organization. By partnering with a select number of vendors who follow agreed-upon talent management and compensation guidelines, the organization can ensure it pays competitive market rates. Organizations that have no such capabilities typically utilize a large number of vendors who charge higher rates. And because no one firm manages these processes, there is no monitoring of standards to ensure these workers are paid and managed appropriately. I have seen organizations who do not strategically manage this workforce pay rates that were more than double the market rates.

The role of the payrolling firm working with an internal recruiting function is to effectively manage those contract workers who are directly sourced by the organization. The savings and benefits associated with these capabilities are significant. Because these individuals are sourced internally, the pay rates the organization would be charged are significantly less than those charged by staffing and consulting firms. It's not uncommon for staffing and consulting firms to charge a markup of 50 percent or more over the individual's pay rate, whereas many payrolling firms charge much lower markups, and some firms charge a flat fee rather than a percent markup, which can result in higher savings.

Looking at current labor force trends, it is a strategic imperative for firms to develop these capabilities. The number of individuals willing to work in multiple employment arrangements is growing. Some of these individuals are long-term employees who are interested in working for the organization after they retire. Transitioning these workers after they formally retire to the payrolling firm as part of a phased retirement program for as long as they can is vital for firms seeking to hold on to workers who have unique skills. There are also many high-skilled employees who decide to go out on their own as independent contractors. And there are many individuals who voluntarily leave their traditional jobs and seek other employment arrangements that provide them with the flexibility they want. Significantly, as this strategically important segment of the labor force continues to grow, the ability to identify and recruit these individuals has never been easier.

Lastly, the role of the talent management function is critical to ensuring these benefits and cost-savings. Working with the other strategic staffing partners, the talent management group can determine the compensation and benefits for these workers based on the strategic needs of the organization and current labor market conditions. In addition, a determination must be made as to how these workers are to be managed both by the organization and the staffing firms. Most important, all these decisions become part of the SLAs entered into with all staffing partners. There also need to be clear policies as to the roles of the staffing firms, client organization, and direct hiring managers. The other real benefits are to monitor how many of these workers are employed by the organization and having data to include when performing workforce analytics.

All in all, organizations need to effectively manage all sources of talent if they are to remain competitive in the 21st century marketplace. The strategic staffing model provides a framework for accomplishing this goal. Organizations that successfully implement this staffing strategy have sophisticated external and internal staffing partners that can recruit and hire top talent. They also have the capability to strategically manage all talent by ensuring there is the right level of investments made in these employment relationships that result in an engaged and productive workforce.

Managing and Engaging a Global Workforce

In the 21st century marketplace, the benefits for organizations that can successfully manage and engage a global workforce are significant. Establishing operations beyond one's borders can help organizations take advantage of global division of labor and improve operational efficiency, expand into new markets, and enhance their product and service offerings. To accomplish these objectives, organizations need to develop and engage mobile talent who have the competencies to work with different cultures and manage the complexities of global work.

Mobilizing Talent

A big challenge for multinational companies is managing a growing number of international assignees who are sent to different countries to either help achieve specific business objectives or for developmental purposes. To ensure these employees are engaged when taking on such a life-altering experience, it is critical for these organizations to have effective policies and programs for managing the selection, training, performance, and repatriation of these employees. However, many multinational firms still do a poor job identifying and selecting internal candidates for international assignments. All too often managers predetermine who they want to send on these international assignments based primarily on their functional expertise.

A 2012 survey of multinational organizations conducted by Brookfield Global Relocation Services reported that only 28 percent of companies indicated that they have formal career or succession management processes in place for managing global talent (Brookfield, 2012). A smaller percentage of respondents (19 percent) said they use candidate assessment tools when evaluating employees for their suitability to go on global assignments. A growing number of organizations (81 percent) noted the importance of providing international assignees cross-cultural training to help them understand and adapt to different cultures.

International Assignee Selection

Whether an organization is sending an employee on an international assignment for business or developmental reasons, it is critical for these individuals to self-select. All too often the decision for selecting an employee for a global assignment is based on who is most qualified or deserving. However, selecting employees who are dealing with pressing personal matters may severely impact their effectiveness and engagement. Given that the number one reason why international assignees fail is due to family problems (Brookfield, 2012), permitting employees to self-select is an effective strategy for ensuring employees are psychologically available for such a challenge.

Equally important is to provide employees with self-assessment tools that can help them explore important personal issues confidentially before making such an important life decision. A number of world-class organizations use the industry-leading Self-Assessment for Global Endeavors (SAGE) for both employees and their families (Caligiuri, 2012). In addition to assessing how one's family and life circumstances, as well as one's career and professional development aspirations, impact their readiness for a global assignment, the SAGE also provides an assessment of the following Big Five personality traits known to impact employees' development and success (Caligiuri, 2012 pg.167):

1. **Sociability and openness to people**—These characteristics directly affect one's ability to initiate contact with others from different cultures. These interactions are critical for development.

2. **Tolerance and flexibility**—These characteristics directly affect assignees' ability to develop positive relationships with colleagues from different parts of the world.

3. **Emotional strength and self-efficacy**—These characteristics impact assignees' ability to feel comfortable and adapt to unfamiliar situations. A high degree of confidence encourages individuals to seek out and feel comfortable in cross-cultural situations. Assignees that have these characteristics are also more resilient when facing negative, embarrassing, or unsuccessful experiences, making it less likely that they will derail the employee.

4. **Curiosity and openness to experience**—These characteristics affect individuals' ability to seek out and embrace new

cross-cultural experiences and accelerate their learning on international assignments.

5. **Reliability and resourcefulness**—These characteristics impact assignees' ability to perform when facing the many challenges of living and working in a different culture.

In addition to selecting candidates who possess these characteristics, other skills important to consider when selecting international assignees who will be managing global operations are presented in the 21st century international assignee manager profile (see Table 7.3) (Briscoe et al., 2009).

Table 7.3 The 21st Century International Assignee Manager Profile

Core Skills	Managerial Implications
Multidimensional perspective	Extensive multiproduct, multifunctional, multi-country, and multi-environment experience
Resourcefulness	Skillful in making connections and getting known and accepted in the host country's political hierarchy
Ability as a team builder	Adept in bringing a culturally diverse working group together to accomplish strategic business objectives of the enterprise
Curiosity and learning	Interest in learning about all aspects of different cultures, foreign countries, and global business
Augmented Skills	**Managerial Implications**
Computer literacy	Comfortable communicating strategic information electronically
Ability as a change agent	Proven track record of success initiating and implementing strategic organizational changes
Visionary skills	Quick to foresee and respond to business opportunities as well as potential political and economic threats in the host country
International business skills	Experienced in conducting and managing business in the global environment

Candidate Database

As the number of international assignees increases, many organizations create candidate databases to help identify employees for both business and developmental global assignments. The database includes employees who have been identified and nominated through the organization's performance management system who have also conducted a self-assessment and have expressed a willingness to go on an international assignment. Often, these databases are part of broader skill-based and competency-based systems that help identify internal talent for open positions or succession planning.

In addition to providing information about employees' technical skills and experience, it can also include information on countries of interest, languages spoken, and time of availability. As a result, organizations can select individuals who have the expertise, management nomination, and desire for an international assignment. Such a process can greatly enhance selected employees' developmental experience, fit and consequently engagement, and performance while on these assignments.

Cultural Agility Training

It is a life-changing event to be sent to live and work in a new country. A big challenge for international assignees is learning how to adapt and be successful in a new culture. Cultural differences impact how people communicate, conduct business, and work. To prepare international assignees for these challenges, many multinational organizations provide cross-cultural training for both employees and family members who accompany them before sending them overseas. Brookfield's 2012 *Global Relocation Trends* reported that 74 percent of organizations provide cross-cultural training for their international assignees; 25 percent of these companies make the training mandatory (Brookfield, 2012).

All too often, many individuals who have been successful working in their home country believe they do not need training to be successful in another country. However, the successful strategies used to manage employees and conduct business in their home country may not be as effective when working with people from different cultures.

Cross-cultural training provides a framework for individuals to understand cultural differences and learn how to adapt their communication and management styles to be effective in these different working environments.

An effective cultural framework explains how cultures differ on multiple dimensions. A good framework begins with Hofstede's (2001) cultural dimensions including the following:

- Power distance
- Individualism versus collectivism
- Uncertainty avoidance
- Masculinity versus femininity

These dimensions highlight significant cultural differences that impact how people should conduct business and manage workers across cultures. For example, a successful manager in a hierarchical organizational structure will feel at home in a high-power distance culture, but will need to adapt when working in a low-power distance culture that prefers an egalitarian work environment. Similarly, a manager who typically motivates employees by praising them in front of their coworkers will be effective in an individualistic culture but will likely embarrass the employee if in a collectivist culture. Someone comfortable with change will excel in a low uncertainty culture but will feel stifled in a high uncertainty culture that is more comfortable maintaining the status quo. Lastly, an employee who has an aggressive and competitive personality will be accepted in a highly masculine culture but will not be as accepted in a low masculine culture that values cooperation.

In addition to Hofstede's cultural dimensions, a good framework should also include Gesteland's (2005) cross-cultural business behaviors:

- Deal focus versus relationship focus
- Informal versus formal cultures
- Rigid-time (monochromic) versus fluid-time (polychromic) cultures
- Expressive versus reserved cultures

When conducting business in a deal-focus culture, it is important to demonstrate your expertise and focus on the bottom line. In a relationship-oriented culture, you must first develop a trusting relationship before conducting business. In an informal culture, people in authority are easily approachable and it's common to address people by their first names. Also, people's titles and dress are not important. In a formal culture, there are often strict protocols when interacting with people deemed to be of a higher status. Showing deference to those in authority is common, and it's important to dress appropriately and call people by their titles. In cultures in which there is a rigid focus on time, time is money, and it is critical to be on time when working or meeting people. Other cultures that have a more fluid time orientation are not as concerned with deadlines and being punctual. In affective and expressive cultures, emotions are openly and naturally expressed verbally and nonverbally; whereas, openly showing one's emotions in a more reserved culture would not be highly looked upon.

Lastly, an effective cultural framework should include how different cultures communicate. Anthropologist Edward T. Hall's (1981) theory of high- and low-context cultures provides an excellent framework, as shown in Table 7.4, for understanding the powerful effect culture has on communication. Some of the unique characteristics of low- and high-context culture communication are presented.

Table 7.4 Culture Communication Styles

High-Context Culture Communication	Low-Context Culture Communication
Indirect style	Direct style
Circular logic	Linear logic
Many nonverbal cues, for example, body language	More focused on words
Listener-oriented	Speaker-oriented
Self-effacement style	Self-enhancement style
Provisional response	Certainty response

Knowing how to effectively communicate in different cultures is critical for developing relationships and managing others. A manager coming from a low-context culture may not understand why an employee from a high-context culture says yes when they actually mean no. Perhaps the employee is looking to save face or is being respectful. In different cultures, the meaning of the message may also change depending on who is delivering it or the context of the situation.

Cross-cultural training is critical for any individual planning to spend time living and working in a new culture. If the international assignee is sent to a different country for developmental purposes, the training can help them effectively communicate and develop relationships with their new colleagues and business associates, thereby enriching their experience. If international assignees are sent to a different country to manage a global business, it is essential for them to learn how to adapt their management style to motivate and engage their workers, thereby ensuring their success.

Predeparture Training/Support

It is equally important to provide international assignees information that can help them navigate all the daily activities of life in a foreign country. It can be a culture shock for many individuals finding themselves in a country with a vastly different culture and way of life. Preparing international assignees beforehand can help them make a smooth and enjoyable transition. From learning which side of the street you drive on and how to order a meal, there are numerous things people take for granted that must be learned when in a different country. A good pretraining program would cover all the following:

- **Language strategy**—Provide basic language training along with translation resources such as books and one of the many language translation apps.
- **Housing**—Identify a place to live before departing. Many multinational organizations have designated living facilities for their international assignees and families.
- **Schools**—Identify quality schools for children who are accompanying international assignees.

- **Compensation and taxes**—Describe how compensation will be impacted by cost-of-living differences, exchange rates, and taxes. Many multinational organizations apply the balance sheet approach to ensure international assignees are kept "whole." This typically requires adjusting wages and/or subsidizing other additional expenses.

- **Benefits**—Communicate what benefits will be available and the processes for receiving them. Identify company-approved local doctors and medical facilities beforehand.

- **Transportation options**—Provide information on public transportation systems, driving regulations, and how to apply for a new driver's license.

- **Security**—Describe what security measures are available and how to contact local law enforcement authorities. Depending on the country, organizations may offer private security along with secured housing and travel.

- **Food and entertainment**—Provide information on local cuisine, places to eat, and places to go for entertainment and cultural experiences.

Given the number one reason why employees on international assignments fail is due to family problems, it is equally important to provide training and assistance to accompanying partners and other family members. Some of the problems international assignees have encountered include dealing with a spouse or partner resistant to relocating, inability of the family to adjust to their new environs, finding suitable education for children, and having to find employment for the trailing spouse (Brookfield, 2012). Organizations that offer training to accompanying family members and provide assistance to address these issues significantly increase the likelihood that international assignees will have a successful and enjoyable experience.

International Assignee Performance Management

Performance objectives must take into account whether the assignment is *demand-driven* (to meet a specific business objective) or *learning-driven* (to develop future global leaders). In addition, consideration must be given to the extent international assignees must immerse themselves in the local culture. For example, sending employees on a global assignment to implement a system may require them to be only tacit transmitters of the corporate culture and uphold corporate norms of behaviors (Caligiuri et al., 2010). However, other employees sent overseas for demand-driven business may need to adapt to the cultural norms of the host country to be effective, for example, those involved with sales and marketing.

For demand-driven assignments, performance criteria should include both specific business objectives and the wanted amount of cultural adaptation. This can help the international assignee to focus on not just what has to be accomplished but how to effectively manage and engage a culturally diverse workforce. For learning-driven assignments, all too often, international assignees' performance is inferred based on how well they achieve business results. However, it's important to have clarity on what are the developmental objectives, such as gaining cross-cultural competencies (for example, tolerance of ambiguity) or international business skills (language fluency or understanding local markets).

Repatriation

There is a significant cost in both time and money in sending an employee to live and work in another country. To ensure there is an acceptable ROI, organizations must have plans in place to strategically manage the repatriation and retention of international assignees. Although the 8 percent annual attrition rate of repatriates is approximately the same rate for all employees at multinational firms (Brookfield, 2012), this rate is high for strategically valuable employees. Given the amount of resources dedicated to the selection, training, and development of these employees, it's critically important for the firm to retain these workers.

Among the international assignees who leave their organization, approximately one-third of them leave within 1 year after repatriation (Brookfield, 2012). Given the increasing demand for talented individuals with global experience, returning expats are highly marketable. It makes no strategic sense to invest so much in the development of talent only to have your competitor hire them away. However, many organizations do not have career plans for individuals who are sent overseas for specific business needs (Kraimer et al., 2009). As a result, there is little thought given to the type of position these employees will receive upon returning from a successful global assignment. If employees are not rewarded with an opportunity that acknowledges their accomplishments, they are more likely to be disengaged and seek such an opportunity elsewhere.

International assignees who are sent on developmental international assignments as part of an effective succession planning program need a clearly defined position for them to return to upon returning to their home country. Typically, this position would give returning employees an opportunity to apply what they learned and continue to develop. Organizations like GE and GM do this well and as a result have a pipeline of highly skilled culturally adept professionals for their future global leadership positions.

8

Conclusion: Achieving Success
in the New Normal

The 21st century presents unparalleled challenges and opportunities for both individuals and organizations. We seem to be moving at an exhausting pace as the fabric of society and the economy is changing before our eyes. All of which has given us our bearings up to this point is now questionable. Indeed, the term *new normal* is an indication we are in new uncharted territory and that the future will look nothing like the present. The only way for individuals to succeed in such a world is to hone their skills and capabilities and be adaptable.

The same holds true for organizations. To succeed in the new normal, organizations need sophisticated strategic planning competencies that can help them navigate turbulent markets and a culture that fosters continuous learning and adaptability. Equally important is having strategic Human Resource (HR) management capabilities necessary for supporting an organizational culture and creating an engaged workforce to achieve strategic business objectives.

Strategic Planning

Given the amount of emphasis on adaptability throughout this book due to the unpredictability of rapidly changing and complex environments, it may seem contradictory to discuss the importance of having effective strategic planning capabilities. However, planning and adaptability go hand in hand. It is critical for organizations to scan, collect, and analyze data to create information and knowledge for deciding how to respond to the multitudes of threats and opportunities of the marketplace. Knowing what to respond to is just as important as having the adaptability to decide how to respond. Organizations that get this right will have a clear strategic advantage competing in the 21ˢᵗ century.

In a 2009 article in the *Balanced Scorecard Report* titled "Dynamic Forecasting: A Planning Innovation for Fast-Changing Times," Bjarte Bogsnes, Vice President of Performance Management Development at Statoil, talks about how budgeting and forecasting concepts invented in the past no longer are as effective in responding to the challenges operating in today's turbulent and dynamic business environment. The old centralized command and control way of forecasting and budgeting is ineffective because it cripples the organization's capability to respond quickly to a changing environment and make quick and effective decisions. He believes the time is ripe for dynamic forecasting. Instead of predefined year-end forecasting in which the time horizon keeps shrinking because the forecast stops at year end, rolling forecasting is much better.

Rolling forecasting has a fixed frequency typically every quarter and fixed-time horizon that perpetually looks five quarters ahead. As a result, the forecasting process is more fluid and permits forecasting data to flow into the system according to natural rhythms and not let important forecasting data pile up only to be analyzed at year end (Bogsnes, 2009). In his book *Talent on Demand: Managing in an Age of Uncertainty* (2008), Peter Cappelli posits an effective forecasting strategy to ask the forecasting team, "What odds would you take if you were betting that the actual demand will turn out to be within 10 percent either way of your forecast?...What are the costs associated with under- and overshooting? What are the alternatives and costs for each?"

All in all, organizations navigating the turbulent markets of the 21ˢᵗ century need sophisticated analytics and models that complement their dynamic strategic planning efforts. The Dow Chemical Company and CapitalOne are two companies using these techniques. The Dow Chemical Company has a sophisticated forecasting model that harnesses the advantage of modern computing power. It aggregates data from its enterprise resource planning (ERP) system and from corporate intelligence initiatives to identify linkages among multiple variables and drivers that impact critical strategic outcomes. For example, it developed models estimating how changes in the political and business climate in their countries of operation impact labor and employment legislation as part of its workforce planning. CapitalOne aggregates real-time product and customer data and, using sophisticated forecasting models, adjusts its operations accordingly (Cappelli, 2008). A big challenge facing forecasting professionals is compiling and analyzing massive amounts of data into useful information.

Data Analytics

Big data is quickly becoming a business priority and a growing and important field of study. In a world in which you are bombarded with information, big data has been used to convey all sorts of concepts, including social media analytics, next-generation data management, and real-time data analysis. In a study of more than 1,000 professionals from 95 countries conducted by the IBM Institute of Business Value and the Saïd Business School at the University of Oxford, nearly two-thirds of respondents reported that the use of information (including big data) and analytics helps their organization create a competitive advantage (Schroeck et al., 2012). The study found that the amount of data collected and analyzed at a growing number of organizations is staggering. For example, a global telecommunications firm collects and analyzes billions of detailed call records each day; an oil exploration company analyzes terabytes of geologic data; and stock exchanges process and analyze millions of transactions per minute.

Although many organizations have been collecting and analyzing data for some time, there are two trends that make this era of big data different. First, virtually everything is digitized, which results in new types of large and real-time data across a spectrum of industries. In addition, much of this is nonstandard data that does not fit neatly into traditional relational databases and warehouses, such as streaming, geospatial, and sensor-generated data. Second, today's organizations have access to advanced technologies and techniques that enable them to extract insights from data with previously unachievable levels of sophistication, accuracy, and speed (Schroeck et al., 2012).

Organizations use big data to predict consumer behavior, optimize their operations, and assess and respond to market trends and competitor moves, to name a few examples. To achieve these objectives using advanced analytics, companies need to develop strengths in three areas, as shown in Table 8.1 (Barton and Court, 2012).

Table 8.1 Areas of Strength

Multiple Data Sources	Prediction and Optimization Models	Organizational Transformation
Creatively source and collect internal and external data.	Focus on the biggest drivers of performance.	Develop simple, understandable tools for employees to use.
Upgrade IT architecture and infrastructure for effective merging of data.	Build models that efficiently factor and balance complexity.	Reconfigure processes and develop capabilities to enable decision-making using tools.

Bryon Schmidt, Cognos Brand Executive, presenting at the IBM Information on Demand 2010 conference, described the characteristics of an "intelligent enterprise" that uses advanced business analytics for decision-making and optimizing performance, as listed in Table 8.2 (Schmidt, 2010).

Table 8.2 Intelligent Enterprise Characteristics

Aware	Leverage internal and external data.
Linked	Connect key financial and sales data.
Precise	Focus only on what is most important.
Questioning	Challenge the status quo on how external data was provided.
Empowering	Automate and orchestrate routine tasks.
Anticipating	Apply models to support what-if analysis.

Scenario Planning

In the past, most strategic plans were created by extrapolating accounting and financial data 2 to 5 years into the future. This data was compared to various ratio models, such as revenues to number of employees to adjust business and staffing plans. For the longest time, these simplistic projections were surprisingly good but became increasingly more unreliable as the environment became more complex. Today, a key component of effective strategic planning is scenario planning. Scenarios include multiple data sources including demographic, social, and political trends, and rather than just extrapolating trends, develop visions for multiple futures.

Scenario planning helps you understand how multiple interdependent trends and events interact and influence one another. For example, an increase in interest rates can lead to a slowing economy, which in turn creates unemployment. One of the pioneers of corporate scenario planning, Paul Schoemaker, recommends first dividing knowledge into two broad categories: (1) things we are confident we know something about and (2) factors we consider uncertain or unknowable. Things we are confident in can be recast as trends recognizing that our world possesses considerable momentum and continuity. For example, we can safely make projections using demographic data and be confident about the substitution effects for certain new technologies. The art of scenario planning entails blending the known and the unknown into a limited number of internally consistent views of the future that span a wide range of possibilities (Schoemaker, 1995).

The effectiveness of scenario planning for business was originally established by Royal Dutch/Shell, which has used scenarios since the early 1970s as part of a process for generating and evaluating its strategic options (Schoemaker et al., 1992). Shell's track record of anticipating and effectively preparing for such industry-altering effects as the Organization of the Petroleum Exporting Countries (OPEC) oil embargo and the eventual overcapacity in the tanker business is legendary. Its success transformed the strategic planning industry. Today, many organizations incorporate Shell's approach to scenario planning, which includes some of the steps shown in Table 8.3.

Table 8.3 Royal Dutch/Shell Scenario Planning Process

1.	Identify drivers for change/assumptions.
2.	Develop viable frameworks.
3.	Identify two or three scenarios.
4.	Communicate the scenarios.
5.	Identify critical outcomes.

1. Identify Assumptions/Drivers for Change

Examining the results of environmental analysis determines which factors/variables will have the biggest impact on the business. The goal is to develop informed assumptions regarding the most significant drivers of change. It's important to focus on the key variables and extend the planning horizon to 10 or more years. By extending the time period, participants are forced to abandon simple extrapolation techniques and think about the alternatives that they may face. This is also called the *brainstorming phase*, which ensures that a complete list of variables are formulated. A common technique is to write all variables on a whiteboard. As in any form of brainstorming, the initial ideas almost invariably stimulate others.

2. Develop Viable Frameworks

After a set of variables/drivers are identified, the next step is to link them together into *event strings* of meaningful frameworks. For example, an increase in oil supply is linked to falling prices, which in turn limits exploration initiatives and reduces profits. The goal is to create seven to nine groupings or mini-scenarios.

3. Identify Two or Three Scenarios

The goal now is to reduce the seven to nine mini-scenarios/groupings to two or three larger scenarios. Not surprisingly, this requires a considerable amount of debate, which typically generates as much light as it does heat. One of the added benefits of this process is participants gain insights into their peers' as well as their own priorities and thinking. Shell's approach is to identify two scenarios that are complementary. The goal is to avoid choosing just one preferred scenario and focus on alternative scenarios that reflect uncertain futures. The two scenarios are required to be equally likely, and between them should cover all the event strings/drivers. It's important that the two scenarios not be labeled as opposites to avoid biasing their acceptance by users. The next step is to have the group test the two scenarios again for viability. Participants must determine if these scenarios make sense based on their logical analysis, or just as likely in terms of their intuition.

4. Communicate the Scenarios

The scenarios now need to be written in the form most suitable for use by the managers who are going to base their strategy on them. Most scenarios are written in word form such as in a series of alternative essays about the future. Scenarios may also include numeric data and/or diagrams or models that predict outcomes.

5. Identify Critical Outcomes

The final stage is to identify the most critical outcomes of these scenarios. Most important is to understand the connecting variables/ drivers that create the scenarios that have the greatest impact on the future of the organization. Armed with a deeper understanding of these scenarios, subsequent strategies can be developed to minimize potential risks and take advantage of potential opportunities rather than just aiming to maximize performance by gambling on one outcome.

Monte Carlo Simulations

Performing Monte Carlo simulations is another valuable technique for managing risk and uncertainty and developing strategic plans. As with scenario planning, it's important not to make important strategic decisions with unknown or unstable variables. In an age of uncertainty, there is variance in most every aspect of life. For example, organizations trying to predict the business climate next year must make assumptions on whether the stock market goes up 20 percent next year or down 20 percent. They must also consider whether there will be a devastating event (black swan) that can drop the market by 50 percent or more. In so doing, they must assign probabilities for each of these events. Thus, it's important to consider the outcomes of various strings of variables/drivers developed in planning sessions based on multiple probability scenarios. The most common approach is to calculate best-case, worst-case, and most-likely-case (average of the two) scenarios.

Monte Carlo simulation is a technique used to model the uncertainty in forecasts and assess the implications of this uncertainty

(Director, 2013). When developing models composed of a string of variables, you have the option to enter not just one estimate for each variable but information about the possible distribution of variables around that estimate. For example, if you forecast revenues based on multiple variables including product price to estimate future staffing needs, you would enter your forecasting model of a string of variables in an Excel spreadsheet. There are Monte Carlo simulations that work as an Excel add-in. You can then enter a range of variables along with their probabilities. You may estimate that there is a 30 percent probability that the product price is $50.00, a 10 percent probability it is $40.00, a 5 percent probability it is $60.00 or $30.00, and so on. You would enter similar values and probabilities for all the other variables in the forecasting model.

The Monte Carlo simulation would then calculate forecasted revenues thousands of times by entering a different value for each variable based on the entered probabilities. Like all forecasts, there are many assumptions, and even the probabilities are based on assumptions. The power of this technique lies in your ability to assess a range of outcomes with associated probabilities. The end result is a probability distribution of all possible outcomes. It will show the most likely outcome as well as the highest outcome (when all variables are most favorable at the same time) and lowest outcome (when all variables are least favorable at the same time) and the probability for each of these outcomes.

It is useful to assess the probabilities of the extreme values. Looking back, it is unfortunately obvious that the financial services industry failed to use such a tool when forecasting prices for mortgage-backed securities. Perhaps if it saw a model that showed the impact of all its assumptions going in the opposite direction, such as housing prices will continue to rise, the industry may have averted countless bankruptcies and the almost total collapse of the financial services industry. Even though the probability of this event would have been small, seeing the possible risk of losing hundreds of billions of dollars would have made someone realize this risk was not worth taking.

Organizational Culture

The notion that organizations have cultures is a relatively recent phenomenon. Prior to the mid-1980s, organizations were simply thought of as rational means for controlling and organizing groups of people. Over time, organizations were thought to have "personalities." Like people, organizations can be rigid or flexible, formal or informal, competitive or cooperative, and so on. *Organizational culture* can be defined as a system of shared meaning held by organizational members that distinguishes the organization from other organizations. Organizational culture can have a significant impact on employee engagement. Organizational culture reflects the unique values and ways of doing business of different companies. Employees who identify with this culture are more committed to helping the organization achieve its goals.

The founders of an organization have a major impact on forming the organization's early culture. In the early stages of an organization's development, the founding managers influence every aspect of the business including setting the firm's vision, how it competes, organizes work, makes decisions, and how business is conducted. They also hire and ultimately reward and retain employees who think and behave like they do. The attraction-selection-attrition (ASA) framework developed by Ben Schneider (1987) describes how organizational cultures develop and get stronger.

First, prospective workers seek and are attracted to organizations that have cultures similar to their own interests and personalities. For example, individuals who like an informal, flexible work environment will likely not be attracted to an organization that is formal and structured. Similarly, a passive person who prefers a cooperative workplace would not be attracted to an organization that is known to have an aggressive and competitive culture. Next, organizations have selection criteria that reinforce the culture. One of the most powerful factors is those who are involved in interviewing and selecting candidates typically prefer people who they feel will "fit in" with the organizational culture. Effective selection criteria should include an assessment of both the person–job and person–organization fit. The selection process is also a two-way process. Not only is management assessing the fit of the candidate, but also candidates are gathering more information about the company to assess how they would fit in at this company. Individuals can assess an organization's culture by gathering information listed in Table 8.4.

Table 8.4 Assessing Organizational Culture

How are people dressed: formal or informal?

How do they communicate?

What is the office layout: cubicles or offices?

How do they pay: straight salary, variable pay, or team pay?

How do they manage time: set hours or flexible hours?

Where do people work: in the office, offsite, or at home?

Who are the founders: What are their personalities and values?

Who are the top managers: What do they look like and how do they behave?

Lastly, a big reason why people leave companies is due to a lack of fit. The attrition rate for those who do not fit with the organization's culture is likely to be much higher than the average rate. Thus, over time, a company is staffed with many like-minded people who have similar values that collectively reinforce the organization's culture. Clearly person–organization fit is needed to ensure employees identify with the organization and are committed to helping the firm achieve its goals. Those employees whose personalities and values are congruent with their organizations are more engaged, have lower turnover, and higher job performance.

In addition to ensuring good person–organization fit, there are known organizational cultural characteristics that are conducive to enhancing employee engagement. One example is a positive organizational culture that organizational behavior researchers describe as one that emphasizes building on employee strengths, rewards more than it punishes, and focuses on individual vitality and growth (Nelson and Cooper, 2007; found in Robbins and Judge, 2008). In the wake of countless scandals and bankruptcies, more people identify with and seek organizations known for creating an ethical organizational culture. Such organizations' top management are visible role models who communicate ethical standards, provide ethical training for all employees, visibly reward ethical behavior and punish unethical behavior, and provide mechanisms for employees to report unethical behavior without fear of reprimand (Robbins and Judge, 2008).

Leadership

Leaders play an important role in creating a high-performing organizational culture that fosters employee engagement. Effective leaders create the type of employee mindset that creates a strategic understanding of each employee's role and customers' and investors' expectations (Becker et al., 2009). In an age of instant communication, corporate transparency from senior management is critical. Sharing information and being more transparent with employees enhances their identification with the organization and sharpens their line-of-sight, helping them understand how their performance is linked to organizational success. Enhancing employees' understanding and identification with organizational goals are known drivers of employee engagement that can give leaders and their organizations a distinctive competitive edge. Executive management at Google embodies this philosophy. According to Shannon Deegan, Director of People Operations at Google, senior management treats employees like owners by "over-communicating," giving them access to strategic company goals and setting a shared vision for what is to be accomplished (Society for Human Resource Management [SHRM] Foundation, 2010).

Many of these attributes are seen in *transformational leaders*. There is a large body of research demonstrating how transformational leadership styles create highly engaged followers. The transformational leaders are best known for harnessing their vision and personality to manage employee expectations, perceptions, and motivation. Four noted characteristics of transformational leadership include (Bass and Riggio, 2006):

- **Idealized influence**—The leaders serve as ideal role models for followers; they demonstrate ethical behaviors and "walk the talk." Followers admire leaders for this.

- **Inspirational motivation**—Transformational leaders have the ability to inspire and motivate followers. Both idealized influence and inspirational motivation combine to what constitutes the transformational leaders' charisma.

- **Individualized consideration**—Transformational leaders have high emotional intelligence and demonstrate genuine real concern for the needs and feelings of followers. This personal attention to all followers is a key element in bringing out their best efforts.

- **Intellectual stimulation**—The leader challenges and engages followers to be innovative and creative. A common misunderstanding is that transformational leaders are "soft," but the truth is that they constantly challenge followers to higher levels of performance.

21st century companies need transformational leaders who can function effectively on a global scale. Leading and engaging culturally diverse groups of individuals around the world requires leaders who have a global mindset and cultural agility competencies who can work effectively as part of a global leadership team. Top organizations that understand the benefits of having an engaged global workforce invest heavily in global leadership development. An effective global leadership development program begins by identifying the competencies required to lead global organizations, creating a process for identifying and selecting leadership candidates, and providing the developmental experiences necessary for creating their leadership pipeline.

Global leadership competencies are found in rare individuals who have a combination of unique personal attributes and extensive developmental experiences. In addition to possessing traditional leadership competencies, these individuals have other competencies that make them effective leading complex global organizations. A study conducted by the Center for Creative Leadership (McCauley, 2006) identified a list of essential leadership competencies that are consistent among many organizations (see Table 8.5).

Table 8.5 Leadership Competencies

Leading the Organization
Managing change
Solving problems and making decisions
Managing politics and influencing others
Taking risks and innovating
Setting vision and strategy
Managing the work
Enhancing business skills and knowledge
Understanding and navigating the organization
Leading the Self
Demonstrating ethics and integrity
Displaying drive and purpose

The challenges of leading global enterprises require leaders who have additional competencies. A study of successful leaders conducted by Morgan McCall and George Hollenback (2002) identified a list of common competencies specific to the global leader (see Table 8.6).

Table 8.6 Global Executive Competencies

Open-minded and flexible in thought and tactics
Cultural interest and sensitivity
Can deal with complexity
Resilient, resourceful, optimistic, and energetic
Honesty and integrity
Stable personal life
Value-added technical or business skills

At top global companies like GE and 3M, global leaders are identified through their succession planning functions. When leadership competencies are identified, employees are evaluated through the performance management process. High-potential employees who exceed performance objectives and have leadership potential go through a more rigorous selection process at an assessment center that entails a battery of tests, self-evaluations, mock assignments, and interviews. Selected individuals are then given a series of developmental assignments designed to develop a pipeline of future global leaders.

A study conducted by the SHRM Foundation of 3M's succession planning program noted five important lessons to consider when developing a program (SHRM Foundation, 2008b):

1. Begin with commitment from the top.

2. Identify and communicate a common set of leadership attributes.

3. Use candid, comprehensive performance reviews.

4. Keep to a regular schedule for performance reviews and identification of talent pools.

5. Link all decisions about talent to the long-term strategy of the organization.

Developmental Cross-Cultural Experiences

Many global organizations have a large number of functional experts and leaders managing complex business operations. These organizations have well-defined career ladders for both technical and managerial employees that provide increasingly greater opportunities to develop their skills. In addition to developing high-potential employees' technical and managerial skills, global organizations also provide cross-cultural experiences for these employees to develop cultural agility competencies necessary for global leadership positions. Multinational organizations provide several opportunities for these developmental experiences, such as those shown in Table 8.7 (Caligiuri, 2012).

Table 8.7 Developmental Cross-Cultural Experiences

Global mentoring programs
Buddy programs
Global rotational programs
Global project teams
International volunteerism programs

Global Mentoring Programs

Mentoring or coaching programs include matching less-experienced employees with successful senior managers. These relationships are valuable resources for employees and provide knowledge about navigating company politics and fitting in with the corporate culture. For international assignees, having a mentor at the host country can greatly enhance their developmental experience. In a study published in the *International Journal of Business Studies*, the authors found that international assignees who had host national mentors enjoyed a variety of career-enhancing benefits from the relationship including gaining in-depth organizational knowledge, improved performance, and greater opportunity for promotion (Carraher et al., 2008).

Buddy Programs

Buddy programs involve the pairing of peer-level employees from different countries to work together to achieve common business objectives. The goal is to have an exchange of knowledge that benefits both employees. IBM's global mentoring programs include connecting employees from emerging markets with peer employees in their developed markets as part of the company's goal of creating a globally integrated enterprise. The program's primary objectives are increasing knowledge sharing, promoting cultural intelligence, and developing talent company-wide by overcoming geographic barriers and fostering cross-border collaboration (IBM.com, 2008).

Global Rotational Programs

Planned rotational global assignments are one of the most common methods at multinational companies for developing high-potential employees for future global leadership positions. These assignments offer employees opportunities to fully immerse themselves in a new culture and develop deep relationships with host country colleagues. Global rotational programs are designed to enhance employees' global business acumen and help build cultural agility competencies. Many leading companies, such as Johnson & Johnson, IBM, Dow, Nokia, and GE, have such programs within their most critical functional areas to help build cross-functional and cultural competence within their firms (Caligiuri, 2012). Employees who are selected for these programs typically rotate through two to three global locations spending between 6 months to 2 years on each assignment. These programs are commonly part of management or leadership training programs that target high-potential early career employees and recent college graduates.

Global Project Teams

An increasing number of organizations rely on global project teams to conduct business around the world. These are typically cross-functional teams of employees from different countries involved in important cross-border business initiatives. Employees who are selected to participate on these teams are given the opportunity to develop cross-cultural competencies, including understanding different cultures, developing contacts who can be valuable resources, and learning how to collaborate and communicate with culturally diverse team members. In addition to providing developmental experiences for selected employees, global project teams are strategically important. For example, at Unilever, global project teams of high-potential employees from around the world work together to collectively investigate trends in emerging markets and develop ways to respond. Teams typically are intact for a few months, and team members work in a variety of modalities including virtually, face-to-face, and collaborating in workshops. Project teams are given the tasks to develop proposals and present their recommendations to Unilever's senior management. The most viable and impactful proposals are then implemented (Gitsham et al., 2011).

International Volunteerism Programs

International volunteerism programs are company-sponsored programs, in which interested, highly skilled employees are given the opportunity to volunteer at targeted nongovernmental organizations (NGOs) in selected countries. Most programs provide employees with time off ranging from a few weeks to several months with regular compensation and benefits. A number of leading organizations such as GlaxoSmithKline, Dow Corning, PepsiCo, FedEx, and IBM have benefited from their international volunteerism programs (Caligiuri, 2012). These programs help organizations achieve a variety of strategic objectives, including increasing their corporate social responsibility reputation, increasing retention and engagement of high-potential employees, and enhancing the attractiveness of the organization among socially conscious workers.

In her new book on *Cultural Agility*, Professor Paula Caligiuri's research confirms the effectiveness of corporate volunteer programs for developing global leaders. Unlike the typical expat business assignment, volunteer programs enable employees to fully immerse in the new environment, gaining deeper insights into the culture and understanding the challenges facing individuals living in the society. These developmental experiences can greatly enhance the volunteer's cultural agility competencies, making them more competent managers and leaders (Caligiuri, 2012).

Flat and Network Structures

Decisions on how to organize and structure work have a big impact on organizational culture and mindset. Employee engagement is enhanced in cultures that encourage collaboration and knowledge sharing in which employees are empowered to make decisions and have developmental opportunities. Flat or network organizational structures help create a work environment that is conducive to these goals. Conversely, hierarchical organizational structures create an atmosphere that discourages collaboration and the free flow of information in which employees have limited autonomy and opportunities to make decisions and develop.

Clearly, those organizations that compete with its intellectual and human capital require a culture that promotes collaboration and knowledge sharing. These organizations' existence is based on creating a continuous learning work environment for all employees. However, like all organizations, to successfully compete, they must properly align the work environment with employee competencies and behaviors. Alignment also is necessary for creating a work environment in which employees feel engaged. Thus, organizations that hire highly skilled employees and develop incentive systems that encourage knowledge sharing will fail if the organizational structure is hierarchical and out of alignment. These employees will likely feel disengaged in such a work environment and will leave for an organization that provides opportunities for them to succeed.

What about those organizations that rely on business strategies that require work to be standardized and controlled? These companies often seek economies of scale or require consistency in delivering their products or services. Many companies that compete this way create hierarchical structures. Does this mean that they can never have engaged employees? Clearly, the answer is no. There are ample ways to create a work environment that enhances engagement regardless of which business strategy a company pursues. Once again, it all starts with alignment. It's critical to select the right workers who are a good fit to work in such a work environment. The types of work behaviors that are typically rewarded include precision and consistency. The important factor is that even in a hierarchical structure, there are ways to structure work to provide employees with flexibility, get them involved in decision-making, and help them to develop.

Organizations that relied on hierarchical structures to organize work in the past now have access to technology that enables production processes to be monitored and controlled. These systems also enable organizations to develop flexible operations that can be customized to meet new customer needs while maintaining the wanted level of consistency and quality standards. And those companies that have engaged employees willing to help achieve these business goals will be the most successful. Nestlé, one of the world's largest food producers, early on recognized the benefits of dismantling rigid hierarchical structures and creating flatter, more flexible organizational structures. By moving in this direction, the company hoped to both enhance employee engagement and gain a competitive edge (Hooijberg et al., 2007).

Nestlé realized there were many shortcomings operating with a traditional hierarchical structure that was limiting growth. These limitations were hindering Nestlé's capability to fully benefit from the knowledge and skills employees bring with them to the workplace. To overcome these limitations, top management approved the design and implementation of the Nestlé on the Move program. The goals of the program were to fundamentally change the mindset of its employees and move toward a performance culture. Their first step was to create a network culture by building more agile and flexible organizational structures. To accomplish this goal, the company created the Nestlé Leadership Program to change the way managers led their people. The program developed managers to encourage employee cooperation, initiative, and alignment with organizational goals. A critical part of this program was changing the employee assessment process. The goals were to enhance employee development and create a culture that encourages knowledge sharing and cooperation.

The second step in their strategy was launching its Develop People initiative, which changed the role of the manager from that of "passive judge" to "committed developer." The essential characteristics of the new performance management plan were to separate performance evaluations and development plans. More important, all developmental discussions were to be totally separate from compensation decisions. The third part of their move to a nonpyramid structure was to focus on long-term career development programs. Although Nestlé had a successful international development program, under the traditional hierarchical structure, there was a silo approach that created vertical career paths that were managed within one region or functional area.

Under the new network structure, the number of organizational levels was reduced, which reduced the number of promotions but increased the number of cross-regional and cross-functional moves. These lateral moves stimulate both employee development and organizational learning. New positions were also created that cut across the organization that required employees to develop new competencies managing projects, leading teams, and understanding how to work across national cultures.

A critical piece of this change initiative was to design a compensation system that was aligned with these new strategic changes. Incentive systems are powerful tools for changing behaviors and shaping a new organizational culture. Thus, Nestlé's fourth step was implementing incentive plans that allowed employees to increase their remuneration without having to be promoted. In addition, a larger part of variable pay was tied to future organizational goals in the form of long-term incentive plans based on equity (Hooijberg et al., 2007). Collectively, these directives and programs have helped Nestlé create a culture that embraces continuous learning, which has greatly contributed to the company maintaining its position as one of the most admired companies in the world.

The layout of employees' workspace is also a reflection of corporate culture. In hierarchical organizations, the size and location of workspace reveal the status and position of employees. Employees working in cubicles are viewed differently than employees working in a corner office. Communication flow is muted and slow as employees typically interact horizontally due to a rigid chain of command. This is your classic command-and-control corporate culture designed to produce standardized work and achieve economies of scale. Such a culture is not conducive to knowledge sharing and can have a negative impact on employee engagement.

Conversely, companies that have open workspaces send a different signal about their corporate culture. There are no status differences because most employees work in identical open workspaces. Such an egalitarian work environment is commonly found in flatter and networked organizational structures. Communication flow is faster and seamless as employees freely interact with one another regardless of their position in the company. This type of culture facilitates knowledge sharing and innovation and has a positive impact on employee engagement.

Creating a work environment that reduces status differences is an easy thing to do to improve employee morale and productivity.

Knowledge Sharing

Organizations that have operations in diverse geographic locations need to overcome these physical barriers that can hinder employee collaboration. These constraints are particularly problematic for managing knowledge workers. A common strategy to facilitate information sharing and collaboration across geographically dispersed knowledge workers is the creation of communities of practice. *Communities of practice* facilitate the finding, sharing, and archiving of information and making expertise and tacit knowledge more explicit. An early example of a community of practice created within a corporation is at Xerox. Xerox client service representatives began exchanging best practices at informal meetings. Seeing the value of these exchanges, Xerox created the Eureka project to facilitate information sharing across its global network of representatives. A database was created that stored technical and client information that was accessible to all field workers throughout the world. Xerox estimated that the efficiencies created as a result of the information sharing saved the corporation approximately $100 million (Brown and Duguid, 2000).

At the World Bank, communities of practice were developed to help employees benefit from each other's advice. The bank uses online tools, social networking, and electronic tools such as videoconferencing and electronic bulletin boards for its urban planners to discuss projects and build relationships across large distances (Matson and Prusak, 2010). At Electronic Arts, online communities were created to coordinate decision-making across its globally distributed organization. These online communities help in knowledge sharing, particularly with best practices, identifying experts, and enhancing decision-making across teams (McKinsey, 2012a).

In a research paper on successfully implementing knowledge management, the American Productivity and Quality Center (APQC) highlighted Chevron Corporation's success in creating and utilizing communities of practice for the development and dissemination of knowledge (APQC, 2000). Chevron, an American multinational energy corporation, formed "best practice teams" that evolved into the formation of various communities of practice throughout the world supporting multiple business units. Chevron's success with communities of practice is attributed to an organizational culture that values continuous learning and teamwork.

To achieve operational excellence, Chevron collected best practice data from other refineries as well as through its own decentralized network of refineries. The end result was the formation of a knowledge management strategy that focused on connections and the concept that ideas and best practices come through customers, partners, and communities. To facilitate knowledge sharing, Chevron created an intranet knowledge map along with improved search portals and tools that connected people with common problems to virtual teams and communities of practice who have ideas and knowledge to help solve them.

They also developed a system called the Chevron Project Development and Execution Process (cped, or chipdip) that is a database of standardized processes used by project managers around the world that has resulted in millions of dollars in project cost-savings. To facilitate the sharing of best practices within its refineries, Chevron created a new role called process masters. These individuals are selected based on their technical expertise and ability to communicate with coworkers. Their objectives are to periodically meet with their respective counterparts around the world to collect and share information (*Training Magazine*, 2001).

A number of communities of practice were created consisting of both internal knowledge sources including project managers, engineers, and consultants, and external knowledge sources including research centers, the APQC, and an array of consulting firms. They also collaborated with Electronic Data Systems (EDS), Chevron's IT outsourcer, and Ernst & Young's knowledge management consortium. Ultimately, best practice teams formed around common business issues that collected and communicated information and made recommendations to help improve the organization.

In all cases, the most rapid expansion of knowledge occurred when senior management was directly involved. In addition to senior management support, successful teams had a support structure consisting of a knowledge management project manager and architect, a database specialist, and a communications specialist. Chevron also publicizes the success of teams on the company's website, in company newsletters and, most important, at executive management meetings.

Chevron's success with transferring best practices helped tremendously when it merged with Texaco. The success of knowledge networks has also spread to other areas throughout the company. There are now networks for new hires that help connect them to other employees around the world who share their experiences about working in their new work environment, and diversity employee networks that facilitate knowledge sharing among likeminded employees (*Training Magazine*, 2001).

Another strategy used by global organizations for increasing collaboration and knowledge sharing among employees who are geographically dispersed is the use of virtual teams. The vast enhancements in computer and communication systems including online applications, cloud computing, and videoconferencing, just to name a few, have enabled dispersed workers to effectively work in virtual teams. Companies such as General Electric, Hewlett Packard, Sun Microsystems, and many other multinational enterprises rely on virtual teams to work on many strategic business objectives (Kirkman et al., 2004).

Although highly engaged virtual teams are a valuable resource at all companies, the potential benefits are magnified in multinational companies (Caligiuri et al., 2010). The first and most obvious benefit is cost-savings. Not having to pay transportation and accommodation expenses to send team members to a single location is a substantial savings. Second, unlike traditional face-to-face meetings that need to be prearranged, virtual teams can quickly respond to pressing events and opportunities. This flexibility is particularly beneficial when those individuals with the needed know-how are not always in the same place. Lastly, virtual teams significantly enhance organizational capabilities by getting together individuals who otherwise would not have an opportunity to work together to share knowledge.

Furthermore, for those employees who want developmental opportunities, working as part of a virtual team on globally important projects with colleagues from around the world is a highly engaging experience. However, given the scope of these projects and challenges of working on geographically and culturally disparate teams, it is critical for organizations to properly select, train, and manage these workers. Some of the best practices at leading multinational companies for managing virtual teams are as follows (Malhotra et al., 2007, Briscoe et al., 2012):

1. **Select appropriate members**—Select individuals based on needed functional expertise, ability to effectively communicate (typically in English), and ability to interact with and work across cultures.

2. **Train virtual team members**—Training should include helping teams develop their social capital, learning how to use technologies that facilitate communication, monitoring group progress, providing constructive feedback, and understanding cultural challenges that can impact team cohesiveness and the ability to effectively communicate.

3. **Establish communication protocols**—To help establish and maintain trust, managers must develop shared norms on how information will be communicated and what information may be shared outside of the team.

4. **Create ground rules for managing conflicts**—Managers need to establish and communicate a formal process for resolving conflicts.

5. **Monitor team progress**—Managers need to ensure team members are actively participating and focused on objectives through the use of IT, reports, and scheduled progress meetings.

6. **Enhance visibility of team members**—Team accomplishments should be recognized and shared with relevant stakeholders.

Strategic HRM Competencies

By now it should be clear that to succeed in the 21st century, organizations need to be strategically adaptable and have highly engaged workers and relationships capable of executing business strategies. As a result, organizations need to have a strategic human resource management (HRM) function that can translate the business strategy into a talent management strategy. As a result, HR professionals need to excel in three domains: operational excellence, relationship management, and change agent.

Researchers at Rutgers University identified two broad competencies that help HR managers to develop effective HR systems: 1) professional HRM capabilities that are related to the delivery of basic HRM practices such as recruiting, selection, compensation, and so on; and 2) business-related capabilities that reflect an understanding of the business and implementation of competitive strategy. Professional HRM capabilities are a necessary, but not sufficient, condition for better firm performance (Huselid et al., 1997).

Due to academic and business partnerships and the multiple ways of transmitting cutting-edge HR research to practitioners, the functional knowledge of HR managers has been enhanced. However, to help their organizations succeed in the new normal, HR managers need to significantly enhance their quantitative and business skills. These skills are necessary if HR professionals are to become true business players that can influence executive management when making critical strategic management decisions. Yet, according to research conducted by McKinsey and the Saratoga Institute, the influence of HR in companies is declining, and many executives do not see HR professionals as having valuable business knowledge or input. To illustrate this point, less than two-thirds of all HR directors in this study reported directly to the CEO (Guthridge et al., 2008).

Organizations like Procter & Gamble require HR managers to have business experience through either working at a plant or working with a key account executive to gain knowledge about a business unit and develop working relationships with business managers. Coca-Cola Enterprises stimulates business knowledge in its HR departments by rotating high-performing line managers into important HR positions for 2 to 3 years to help HR professionals develop better business skills and enhance the overall credibility of the HR department (Guthridge et al., 2008).

As shown in the employee engagement framework in Chapter 5, "Leveraging What We Know: An Employee Engagement Framework," (see Figure 5.1), it's critical for HR to understand the linkages among HR systems, employee engagement, and strategic and financial outcomes. Drawing from research on the differentiated workforce, an important first step is to understand who are the A, B, and C positions and players (Becker et al., 2009). "A" positions have direct impact on the firm's competitive advantage. An important feature of these positions is high performance variability. Great performers in these positions can have a positive impact on an organization's bottom line, whereas low performers can have a devastating impact. Thus, it is critical to have the most competent and engaged employees in these positions. In other words, you want "A players" in "A positions" (Huselid et al., 2005a).

"B" positions have an indirect impact on strategic outcomes. Many of these positions are in support roles for value-creating positions. These can also be positions that have a strategic impact but exhibit little performance variability. It is equally important to have competent and engaged employees in these positions because these positions are critical for minimizing downsize risk. In other words, although a high performer may not have a significant impact on competitive advantage, a low performer can negatively impact the bottom line.

Lastly, "C" positions have little strategic impact but may be required for the firm to function. These positions are prime candidates for outsourcing. The key for strategic HRM professionals is knowing how these positions impact strategic outcomes and the importance of disproportionally investing in these different employment relationships. This knowledge is critical when analyzing employee engagement results.

Analyzing Employee Engagement Results

Although the evidence linking employee engagement with strategic outcomes is compelling, too many organizations look to cut corners and take the easy way out. Organizations not willing to put the time and effort to strategically analyze their employee engagement surveys often favor the concise "best practice" approach that is hawked by many consulting firms. The lure of the best practice approach is administering employee surveys using engagement measures with as few questions as possible that can be averaged and compared to other firms. My guess is the appeal of such an approach is based on the assumption that employees and managers will be turned off having to answer and interpret too many questions. As Director for the Center for Human Resource Strategy at Rutgers University, I heard many firms praise the benefits of benchmarking their parsimonious engagement survey results with their industry competitors.

My response to such a strategy, or lack thereof, is you should not be benchmarking with other companies but should be benchmarking against your own business strategy and culture. What is the benefit of knowing that the average engagement score of a group of companies you are benchmarking against is 70 percent compared to your company's average score of 80 percent? Sure, that may make you feel better and it's an easy message to send to managers and employees, but does the answer actually provide any strategic value? The more interesting questions to ask are which employees in your company are most positive (are all your "A" players below the average and your "B" players above the average?), what are the different drivers impacting positive responses for different employees, and does a positive score on this question impact organizational strategic outcomes?

The answer to these more important questions requires a more thoughtful approach to administering and interpreting employee engagement surveys. The key is to list the necessary questions that reflect the measures, drivers, and different outcomes of employee engagement so that a thorough strategic analysis of the data can be performed. To gain a "seat at the table," HR professionals need to embrace analytics, particularly as a predictive model. Having an ability to articulate the current state and predict the future impact of human capital initiatives in business terms, as well as make data-driven decisions, are necessary for creating HR strategies that make an impact on the business.

The capabilities for organizations to collect and analyze data have never been as great as they are today. Workforce analytics is an important and growing function within many organizations. Driving forces behind this "big data" revolution are advances in integrated HR and business systems and cloud computing. Through their online résumé, applicant tracking, onboarding, payroll, benefits, performance management, training, and succession planning systems, organizations collect streams of real-time employee data. Organizations also collect employee data through various inventory systems that collect skills and competency data. Lastly, a massive amount of employee data is collected through ongoing engagement and organizational climate surveys. Similarly, there is a tremendous amount of business and financial data collected on customer satisfaction, product quality, productivity, revenue, costs, profits, market share and, for publically held organizations, stock price and earnings per share.

In the not-too-distant past, all this data was collected separately either manually or in batch systems. Today, this data is collected through integrated online and self-service systems. Most significant is the capability for almost any organization to store massive amounts of data in relational databases utilizing sophisticated computer applications that can slice, dice, analyze, and report the data in a multitude of formats. The ability to do this is no longer just the domain of large organizations that have the resources to make such large investments. Today, there are a number of companies that offer a variety of hosted computer platforms that are accessible through cloud computing that provide these capabilities to organizations that either cannot or do not want to invest the millions of dollars to develop their own computer systems and applications.

However, what has not changed in spite of all the developments increasing organizations' abilities to collect and analyze data is the old adage "garbage in, garbage out." If the data you collect is not useful, then even with all the computing power in the world, you cannot transform this information into knowledge. This is most evident in how organizations decide on what data to collect in employee engagement surveys and how they analyze and make strategic decisions using these data. Many of the organizations that I have worked with focus too much on their employee engagement reports and not enough attention on what data to collect and how to transform the information collected into meaningful business results. A summary of the problems I have encountered are presented in Table 8.8.

Table 8.8 Problems Analyzing Employee Engagement Data

Failing to separate the drivers, measures, and outcomes of engagement
Focusing too much on the number rather than the usefulness of survey questions
Reporting aggregate survey results rather than differentiating results by positions and employee groups
Wanting to benchmark survey results against other companies rather than benchmarking against their own business strategy
Pursuing a one-size-fits-all response to survey results rather than assessing the different drivers of engagement at the individual level
Failing to make valid linkages between employee survey results and strategic business and financial outcomes

Failing to Separate the Drivers, Measures, and Outcomes of Engagement

To use the most parsimonious measure of employee engagement, many organizations do not have enough information that can be analyzed and transformed into useful knowledge that can impact individual and organizational outcomes. Many of the common measures of engagement include drivers of engagement (for example, supportive management, developmental opportunities, and so on) as well as a measure of engagement (for example, satisfaction, commitment, and so on), and outcomes of engagement (for example, helping behavior, volunteering, and so on). Such an overall measure of engagement provides little information for understanding how different employees might respond to different drivers of engagement.

By developing separate, more comprehensive measures of the drivers, specific measures, and outcomes of engagement, organizations can better understand the dynamics of engagement at the individual level. As a result, organizations can analyze and target the specific practices and programs that have the greatest impact on engagement and performance levels for different groups of workers. It's a strategic mistake to think that all workers are motivated by the same drivers. For some workers, there may be no correlation between developmental programs and engagement, whereas for others there may be a strong and significant relationship. Furthermore, it is worth analyzing the different employee outcomes of engagement. For example, some drivers may have a moderate impact on engagement resulting in high levels of job performance but no extra role behavior.

Perhaps it made business sense in the past to keep the number of variables in employee surveys to a minimum given the difficulty and complexity for analyzing these data. However, given the advances in computer technology, it is doable to perform these complex operations. In fact, by expanding the number of variables and performing sophisticated data analysis techniques, organizations can gain valuable knowledge that can significantly increase their return on investment (ROI) in costly employee engagement surveys.

Focusing Too Much on the Number Rather Than the Usefulness of Survey Questions

Closely related to the preceding problem is the desire to keep the total number of survey questions to a minimum, which in turn reduces the quality and usefulness of survey results. Here, organizations need to strike a balance between lengthy traditional academic surveys and shortened surveys pitched by internal and external consultants. The problem with academic surveys is the overemphasis on developing valid scales and measures of variables that are necessary to publish survey results in academic journals. Such surveys often require multiple measures for each variable that result in long surveys with many redundant questions. Conversely, many consultant surveys strive to provide significant insights using the fewest possible questions. Knowing that many companies like surveys with the fewest possible questions, there seems to be a race among consulting firms to see who can create the most parsimonious employee engagement survey.

Clearly, there are many internal and external consulting groups that strike this balance. The goal is to ask the right amount of questions needed to perform the type of analyses that can help the organization make strategic decisions that impact individual and organizational outcomes. There is no magic number of questions. I've seen employee surveys range from 12 to 150 questions. A good balance is between 50 and 75 questions. The goal is to ask the right questions to understand which drivers have the biggest impact on employee engagement for different employees. Equally important is to ask enough questions to get a true measure of engagement and different questions that reflect the possible behavioral outcomes of engagement.

Organizations that develop online employee surveys have a distinct advantage in accomplishing these goals. Online surveys can be designed to be completed incrementally over a set period of time. After employees log in and begin answering survey questions, they can stop and save results and come back and finish at their leisure. The best online surveys permit employees to access the survey using multiple platforms, such as a work or home computer, or a mobile device such as a smartphone or tablet.

Reporting Aggregate Survey Results Rather Than Differentiating Results by Positions and Employee Groups

The problem with reporting aggregate survey results is having to make strategic decisions using averaged data. For example, indicating that, on average, 75 percent of employees were satisfied or very satisfied with a particular program provides little information that can help companies develop targeted employee engagement strategies. Averages can be problematic when the data is skewed or when there are countervailing outliers. I remember a statistics professor of mine joking that you can have your head in an oven and feet in a freezer and on average you are doing fine.

What if I told you that a deeper analysis of employees' responses indicates that 90 percent of employees in staff positions rated a program as satisfied or very satisfied and only 40 percent of employees in strategic positions rated the programs as satisfied or higher? By reporting that 75 percent or higher was satisfied paints a different picture. The same may be true among different employee groups. Perhaps 90 percent of Gen Y employees were positive about a program, but only 40 percent of baby boomers felt that way. If management interpreted these survey results as the vast majority of employees will be satisfied if we expand this program, they would be making a classic mistake as a result of using weighted averaged survey results.

Thus, organizations that conduct employee engagement surveys need to develop a coding system that will enable them to analyze and differentiate survey results in meaningful ways. A typical coding system would include a way of determining the job position, work unit, and location of each respondent. Demographic information can be captured by asking employees to voluntarily provide this information. This can easily be collected while ensuring the anonymity of each employee completing a survey. Whether online or mailed, surveys need to be coded and sent directly to each employee. Employees need to be assured that no individual survey will be reported in any analysis of less than five surveys, which is necessary to ensure their confidentiality.

Wanting to Benchmark Survey Results Against Other Companies Rather Than Benchmarking Against Their Own Business Strategy

Organizations that focus more on how their employee engagement survey results stack up against other companies' results rather than assessing how well they are managing their own employees to execute their business strategy are making a perilous mistake. All too often, management is more interested in seeing fancy colorful reports that compare their results to benchmark companies. An entire employee engagement industry has been created to accommodate these misguided desires. In fact, this is why so many consulting firms create standard measures so that they can easily compare companies' results. Benchmarking is also popular at companies that compile aggregate survey results.

Because they cannot differentiate employees' responses, the next best strategy is to see how their aggregate results compare to other companies' aggregate results. Thus, what are being benchmarked are one company's average survey results against average survey results of multiple other companies. In addition to the problem of using weighted-average data, there is the problem of making the wrong comparisons.

Every company has unique characteristics and different strengths and weaknesses. Companies can differ on a range of dimensions including size, business strategy, core competencies, organizational culture, employee demographics, geographic locations, financial resources, technological capabilities, and HRM. As a result, even companies that follow similar business strategies and compete in the same industry may have different linkages between drivers and outcomes of employee engagement.

The best benchmark is an organization's own employees. Specifically, organizations must assess whether those employees who have unique skills and those who add the most value are engaged. If these employees are not engaged, it will be highly unlikely that the company will be successful regardless of how well it looks in a benchmark report.

Pursuing a One-Size-Fits-All Response to Survey Results Rather Than Assessing the Different Drivers of Engagement at the Individual Level

Firms that aggregate employee survey data have no choice but to pursue a one-size-fits-all strategy when developing programs and policies in response to survey findings. Companies that rely on benchmark data are also likely to have a one-size-fits-all approach by copying the "best practices" at those companies that have the highest scores. Organizations that take such a blunt approach will be at a competitive disadvantage compared to those organizations that take a sharper, more strategic approach. Considering the amount of time, money, and other resources that are used to create, administer, analyze, and report survey findings, a one-size-fits-all strategy significantly reduces the ROI of these engagement initiatives.

Yet this is the approach taken at many organizations. Thus, it's not surprising that one of the biggest complaints that employees have about engagement surveys is not how many questions they must answer, but their perception that the company is not effectively responding to what they are telling them. Perhaps in a far-gone era when companies managed a more stable and homogenous workforce, developing general programs and practices made economic sense. However, we now live and work in a much more diverse and dynamic world. Just as companies need to understand their customers and differentiate how they meet their different needs, so it is with their employees. In almost every aspect of business, there is a movement toward customization. The most successful companies continuously tailor their products and services to specific market segments, and develop targeted differentiated management programs and practices designed to manage and engage different groups of workers.

Failing to Make Valid Linkages Between Employee Survey Results and Strategic Business and Financial Outcomes

Finally, the most effective way to assess employee engagement results is to measure the impact they have on strategic business and financial outcomes. Once again, organizations that cannot differentiate survey results are at a strategic disadvantage. Not only are they unable to assess how different employees are performing, but they also often do not have enough data to draw valid conclusions between employee survey results and organizational outcomes.

For example, an analysis of employee engagement survey results may show there is no relationship between the level of employee engagement and strategic outcomes. There are three possible reasons for results like these. One, the actual measure of engagement may be flawed. The best measure is one that has the least amount of noise. Rather than including conditions and other aspects of engagement, the measure should simply reflect the psychological state of engagement. There is a large body of research demonstrating a strong relationship between employees who feel energized, involved, and committed at work and their job performance.

Second, the problem may be the result of analyzing aggregate data. As previously discussed, a high average score may mute significant variances among different groups of employees. Assessing average scores fails to acknowledge that some employees have a stronger impact on strategic outcomes than others. A high average engagement score may not be correlated with strategic outcomes if the most valuable employees in the group have low engagement scores. Organizations that differentiate engagement scores can see relationships among the data that can help management make well-informed decisions.

Third, there may not be enough data to make valid conclusions. Often, the measures of strategic outcomes (for example, customer satisfaction, product quality, and employee productivity) are compiled at high organizational levels, such as divisional or geographical. As a result, there are too few comparisons to make valid conclusions regarding employee engagement–performance relationships. Given that it is desirable to have at least 30 comparisons to ensure a high degree of confidence in the analysis, it's important to use data compiled at lower levels of the organization, such as the business unit. Once again, this can be accomplished by properly coding the surveys.

All in all, the credibility of engagement initiatives as well as those who are involved is in jeopardy when surveys are poorly designed and analyzed. Management will be less willing to make strategic investments based on questionable results—and rightly so. After investing a significant amount of time and money, the outcome will be a dusty binder of reports on a shelf and a lost opportunity to make a significant impact on the business. Alternatively, organizations that strategically gather and analyze credible employee engagement data will have a distinct competitive advantage managing their most important asset: their human capital.

Not surprisingly, Google is an example of a company that takes such a strategic approach utilizing employee engagement data to help maximize strategic outcomes. At the 2010 Thought Leaders Retreat sponsored by the SHRM Foundation, Shannon Deegan, Director of People Operations at Google, talked about how Google surveys employees annually to identify the factors that engage employees and drive business outcomes. She described how developing the survey is a rigorous process involving complex formulas. In all, Google's employee survey has 75 questions in 13 survey dimensions that enable it to identify specific factors that keep employees motivated and performing at high levels. The measures of success are based on employee retention rates and innovation, which in turn impact measurable financial objectives (SHRM Foundation, 2010).

HRM Practices

There has been a significant shift in various HR practices in response to the challenges of engaging workers in the 21st century. World-class organizations that have organizational adaptability competencies and engaged employees have changed their focus on a series of management practices, such as those presented in Table 8.9.

Table 8.9 Shifting Focus on Management Practices

Planning			Job and Organization Design		
Short term	→	Long term	Narrow jobs	→	Broad jobs
Explicit analysis	→	Implicit analysis	Low involvement	→	High involvement
Extrapolating trends	→	Scenario analysis	Centralization	→	Flat/network structures
Static budgets	→	Dynamic budgeting	Top down	→	Bottom up
			Single decision maker	→	Multiple decision makers
Staffing			**Performance Management**		
Skills-based	→	Competency-based	Once a year	→	Ongoing
Job fit	→	Job and organization fit	Behavioral criteria	→	Results criteria
Single criterion	→	Multiple criteria	Remedial	→	Developmental
Upward movements	→	Lateral movements	Single evaluator	→	Multiple evaluators
Internal sources	→	Multiple sources	Individual focus	→	Group focus
			Low employee input	→	High employee input

Compensation		Training and Development	
Base salary	→ Variable pay	Narrow application	→ Broad application
Standard benefits	→ Flexible benefits	Unplanned	→ Planned
Internal equity	→ External equity	Standard approach	→ Custom approach
Short-term incentives	→ Long-term incentives	Few training options	→ Many training options
Few perks	→ Many perks	Individual focus	→ Group/organization focus

Another noteworthy trend in strategic HRM is the development of sophisticated models for measuring HR's impact on strategic and financial outcomes. Just as there is not a single set of practices for engaging a diverse workforce, there is no single set of measures to assess the effectiveness of HR and engagement practices. Organizations differ on many dimensions including cultural and competitive advantage.

Each organization's measure of success is different given the unique characteristics and competencies. Walmart may measure operational efficiencies, logistics, and cost reductions, whereas Apple may measure knowledge sharing, creativity, and product development. The challenge for management is to understand just how the organization achieves these goals through its employees. Thus, many of the traditional measures used to assess HR's effectiveness including cost per hire, expense ratios, turnover rates, and so on are insufficient because they do not capture how various management practices impact employee engagement and specific strategic outcomes. What good is a cost-effective HR strategy that fails to hire and engage employees necessary for executing the strategic objectives of the organization?

One of the best models for assessing how well a firm's human capital executes strategy is found in the book *The Workforce Scorecard: Managing Human Capital to Execute Strategy* (Huselid et al., 2005b). Their model demonstrates the linkages among the HR Scorecard, Workforce Scorecard, and Balanced Scorecard. Within this model, the true measure of HRM's success consists of specific customer, operational, and financial objectives. These objectives are unique to each organization based on how they choose to compete. These in turn are translated into specific workforce measures including the needed competencies, behaviors, mindset, and culture necessary to achieve these business outcomes. Lastly, the HR scorecard identifies whether there are appropriate HR practices and programs that are internally and externally aligned necessary to create a competent and engaged workforce that can effectively execute the business strategy.

Public Policies

The structural shifts responsible for the social and economic new realities of the 21st century require changes not only in organizational structures and talent management systems, but also in public policies. Indeed, the 21st century workplace is like no other in the history of management. The technological, global, economic, and demographic trends are transforming work systems and the definition of what is an employee, as older bureaucratic work structures are replaced with decentralized networks. There is a clear recognition among businesses, employees, and government that the overall demographics and needs of the workforce have changed. Public policy makers need to take note of the workforce trends presented in Chapter 2, "The 21st Century Workforce," which are summarized here.

In most U.S. households today, both men and women work, leaving less time to take care of daily tasks. Women are now the breadwinners or co-breadwinners in more than two-thirds of U.S. households and represent nearly one-half of all U.S. workers. As the average age of the population continues to increase, nearly 40 percent of employed people are responsible for aging family members. Thus, there is a rapidly growing need for support and flexibility to help workers balance work and life needs. And the challenges facing low-skilled, low-income workers are even greater as they struggle just to make ends meet. Lastly, in today's complex and changing workplace, workers need to continually update their skills if only they can find the time and money to pursue their education.

Yet many of the U.S. laws and regulations governing today's workplace were developed during the New Deal era of the 1930s. New Deal legislation was developed during a time when the typical breadwinner was a male employee working in a regular full-time job, and a single employer was the primary mechanism through which social benefits reach that employee. Indeed, subsequent employment regulations have expanded the role of the employer as the primary provider of an array of benefits including health insurance, pensions, and training and development. Clearly, these regulations are all predicated on a work environment in which employees have long-term relationships with a single employer, a clear definition as to who is the responsible employer, and a clear definition of who is and who is not an employee (Burton et al., 2004).

These assumptions about stable employer–employee relationships do not reflect the realities of today's work environment. The traditional employer–employee relationship of the past in which there was an exchange of worker loyalty for job security is long gone. Today, organizations hire both full-time and part-time employees who work in traditional as well as alternative work arrangements. There is also a growing number of contract human capital including temporary employees, consultants, independent contractors, and so on who are hired for both short-term and long-term project work. By the end of this decade, it's projected that these nontraditional workers will comprise more than 30 percent of the workforce.

Public policies need to evolve just as the economy and workforce have evolved. We live and work in a highly mobile environment in which there is a constant exchange of work for hire. Organizations have access to a wide range of talent throughout the world and move and redeploy workers where they are needed. Furthermore, organizations must be adaptable and align their labor needs with fluctuating business needs by engaging multiple sources of talent. In a constantly changing work environment in which companies come and go and skills quickly become obsolete, workers also need to be adaptable and continue to develop their skills, often by changing jobs or careers. And as people live and work longer, it's not uncommon for them to move in and out of the labor force throughout their working lives.

One trend discussed at length in this book that needs to be addressed by government policy makers is the impending impact of

79 million baby boomers retiring from the workplace. When Social Security was created in 1935, the average life expectancy of retiring workers was significantly lower and the ratio of workers to beneficiaries was significantly higher than it is today. Looking over the next two decades, these continuing negative trends will put a tremendous strain on the program. Research shows that by increasing the median retirement age by 2 years over the next decade, $13 trillion can be added to real U.S. gross domestic product (GDP) over the next 30 years. An added benefit would be an estimated 50 percent reduction in the number of baby boomers who have insufficient funds available for retirement (Beinhocker et al., 2008). Increasing the retirement age can also help keep Social Security solvent if government payments are delayed while payroll taxes increase.

The system also needs to be changed to reflect that many of today's workers work many more years than previous generations. The current Social Security system calculates retirement benefits based on 35 years of work. Thus, workers are not motivated to work beyond 35 years because they would have to continue to pay Social Security taxes with little added benefit. One solution would be to extend the number of years from 35 to 40 and eliminate the payroll tax if workers choose to work beyond 40 years. The elimination of these payroll taxes would also incentivize employers to retain and hire older workers.

Major reforms are also needed in pension policies that will permit workers who collect a pension to continue working. There is also a need for new worker associations in which membership and benefits would be independent of a particular employment relationship. These associations can be workers' secondary sources for health and pension benefits to protect individuals who move from employer to employer from losing benefits that otherwise would be provided by their former employers. These associations can also help workers retrain and learn new skills that can facilitate the movement and continuity of workers' employment.

There is also a need to increase U.S. competitiveness to ensure we continue to be a world economic leader that's necessary to attract and develop new businesses that will create the jobs needed to hire and engage the 21st century workforce. Though we keep hearing how the government may have to increase taxes to help reduce the staggering national debt, the Business Roundtable is lobbying for lower corporate taxes to encourage companies to move and keep operations in the United States. The 39.2 percent combined 2011 U.S. corporate tax rate that includes federal (35 percent) and state taxes is the highest among industrialized nations. Though the effective tax rate, which includes deductions and tax credits, is much lower at approximately 27 percent, it is still much higher than the average 19.5 percent of other developed nations (Business Roundtable, 2011).

The United States also needs to make significant investments to promote a more highly skilled workforce. The U.S. immigration policies regarding highly talented individuals who are trained by our world-renowned universities must be reformed. Intel Vice President Peter Cleveland estimates they are seeking 4,000 to 5,000 engineering and other skilled workers, whereas U.S. immigration law imposes strict annual limits on the number of workers from each country who are eligible for permanent residency. Cleveland laments that the cap hurts highly skilled workers from countries like India whose quotas are reached first. The policy, he says, reduces the pool of qualified foreign candidates, many of whom return home after graduating from U.S. universities, and harms existing workers who are waiting to be promoted. He lamented there are 2,300 people at Intel waiting in a green-card line, and it's discouraging for them (Davidson, 2012).

The National Academy of Science Committee on Prospering in the Global Economy of the 21st Century has highlighted the urgency for the United States to reform the current limiting immigration policies for highly skilled immigrants. The committee recommends instituting a new skills-based, preferential immigration option that entails increasing the number of H-1B visas by 10,000 primarily for science and engineering applicants with doctorates from U.S. universities. It also recommends providing a 1-year automatic visa extension to international students who receive PhDs or the equivalent in the high-demand degrees of science, engineering, mathematics, or other fields of national need at qualified U.S. institutions to remain in the United States to seek employment.

Lastly, the United States needs to transform its educational system. It needs to do a better job preparing students for 21st century jobs. Greater investments are needed to expand research and teaching resources in the sciences, technology, engineering, and mathematics disciplines and provide scholarships for students interested in these fields. Other investments are needed to enhance the effectiveness of community colleges and to offer more vocational training to students who are not interested in an academic degree.

Yes, we do live in interesting times. We seem to be living at the edge of chaos in which governments, organizations, and individuals need a solid foundation by developing the right competencies and capabilities to interpret and respond to the multitude of challenges facing society, while simultaneously becoming adaptable. If we are to succeed, we need people to invest in themselves including their health and human capital, governments to create regulations and make the necessary investments in infrastructure, resources, institutions that support these goals, and organizations that invest in strategic management capabilities necessary to create adaptable organizations that effectively engage a highly diverse workforce and multiple sources of talent.

Bibliography

Adams, J. 1965. "Inequity in social exchanges." In L. Berkowitz (Ed.), *Advances in Experimental Social Psychology*, Vol. 2, New York: Academic Press.

Agrawal, Vivek; Farrell, Diana; and Remes, Jaana. 2003. "Offshoring and beyond." *McKinsey Quarterly*; December. Retrieved May 14, 2012 at www.mckinseyquarterly.com/Offshoring_and_beyond_1367.

Allen, F. A. 2012. "You can only win in sports, or anywhere else, if you're ready for chaos." *Forbes*. Retrieved February 26, 2013 at http://forbes.com/sites/frederickallen/2012/08/14/you-can-only-win-in-sports-or-anywhere-else-if-youre-ready-for-chaos.

Allen, J. R. 1966. *Personnel Administration: Changing Scope and Organization*. New York: National Industrial Conference Board, No. 203.

Amabile, T. M. 1988. "A model of creativity and innovation in organizations." In B. M. Staw and L. L. Cummings (Eds.), *Research in Organizational Behavior*, 10:123–167. Greenwich, CT: JAI Press.

American Savings Education Council & AARP. 2008. "Preparing for Their Future: A Look at the Financial State of Gen X and Gen Y." Retrieved March 2012 at http://assets.aarp.org/rgcenter/econ/preparing_future.pdf.

Andrews, Michelle. 2007. "Employers roll out aggressive wellness programs." *U.S. News and World Report*. Retrieved March 20, 2013 at http://health.usnews.com/health-news/health-plans/articles/2007/10/25/americas-best-health-plans_print.html.

Aon Hewitt. 2012. "Making Employee Engagement Happen: Best Practices from Best Employers." Retrieved March 2013 at www.aon.com/attachments/human-capital-consulting/2012_Making_Employee_Engagement_Happen_Best_Practices_from_Best_Employers_white_paper.pdf.

[APQC] American Productivity and Quality Center. 2000. "Successfully Implementing Knowledge Management: Chevron Knowledge Management." Retrieved March 20, 2013 at http://xa.yimg.com/kq/groups/22235918/526308274/name/Chevron.pdf.

Arndt, M. and Einhorn, B. 2010. "The 50 most innovative companies." *Bloomberg Businessweek Magazine*, April 25.

Arthur, J. B. 1994. "Effects of human resource systems on manufacturing performance and turnover." *Academy of Management Journal*, 37:670–687.

Ashford, S. J.; Rothbard, N. P.; Piderit, S. K.; and Dutton, J. E. 1998. "Out on a limb: The role of context and impression management in selling gender-equity issues." *Administrative Science Quarterly*, 43:23–57.

Augustine, Norman R. 2007. *Is America Falling Off the Flat Earth?* National Academy of Sciences, National Academy of Engineering, Institute of Medicine. Washington DC: National Academies Press.

Auckland, Louis van Wyk. "JetBlue's Reservations Staff Embrace Teleworking." *Computer World*, November 20, 2008.

Avolio, B. J. and Bass, B. M. 1988. "Transformational leadership, charisma, and beyond." In J. G. Hunt, B. R. Baliga, H. P. Dachler, and C. A. Schriesheim (Eds.), *Emerging Leadership Vitas* (29–49). Lexington, MA: Lexington Books.

Bakker, A. B. and Schaufeli, W. B. 2008. "Positive organizational behavior: Engaged employees on flourishing organizations." *Journal of Organizational Behavior*, 29:147–154.

Bandura, A. 1977. "Self-efficacy: Toward a unifying theory of behavioral change." *Psychological Review*, 84(2):191–215.

Barford, Ian N. and Hester, Patrick T. 2011. "Analysis of generation Y workforce motivation using multiattribute utility theory." *Defense Acquisition Review Journal*, 18(1):63–80.

Barnett, Rosalind C.; Gareis, Karen C.; and Carr, Phyllis L. 2005. "Career satisfaction and retention of a sample of women physicians who work reduced hours." *Journal of Women's Health*, 14(2):146–153.

Barney, J. 1991. "Firm resources and sustained competitive advantage." *Journal of Management*, 17:99–129.

Barsh, Joanna. 2008. "Innovative management: A conversation with Gary Hamel and Lowell Bryan." *McKinsey Quarterly*, 2008:1–10.

Barton, Dominic and Court, David. 2012. "Making advanced analytics work for you." *Harvard Business Review*, October. Retrieved May 15, 2013 at http://hbr.org/2012/10/making-advanced-analytics-work-for-you/.

Bass, Bernard M. and Riggio, Ronald E. 2006. *Transformational Leadership, 2nd Edition*, Mahwah, NJ: Lawrence Erlbaum Associates, Inc.

Baum, Sandy and Payea, Kathy. 2004. *Education Pays: The Benefits of Higher Education for Individuals and Society.* The College Board.

Becker, B. E.; Huselid, M. A.; and Beatty, R. W. 2009. *The Differentiated Workforce*, Boston, MA: Harvard Business Press.

Becker, H. S. 1960. "Notes on the concept of commitment." *American Journal of Sociology*, 66:32–42.

Beinhocker, Eric D.; Farrell, Diana; and Greenberg, Ezra. 2008. "Why baby boomers will need to work longer." *McKinsey Quarterly*, November.

Beinhocker, Eric D. 1997. "Strategy at the edge of chaos." *McKinsey Quarterly*, Number 1.

Benko, Cathleen and Anderson, Molly. 2010a. *The Changing World of Work.* Harvard Business Review Press: Boston, MA.

Benko, Cathleen and Anderson, Molly. 2010b. *The Changing World of Work.* Harvard Business Review Press: Boston, MA; and Eric D. Beinhocker, Diana Farell, and Ezra Greenberg, "Why baby boomers will need to live longer." *McKinsey Quarterly*, November 2008.

Benko, Cathleen and Anderson, Molly. 2010c. *The Changing World of Work.* Harvard Business Review Press: Boston, MA; and Families and Work Institute, 2006. *Gender and Generations in the Workplace: An Issues Brief.* New York: Families and Work Institute.

Benko, Cathleen and Anderson, Molly. 2010d. *The Changing World of Work.* Harvard Business Review Press: Boston, MA; and WorldAtWork, 2009. *Telework Trendlines.* Scottsdale, AZ.

Benko, Cathleen and Anderson, Molly. 2010e. *The Changing World of Work.* Harvard Business Review Press: Boston, MA; and Louis van Wyk Auckland, "JetBlue's Reservations Staff Embrace Teleworking." *Computer World*, November 20, 2008; and Chuck Salter, "Calling JetBlue." *Fast Company*, December 19, 2007.

Berube, Alan; Frey, William; Singer, Audrey; and Wilson, Jill. 2011. "Five Things the Census Revealed About America." *The Brookings Institution*, December. Retrieved May 15, 2012 at www.brookings.edu/opinions/2011/1220_census_demographics.aspx#5.

Bies, R. J and Moag, J. F. 1986. "Interactional justice: Communication criteria of fairness." In Lewicki, R. J.; Sheppard, B. H.; and Bazerman, M.H. (Eds.), *Research on Negotiations in Organizations*, 43–55, Greenwich, CT: JAI Press.

Bisson, Peter; Kirkland, Rik; and Stephenson, Elizabeth. 2010. "The great rebalancing." *McKinsey Quarterly*, June.

Blau, P. 1964. *Exchange and Power in Social Life*. New York: Wiley.

Bogsnes, Bjarte. 2009. "Dynamic forecasting: A planning innovation for fast-changing times." *Balanced Scorecard Report*, Harvard Business Publishing.

Bollier, David. 2011. *The Future of Work*. Washington, DC: The Aspen Institute.

Bond, James T.; Galinsky, Ellen; and Hill, Jeffery. 2002. "When Work Works." *Family and Work Institute Research Findings*. Retrieved March 1, 2013 at www.familiesandwork.org/3w/research/downloads/3wes.pdf.

Bono, J. E. and Judge, T. A. 2003. "Self-concordance at work: Toward understanding the motivational effects of transformational leaders." *Academy of Management Journal*, 46:554–571.

Borman, W. and Motowildo, S. 1997. "Task performance and contextual performance: The meaning for personnel selection research." *Human Performance*, 10(2):99–109.

Briscoe, D.; Schuler, R.; and Tarique, I. 2012. *International Human Resource Management Policies and Practices for Multinational Enterprises, 4th Edition*. New York: Routledge.

Briscoe, D.; Schuler, R.; and Claus, L. 2009. *International Human Resource Management, 3rd Edition*, New York: Routledge.

Britt, T. W. 2003. "Black hawk down at work." *Harvard Business Review*, 81:16–17.

Brookfield Global Relocation Services. 2012. "Global Relocation Trends 2012 Survey Report." Retrieved April 13, 2013 at http://knowledge.brookfieldgrs.com/content/insights_ideas-2012_GRTS.

Broschak, J. P. and Davis-Blake, A. 2006. "Mixing standard work and non-standard deals: The consequences of heterogeneity in employment arrangements." *Academy of Management Journal*, 49(2):371–393.

Brown, Kathi S. 2005. "Attitudes of Individuals 50 and Older Toward Phased Retirement." Washington DC: AARP Knowledge Management.

Brown, John S. and Duguid, Paul. 2000. "Balancing act: How to capture knowledge without killing it." *Harvard Business Review*, October 16.

Brown, S. P. 1996. "A meta-analysis and review of organizational research on job involvement." *Psychological Bulletin*, 120:235–255.

Buckingham, M. and Coffman, C. 1999. *First Break All the Rules*. New York: Simon & Schuster.

Bughin, Jacques; Chul, Michael; and Manyika James. 2010. "Clouds, big data, and smart assets: Ten tech-enabled business trends to watch." *McKinsey Quarterly*, August.

Bureau of Economic Analysis. 2013. Fourth quarter GDP news release. Retrieved March 8, 2013 at www.bea.gov/newsreleases/national/gdp/gdpnewsrelease.htm.

Bureau of Economic Analysis. 2012. Table 1.1.5 Gross Domestic Product, April. Retrieved April 29, 2012 at www.bea.gov/iTable/iTable.cfm?ReqID=9&step=1.

Bureau of Labor Statistics, U.S. Department of Labor. 2013. "The Employment Situation." Released March 8. Retrieved March 8, 2013 at www.bls.gov/news.release/empsit.nr0.htm.

Bureau of Labor Statistics, U.S. Department of Labor. 2012. "The Employment Situation." Released March 12. Retrieved April 20, 2012 at www.bls.gov/news.release/pdf/empsit.pdf.

Bureau of Labor Statistics, U.S. Department of Labor. 2011. "Women in the Labor Force: A Databook." Labor Force Statistics from the Current Population Survey. Retrieved June 26, 2012 at www.bls.gov/cps/wlf-databook2011.htm.

Bureau of Labor Statistics, U.S. Department of Labor. 2010a. "Employee Tenure in 2010." Retrieved May 15, 2012 at www.bls.gov/news.release/pdf/tenure.pdf.

Bureau of Labor Statistics, U.S. Department of Labor. 2010b. "Employment Characteristics of Families." Current Population Survey. Retrieved April 2012 at www.bls.gov/cps.

Bureau of Labor Statistics, U.S. Department of Labor. 2009a. 2008–2018 Job Outlook. Retrieved from www.bls.gov/oco/oco2003.htm.

Bureau of Labor Statistics, U.S. Department of Labor. 2009b. "Pension and Welfare Benefits Administration." Retrieved from www.dol.gov/ebsa/regs/AOs/settlor_guidance.html.

Bureau of Labor Statistics, U.S. Department of Labor. 2008. "Older Workers: Are There More Older People in the Workplace?" July. Retrieved May 25, 2013 at www.bls.gov/spotlight/2008/older_workers/.

Bureau of Labor Statistics, U.S. Department of Labor. 2007. "Human Resources, Training, and Labor Relations Managers and Specialists." Retrieved from www.bls.gov/oco/ocos021.htm.

Bureau of Labor Statistics, U.S. Department of Labor. 2005. "Contingent and Alternative Employment Arrangements," February. Current Population Survey. Retrieved April 5, 2012 at www.bls.gov/news.release/pdf/conemp.pdf.

Burton, D.; Bidwell, M.; Fernandez-Mateo, I.; and Kochan, T. SA. 2004. "HRM Challenges for Managing Varied Employment Relationships: IT Employees, Independent Contractors, and Consultants." Cambridge, MA: MIT Institute of Work and Employment Relations.

Business Roundtable. 2011. "Taxation of American Companies in the Global Marketplace: A Primer." Available at http://businessroundtable.org/studies-and-reports/taxation-of-american-companies-in-the-global-marketplace-a-primer/.

Butrica, Barbara A.; Johnson, Richard W.; Smith, Karen E.; and Steuerle, C. Eugene. 2004. "Does Work Pay at Older Age?" Washington, DC: The Urban Institute.

Byun, Kathryn J. and Frey, Christopher. 2012. "The U.S. Economy in 2020: Recovery in Uncertain Times," *Bureau of Labor Statistics, Monthly Labor Review*, January.

Caligiuri, Paula. 2012. *Cultural Agility: Building a Pipeline of Successful Global Professionals.* San Franciso, CA: Jossey-Bass.

Caligiuri, Paula; Lepak, David; and Bonache, Jaime. 2010. *Managing the Global Workforce.* United Kingdom: John Wiley & Sons.

Callanan, Gerard A. and Greenhaus, Jeffrey H. 2008. "The baby boom generation and career management: A call to action." *Advances in Developing Human Resources*, 10(1):70–85.

Calvo, Esteban. 2006. *Does Working Longer Make People Healthier and Happier?* Work Opportunities for Older Americans, Series 2. Chestnut Hill, MA: Center for Retirement Research at Boston College.

Camarota, Steven A. 2007. "Immigrants in the United States, 2007: A Profile of America's Foreign-Born Population." *Center for Immigration Studies*, November.

Cappelli, Peter. 2008. *Talent on Demand: Managing in an Age of Uncertainty.* Boston, MA: Harvard Business Press.

Cappelli, P.; Pfau, B. N.; and Kay, I. T. 2001. *The Human Capital Edge: 21 People Management Practices Your Company Must Implement (or Avoid) to Maximize Shareholder Value.* New York: McGraw-Hill.

Cappelli, Peter. 1999. *The New Deal at Work: Managing the Market-Driven Workforce.* Boston, MA: Harvard Business Press.

Carraher, Shawn; Sullivan, Sherry E.; and Crocitto, Madeline. 2008. "Mentoring across global boundaries: An empirical examination of home and host country mentors on expatriate career outcomes." *International Journal of Business Studies*, 39(8):1310–1326.

Casner-Lotto, J. and Barrington, L. 2006. "Are They Really Ready to Work?" United States: The Conference Board, Corporate Voices for Working Families, Partnership for 21st Century Skills and Society for Human Resource Management (SHRM).

Central Intelligence Agency. 2010. *The World Factbook.* Washington, DC. Retrieved April 16, 2013 at https://www.cia.gov/library/publications/the-world-factbook/index.html.

Cermak, Jenny and McGurk, Monika. 2010. "Putting a value on training." *McKinsey Quarterly.* July:1–5.

Cohn, D'Vera. 2010. "Is the Great Recession Linked to a Decline in Marriage?" *Pew Research Center*, October. Retrieved May 15, 2012 at www.pewsocialtrends.org/2010/10/22/is-the-great-recession-linked-to-a-decline-in-marriage/.

Cohn, D'Vera and Taylor, Paul. 2010. "Baby Boomers Approach 65–Glumly: Survey Findings about America's Largest Generation." *Pew Research Center*, 20 December:1–7.

Colquitt, J.; Conlon, D.; Wesson, M.; Porter, C.; and Ng, Y. 2001. "Justice at the millennium: A meta-analytic review of 25 years of organizational justice research." *Journal of Applied Psychology*, 86:425–445.

Committee on Prospering in the Global Academy of the 21st Century: An Agenda for American Science and Technology. 2007. *Rising Above the Gathering Storm*, Washington, DC: The National Academies Press.

Conger, J. A. and Kanungo, R. N. 1988. "The empowerment process: Integrating theory and practice." *Academy of Management Review*, 13(3): 471–482.

Conlin, Michelle. 2006. "Smashing the clock." *Bloomberg Businessweek Magazine.* December 10. Retrieved February 27 at www.businessweek.com/stories/2006-12-10/smashing-the-clock.

Costa, P. T., Jr. and McCrae, R. R. 1985. *The NEO Personality Inventory Manual.* Odessa, FL: Psychological Assessment Resources.

Court, David and Narasimhan, Laxman. 2010. "Capturing the world's emerging middle class." *McKinsey Quarterly*, July. Retrieved March 30, 2012 at www.mckinseyquarterly.com/capturing_the_worlds_emerging_middle_class_2639.

Court, David; Farrell, Diana; Forsyth, John; and Hollenbach, David. 2007. "Serving aging baby boomers." *McKinsey Quarterly.* November. Retrieved May 15, 2012 at www.mckinseyquarterly.com/Serving_aging_baby_boomers_2068.

Crant, J. 2000. "Proactive behavior in organizations." *Journal of Management*, 26(3):435–462.

Crumpacker, Martha and Crumpacker, Jill M. 2007. "Succession planning and generational stereotypes: Should HR consider age-based values and attitudes a relevant factor or a passing fad?" *Public Personnel Management*, 36(4):349–369.

Csikszentmihalyi, M. 1990. *Flow: The Psychology of Optimal Experience.* New York: Harper & Row.

Davidson, Paul. 2012. "U.S. businesses seek a more competitive economy." *USA Today*, November 8.

Davis, Andrea. 2012. "2012 Benny Award Winner: Aetna Makes Financial Wellness Part of Its Culture." *Employee Benefit News Online*, September 1. Retrieved March 21, 2013 at http://ebn.benefitnews.com/news/aetna-carol-klusek-benny-award-retirement-2727080-1.html.

Deci, E. L.; Connell, J. P.; and Ryan, R. M. 1989. "Self-determination in a work organization." *Journal of Applied Psychology*, 74(4):580–590.

Deci, E. L. and Ryan, R. M. 1987. "The support of autonomy and the control of behavior." *Journal of Personality and Social Psychology*, 53(6):1014–1037.

De Lisser, E. 1999. "Update on small business: Firms with virtual environments appeal to workers." *The Wall Street Journal*, April 17, 1999. B2.

Deloitte.com. 2012. "Life and Family: Keeping a Happy Balance." Retrieved June 6, 2013 at http://mycareer.deloitte.com/us/en/life-at-deloitte/worklifefit/benefits/life-and-family#.

Demerouti, E.; Bakker, A.B.; Nachreiner, F.; and Schaufeli, W. B. 2001. "The job demands-resources model of burnout." *Journal of Applied Psychology*, 86:499–512.

Destro, Jeanne. 2012. "Review: 'Automate This' Probes Math in Global Training." *USA Today*, Sept. 16, 2012. http://usatoday30.usatoday.com/money/business/story/2012/09/16/review-automate-this-probes-math-in-global-trading/57782600/1.

Dill, W. R.; Gaver, W. P.; and Weber, W. L. 1966. "Models and modeling for manpower planning." *Management Science*, 13(4):88–89.

Director, S. 2013. *Financial Analysis for HR Managers*. Upper Saddle River, NJ: FT Press.

Dobbs, Richard; Lund, Susan; and Madgavkar, Anu. 2012. "Talent tensions ahead: A CEO briefing." *McKinsey Quarterly*, McKinsey Global Institute, November.

Dvir, T.; Eden, D.; Avolio, B. J.; and Shamir, B. 2002. "Impact of transformational leadership on follower development and performance." *Academy of Management Journal*, 45:735–744.

The Economist. 2009. "Women in the workforce." December 30. Retrieved April 6, 2012 at www.economist.com/node/15174418.

Edmondson, A. C. 1999. "Psychological safety and learning behavior in work teams." *Administrative Science Quarterly*, 44(2):350–383.

Educational Testing Service. 2007. "America's Perfect Storm: Three Forces Changing Our Nation's Future."

Edwards, J. and Rothbard, N. 2000. "Mechanisms linking work and family: Clarifying the relationship between work and family constructs." *Academy of Management Review*, 25(1):178–199.

VanDerhei, Jack and Copeland, Craig. 2010. "The EBRI Retirement Readiness Rating: Retirement Income Preparation and Future Prospects." Employee Benefit Research Institute (EBRI). July, No. 344. Retrieved at www.ebri.org/pdf/briefspdf/EBRI_IB_07-2010_No344_RRR-RSPM.pdf.

Erickson, Tamara. 2010. "Restore trust with employees? Forget about it." *Harvard Business Review*, May.

Ernst & Young. 2010. "Managing Today's Global Workforce: Elevating Talent Management to Improve Business." Ernst & Young LLP, May. Retrieved September 29, 2012 at www.ey.com/Publication/vwLUAssets/ Managing_Todays_Global_workforce/$FILE/Managing_Todays_Global_ workforce.pdf.

Ernst & Young. 2006. "The Aging of the U.S. Workforce: Employer Challenges and Responses." Available at http://theworkpaper.ey.com/national/ alumni.nsf/admin/sectiondocs/D9D0E8724FEB2B5785256DF900592BF9/ $file/AgingUSWorkforceEmployerChallenges.pdf.

Families and Work Institute, 2006. *Gender and Generations in the Workplace: An Issues Brief.* New York: Families and Work Institute.

Farrell, Diana; Beinhocker, Eric; Greenberg, Ezra; Shukla, Suruchi; Ablett, Jonathan; and Greene, Geoffrey. 2008. "Talkin' 'bout my generation: The economic impact of aging US baby boomers." *McKinsey & Company Global Institute*.

Farrell, Diana and Grant, Andrew. 2005. "China's looming talent shortage." *McKinsey Quarterly*, November. Retrieved May 14, 2012 at www. mckinseyquarterly.com/Chinas_looming_talent_shortage_1685.

Farrell, Diana; Laboissiere, Marta A.; and Rosenfeld, J. 2005. "Sizing the emerging global labor market." *McKinsey Quarterly*, Number 3.

Federal Reserve Statistical Release. 2013. "Flows of Funds Accounts of the United States." Board of Governors of the Federal Reserve System, Washington, DC.

Field, Jonathan. 2012. "Superstars 2012: Aetna's Three-Pronged Approach Wellness." *The Institute of Health Care Consumerism (online)*. Retrieved March 21, 2013 at www.theihcc.com/en/communities/population_health_and_wellness/superstars-2012-aetna%E2%80%99s-three-pronged-approach-to-_hb8e4g0i.html.

Fleming, J. H.; Coffman, C.; and Harter, J. K. 2005. "Manage your human sigma." *Harvard Business Review*, July–August: 1–8.

Freidman, George. 2011. *The Next Decade*. New York: Doubleday.

Frese, M. and Fay, D. 2001. "Personal initiative (PI): An active performance concept for work in the 21st century." In B. M. Staw and R. M. Sutton (Eds.), *Research in Organizational Behavior*, 23:133–187.

Friedberg, Leora and Webb, Anthony. 2005. "Retirement and the evolution of pension structure." *Journal of Human Resources*, 40(2):281–308.

Fry, Richard and Cohn, D'Vera. 2011. "Living Together: The Economics of Cohabitation." *Pew Research Center*. Retrieved May 15, 2012 at www.pewsocialtrends.org/2011/06/27/living-together-the-economics-of-cohabitation/2/.

Fulmer, R.; Gibbs, P. A.; and Goldsmith, M. 2000. "Developing leaders: How winning companies keep on winning." *Sloan Management Review*, 42(1).

Gagne, M. and Deci, E. L. 2005. "Self-determination theory and work motivation." *Journal of Organizational Behavior*, 26:332–362.

Galama, T. and Hosek, J. 2008. *U.S. Competitiveness in Science and Technology*. Rand Corporation. Retrieved at www.rand.org/pubs/monographs.

Galinsky, Ellen; Aumann, Kerstin; and Bond, James. 2009. *Times Are Changing: Gender and Generation at Work and at Home*. New York: Families and Work Institute.

Gesteland, Richard R. 2005. *Cross-Cultural Business Behavior: Selling, Sourcing, and Managing Across Cultures, 4th Edition*, Copenhagen: Business School Press.

Ghemawat, P. 2001. "Distance still matters: The hard reality of global expansion." *Harvard Business Review*, September: 1–10.

Gibbons, John. 2006. "Employee Engagement, a Review of Current Research and Its Implications." *The Conference Board*, November.

Gilbert, Jay. 2011. "The millennials: A new generation of employees, a new set of engagement policies." *Ivey Business Journal.* Retrieved May 16, 2012 at www.iveybusinessjournal.com/topics/the-workplace/the-millennials-a-new-generation-of-employees-a-new-set-of-engagement-policies.

Gitsham, Matthew; Pegg, Mark; and Culpin, Vicki. 2011. "The shifting landscape of global challenges in the 21st century: What this means for what businesses want from tomorrow's leaders, and the implications for management learning." *Business Leadership Review*, 8(2):1–15.

Goldstone, Jack. 2010. "The new population bomb." *Foreign Affairs*, 89.

Goodspeed, Linda. 2011. "IBM Wellness Program works one employee at a time." *Boston Business Journal.* Retrieved March 20, 2013 at www.bizjournals.com/boston/print-edition/2011/04/15/ibm-wellness-program-works-one.html?page=all April 15.

Graham, J. W. 1986. "Principled organizational dissent: A theoretical essay." In B. M. Staw and L. L. Cummings (Eds.), *Research in Organizational Behavior*, 8:1–52. Greenwich, CN: JAI Press, Inc.

Greenberg, J. 1990. "Organizational justice: yesterday, today, and tomorrow." *Journal of Management*, 16:399–432.

Griffin, M. A.; Neal, A.; and Parker, S. 2007. "A new model of work role performance: Positive behavior in uncertain and interdependent contexts." *Academy of Management Journal*, 50(2):327–347.

Guthridge, Matthew; Komm, Asmus, B.; and Lawson, Emily. 2008. "Making talent a strategic priority." *McKinsey Quarterly*, Vol 1.

Hackman, J. R. and Lawler, E. E. 1971. "Employee reactions to job characteristics." *Journal of Applied Psychology*, 55(3):259–286.

Hackman, J. R. and Oldham, G. R. 1980. *Work Redesign*. Reading, MA: Addison-Wesley.

Hackman, J. R. and Oldham, G. R. 1976. "Motivation through the design of work: Test of a theory." *Organizational Behavior & Human Performance*, 16:250–279.

Hall, Edward T. 1981. *Beyond Culture*. New York: Anchor Books.

Hamel, Gary, and Prahalad, C. K. 1994. *Competing for the Future*. Boston, MA: Harvard Business School Press.

Harnish, Tom, and Lister, Kate. 2010. *Workshifting Benefits: The Bottom Line*. Retrieved May 14, 2012 at www.workshifting.com/downloads/downloads/Workshifting%20Benefits-The%20Bottom%20Line.pdf.

Harter, J. K.; Schmidt, F. L.; and Hayes, T. L. 2002. "Business-unit-level relationship between employee satisfaction, employee engagement, and business outcomes: A meta-analysis." *Journal of Applied Psychology*, 87(2):268–279.

Hartley, D. 2010. Eli Lilly & Co.'s OLA Lilly. *Diversity Executive*, 3.

Harvey, C. P. and Allard, M. J. 2011. *Understanding & Managing Diversity: Readings, Cases, & Diversity*. Boston, MA: Prentice Hall.

Hawksworth, John, 2006. "The World in 2050." *PricewaterhouseCoopers Report*, March.

The Health Project. 2010. "IBM-Wellness for Life." Retrieved March 20, 2013 at www.sph.emory.edu/healthproject/past_winners/year/2008/ibm/ description.html. National Health Awards, 2008.

Henderson, Richard. 2012. "Industry Employment and Output Projections to 2012." *Bureau of Labor Statistics Monthly Labor Review*, January.

Hewitt Associates LLC. 2005. "Employee Engagement." Retrieved April 29, 2005 at http://was4.hewitt.com/hewitt/services/talent/subtalent/ee_ engagement.htm.

Hewlett, Sylvia Ann. 2012. "Strengthen Your Workforce Through Volunteer Programs." *Harvard Business Review HBR Blog Network*. Retrieved February 26, 2013 at http://blogs.hbr.org/hbr/hewlett/2012/03/strengthen_ your_workforce_thro.html.

Hewlett, Sylvia Ann; Sherbin, Laura; and Sumberg, Karen. 2009. "How gen Y and boomers will reshape your agenda." *Harvard Business Review*, July–August.

Hewlett, Sylvia Ann. 2009. "Flex Time: A Recession Triple Win." *Harvard Business Review HBR Blog Network*. Retrieved May 16, 2012 at http:// blogs.hbr.org/hbr/hewlett/2009/08/time_as_currency.html.

Heyn, Lisa. 2012. "Coalition of Interest Groups Urges House to Make Available More Visas to Foreign STEM-Graduates." *Alliance for International Education and Cultural Exchange*. Based on a CQ.com report. Retrieved September 10, 2012 at www.alliance-exchange.org/policy-monitor/07/16/2012/coalition-interest-groups-urges-house-make-available-more-visas-foreign-st.

Hinssen, Peter. 2010. "The New Normal: Explore the Limits of the Digital World." Gent, Belgium: Mach Media.

Hirschfeld, R. and Thomas, C. R. 2008. "Representations of trait engagement: Integration, additions, and mechanisms." *Industrial and Organizational Psychology*, 1(1):63–66.

Hofstede, G. 2001. *Culture and Organizations: Comparing Values, Behaviors, Institutions, and Organizations Across Nations, 2nd Edition.* Thousand Oaks, CA: Sage.

Hooijberg, Robert; Hunt, James G.; Antonakis, John; Boal, Kimberly B.; and Lance, Nancy. 2007. "Being There Even When You Are Not: Leading through Strategy, Structures, and Systems." Chapter 3. In Paul V. Broeckx, *Nestlé on the Move.* UK: Emerald Group Publishing Limited.

Huselid, M. A. 1995. "The impact of human resource management practices on turnover, productivity, and corporate financial performance." *Academy of Management Journal*, 38:835–854.

Huselid, M. A.; Becker, B. E.; and Beatty, R. W. 2005a. "A players or A positions? The strategic logic of workforce management." *Harvard Business Review*, December.

Huselid, M. A.; Becker, B. E.; and Beatty, R. W. 2005b. *The Workforce Scorecard: Managing Human Capital to Execute Strategy.* Boston, MA: Harvard Business School Press, pg. 4.

Huselid, M. A.; Jackson, S. E.; and Schuler, R. S. 1997. "Technical and strategic human resource management effectiveness as determinants of firm performance." *Academy of Management Journal*, 40(1):171–188.

IBM. 2010. "Working Beyond Borders. Insights from the Chief Human Resource Officer Study," pg. 59. Retrieved April 16, 2013 at http://public.dhe.ibm.com/common/ssi/ecm/en/gbe03353usen/GBE03353USEN.PDF.

IBM. 2008. *Unlocking the DNA of the Adaptable Workforce: The IBM Global Human Capital Study.* Armonk, New York: IBM, pg. 30.

IBM.com. 2008. "Global Mentoring: IBMers Learning from Each Other." Retrieved May 9, 2013 at www.ibm.com/ibm/responsibility/mentoring.shtml.

International Energy Agency. 2012. "World Energy Outlook 2012." Retrieved January 8, 2013 at http://iea.org/publications/freepublications/publication/English.pdf.

Jayson, Sharon. 2012. "Burnout up among employees." *USA Today*. October 24. Retrieved February 27, 2013 at www.usatoday.com/story/news/nation/2012/10/23/stress-burnout-employees/1651897/.

Johnson, Richard W. 2010. "Phased Retirement and Workplace Flexibility for Older Adults: Opportunities and Challenges." *Alfred P. Sloan Foundation*, November 29–30.

Johnson, Richard W. and Steuerle, Eugene. 2004. "Promoting work at older ages: The role of hybrid pension plans in an aging population." *Journal of Pension Economics and Finance*, 3(3):315–337.

Jones, C. 2004. "Teleworking: The Quiet Revolution." Report published by the Gartner Group.

Judge, T. A.; Thoresen, C. J.; Bono, J. E.; and Patton, G. K. 2001. "The job satisfaction–job performance relationship: A qualitative and quantitative review." *Psychological Bulletin*, 127(3):376–407.

Kahn, W. A. 1990. "Psychological conditions of personal engagement and disengagement at work." *Academy of Management Journal*, 33:692–724.

Kanter, R. M. 1989. *When Giants Learn to Dance: Mastering the Challenge of Strategy, Management, and Careers in the 1990s*. New York: Simon & Schuster.

Kanungo, R. N. 1982. "Measurement of job and work involvement." *Journal of Applied Psychology*, 67:341–349.

Keene, J. 2006. "Age discrimination." In J. H. Greenhaus and G. A. Callanan (Eds.), *Encyclopedia of Career Development*, 1:10–14. Thousand Oaks, CA: Sage.

Keller, Scott and Price, Colin. 2011. "Organizational health: The ultimate competitive advantage." *McKinsey Quarterly*, June:1–13.

Kirkman, B. L.; Rosen, B.; Tesluk, P. E.; and Gibson, C. B. 2004. "The impact of team empowerment on virtual team performance: The moderating influence of face-to-face interaction." *Academy of Management Journal*, 2:175–192.

Kirsch, Irwin; Braun, Henry; Yamamoto, Kentaro; and Sum, Andrew. 2007. "America's Perfect Storm: Three Forces Changing Our Nation's Future." Educational Testing Service (ETS). Retrieved March 20, 2012 at www.ets. org/Media/Education_Topics/pdf/AmericasPerfectStorm.pdf.

Kouzes, J. M.; and Posner, B. Z. 1987. *The Leadership Challenge*. San Francisco, CA: Jossey-Bass.

Kraimer, Maria; Shaffer, Margaret; and Bolino, Mark. 2009. "The influence of expatriate and repatriate experiences on career advancement and repatriate retention." *Human Resource Management*, 48(1):27–47.

Lane, Kevin and Pollner, Florian. 2008. "How to address China's growing talent shortage." *McKinsey Quarterly*, July. Retrieved May 14, 2012 at www.mckinseyquarterly.com/How_to_address_Chinas_growing_talent_shortage_2156.

Lannquist, Yolanda. 2012. "A Perfect Storm: Europe's Looming Pension Crisis." *The Conference Board*, No. 372, January. Available at www.conference-board.org/publications/publicationdetail.cfm?publicationid=2079.

Laudicina, P. A. 2005. *World Out of Balance: Navigating Global Risks to Seize Competitive Advantage.* New York: McGraw-Hill, pg. 76.

Lawler, E. E. 1992. *The Ultimate Advantage: Creating the High-Involvement Organization.* San Francisco, CA: Jossey-Bass.

Lee, Marlene A. and Mather, Mark. 2008. "U.S. labor force trends." Population Reference Bureau. *Population Bulletin*, 63(2):2–16.

Lepak, David P.; Takeuchi, Riki; and Snell, Scott A. 2003. "Employment flexibility and firm performance: Examining the interaction effects of employment mode, environmental dynamics, and technological intensity." *Journal of Management*, 29(5):681–703.

Lepak, D. P. and Snell, S. A. 1999. "The human resource architect: Toward a theory of human capital allocation and development." *Academy of Management Review*, 24:31–48.

Levanthal, G. S. 1980. "What should be done with equity theory? New approaches to the study of fairness in social relationships." In Gergen, K., Greenberg, M., and Willis, R. (Eds.), *Social Exchange: Advances in Theory and Research*, 27–55, New York: Academic Press.

Levine, Arthur and Dean, Diane R. 2012. *Generation on a Tightrope: A Portrait of Today's College Student.* San Francisco, CA: Jossey-Bass.

Light, Joe and Silverman, Rachel Emma. 2011. "Generation jobless: Students pick easier majors despite less pay." *The Wall Street Journal*, 9 November.

Lockard, C. B. and Wolf, M. 2012. "Occupational Employment Projections to 2020." *Bureau of Labor Statistics Monthly Labor Review*, January.

Locke, E. A. and Latham, G. P. 1990. *A Theory of Goal Setting and Task Performance.* Englewood Cliffs, NJ: Prentice Hall.

Lund, Susan; Manyika, James; and Ramaswamy, Sree. 2012. "Preparing for a new era of work." *McKinsey Quarterly*, November.

MacDuffie, John Paul. 2007. "HRM and distributed work." *The Academy of Management Annals*, 1(1):549–615.

Macey, W. H. and Schneider, B. 2008. "The meaning of employee engagement." *Industrial and Organizational Psychology*, 1:3–30.

MacMillan, Douglas. 2008. "Issue: Retiring employees, lost knowledge." *Bloomberg Businessweek*, November 20. Retrieved March 2, 2013 at www.businessweek.com/stories/2008-08-20/issue-retiring-employees-lost-knowledgebusinessweek-business-news-stock-market-and-financial-advice.

Makridakis, Spyros; Hogarth, Robin M.; and Gaba, Anil. 2010. "Why forecasts fail: What to do instead." *MIT Sloan Management Review*, 51(2).

Malhotra, A.; Majchrzak, A.; and Rosen, B. 2007. "Practices of effective virtual teams." *Academy of Management Persepectives*, 21:61–70.

Malcolm, Hadley. 2012. "Future of shopping? A brave new world." *USA TODAY*, September 15.

Manpower Group. 2011. "Talent Shortage Survey Results." Retrieved April 14, 2012 at http://us.manpower.com/us/en/multimedia/2011-Talent-Shortage-Survey.pdf.

Martinez, Gladys; Daniels, Kimberly; and Chandra, Anjani. 2012. "Fertility of men and women aged 15–44 years in the United States: National survey of family growth 2006-2010." *National Health Statistics Reports*, 51, April 12.

Maslach, C.; Schaufeli, W. B.; and Leiter, M. P. 2001. "Job burnout." *Annual Review Psychology*, 52:397–422.

Masters, Brooke. 2009. "Rise of the headhunter." *Financial Times*. March 30. Referred to in Mitchell, Charles; Ray, Rebecca L.; and van Ark, Bart. 2012. "The Conference Board CEO Challenge." *The Conference Board.*

Masterson, S. S.; Lewis, K.; Goldman, B. M.; and Taylor, M. S. 2000. "Integrating justice and social exchange: The differing effects of fair procedures and treatment on work relationships." *Academy of Management Journal*, 43:738–48.

Mathieu, J. E.; Gilson, L. L.; and Ruddy, T. M. 2006. "Empowerment and team effectiveness: An empirical test of an integrated model." *Journal of Applied Psychology*, 91(1):97–108.

Matson, Eric and Prusak, Laurence. 2010. "Boosting the productivity of knowledge workers." *McKinsey Quarterly*, 1–4.

May, D. R.; Gilson, R. L.; and Harter, L. H. 2004. "The psychological conditions of meaningfulness, safety and availability, and the engagement of the human spirit at work." *Journal of Occupational and Organizational Psychology*, 77(1):11–37.

McCall, Morgan and Hollenback, George. 2002. "Developing Global Executives: The Lessons of International Experience." Boston, MA: Harvard Business School Publishing. Retrieved May 3, 2013 at www.shrm.org/Research/Articles/Articles/Pages/LeadershipCompetencies.aspx.

McCauley, Cynthia D. 2006. "Developmental Assignments Creating Learning Experiences Without Changing Jobs." Greensboro, N.C.: Center for Creative Leadership Press. Retrieved May 3, 2013 at www.shrm.org/Research/Articles/Articles/Pages/LeadershipCompetencies.aspx.

McKinsey & Company. 2012a. "Listening to employees: The 'Beyond Bureaucracy' M-Prize winners." *McKinsey Quarterly*, March, 1–4.

McKinsey & Company. 2012b. McKinsey Global Survey Results. "Minding Your Digital Business."

McKinsey & Company. 2010. McKinsey Global Survey Results. "Innovation and Commercialization."

McKinsey & Company, Social Sector Office. April 2009. "The Economic Impact of the Achievement Gap in America's Schools." New York: McKinsey & Company.

McKinsey Global Institute. June 2009a. "Changing the Fortunes of America's Workforce: A Human Capital Challenge," and using data from Current Population Survey and Bureau of Labor Statistics.

McKinsey Global Institute. June 2009b. "Changing the Fortunes of America's Workforce: A Human Capital Challenge," and TradeStats Express, Office of Trade and Industry Information, International Trade Association, Department of Commerce, BEA.

Meister, Jeanne C. and Willyerd, Karie. 2010. *The 2020 Workplace*. New York: HarperCollins.

Meyer, J. P. and Allen, N. 1997. *Commitment in the Workplace: Theory, Research, and Application*. Thousand Oaks, CA: Sage.

Meyer, J. P. and Allen, N. 1991. "The three-component conceptualization of organizational commitment." *Human Resource Management Review*, 1(1):61–89.

Meyer, J. P.; Paunonen, S. V.; Gellatly, I. R.; Goffin, R. D.; and Jackson, D. N. 1989. "Organizational commitment and job performance: It's the nature of commitment that counts." *Journal of Applied Psychology*, 74:152–156.

Miles, R. E. and Snow, C. C. 1978. *Organizational Strategy, Structure, and Processes*. New York: McGraw-Hill.

Miller, Jody. 2005. "Get A Life!" *Fortune Magazine*. 28 November. Retrieved January 29, 2013 at http://money.cnn.com/magazines/fortune/fortune_archive/2005/11/28/8361955/index.htm.

Mitchell, Charles. 2011. "Giving the Working Poor a Working Chance." *The Conference Board, Council Perspectives*, TCBCP027, February.

Mitchell, Charles; Ray, Rebecca L.; and van Ark, Bart. 2012. "The Conference Board CEO Challenge." *The Conference Board*.

Morris, J. A. and Feldman, D. C. 1996. "The dimensions, antecedents, and consequences of emotional labor." *Academy of Management Review*, 21(4):986–1010.

Morrison, E. W. and Robinson, S. L. 1997. "When employees feel betrayed: A model of how psychological contract violation develops." *Academy of Management Review*, 22:226–256.

Mullaney, Tim. 2012. "Jobs flight: Haves vs. have-nots." *USATODAY. com*. Retrieved February 27, 2013 at http://usatoday.com/money/business/story/2012/09/14/jobs-haves-vs-the-have-nots.

MyCareer/Deloitte.com. 2012. "Life and Family: Keeping a Happy Balance." Retrieved June 6, 2013 at http://mycareer.deloitte.com/us/en/life-at-deloitte/worklifefit/benefits/life-and-family#.

My Family Care Whitepaper. 2011. "P&G: Setting the Gold Standard in Family Friendly Working." *My Family Care*. Retrieved March 5, 2013 at https://www.myfamilycare.co.uk/case-studies-and-downloads/articles-white-papers.html.

National Science Board, Science and Engineering Indicators. 2012. Arlington, VA: National Science Foundation. Retrieved from www.nsf.gov/statistics/seind12/.

National Science Board, Science and Engineering Indicators. 2004. "An Emerging and Critical Problem of the Science and Engineering Labor Force." Arlington, VA: National Science Foundation.

Nelson, D. L. and Cooper, C. L. (Eds.). 2007. *Positive Organizational Behavior.* London: Sage. Found in Robbins, S. P. and Judge, T. A. 2008. *Organizational Behavior, 13th Edition*, Upper Saddle River, NJ: Pearson Education, Inc.

Nestlé. 2003. "The Nestlé People Development Review." Retrieved April 10, 2013 at www.nestle.com/asset-library/Documents/Library/Documents/People/People-Development-Review-EN.pdf.

Newman, D. and Harrison, D. 2008. "Been there, bottled that: Are state and behavioral work engagement new and useful construct 'wines'?" *Industrial and Organizational Psychology*, 1:3–30.

Norris, Floyd. 2012. "Private pension plans, even at big companies, may be underfunded." *The New York Times*, July 20. Retrieved September 19 at www.nytimes.com/2012/07/21/business/pension-plans-increasingly-under-funded-at-largest-companies.html.

[OECD] Organization for Economic Cooperation and Development. 2008. "The Global Competition for Talent Mobility of the Highly Skilled." Retrieved March 30, 2012 at www.oecd.org/dataoecd/55/3/41362303.pdf.

OECD. 2011. "Society at a Glance 2011: OECD Social Indicators." Available at www.oecd.org/social/soc/47571423.pdf.

O'Neil, Jim and Stupnytska, Anna. 2009. "The Long-Term Outlook for the BRICs and N-11 post crisis." Goldman Sachs Global Economics Paper No: 192. Retrieved March 26, 2012 from www.goldmansachs.com/our-thinking/brics/brics-reports-pdfs/long-term-outlook.pdf.

Oracle. 2010. "Successfully Executing and Managing Contingent Workforce Strategy." *Oracle White Paper*. Available at www.oracle.com/us/products/applications/ebusiness/psft-contingent-workforce-406025.pdf.

Organ, D. W. 1997. "Organizational citizenship behavior: It's construct cleanup time." *High Performance*, 10:85–97.

Organ, D. W. 1988. *Organizational Citizenship Behavior: The Good Soldier Syndrome*. Lexington, MA: Lexington Books.

Organ, D. W.; Podsakoff, P. M.; and MacKenzie S. P. 2006. *Organizational Citizenship Behavior: Its Nature, Antecedents, and Consequences*. London: Sage Publications.

Organ, D. W. and Ryan, K. 1995. "A meta-analytic review of attitudinal and dispositional predictors of organizational citizenship behavior." *Personnel Psychology*, 48:775–802.

Osterman, P. 1987. "Choice of employment systems in industrial relations." *Industrial Relations Review*, 26:48–63.

Passel, Jeffrey S. and Cohn, D'Vera. 2008. "U.S. Population Projections: 2005–2050." *Pew Research Center*, February.

Peters, Thomas J. and Waterman Jr., Robert H. 2004. *In Search of Excellence: Lessons from America's Best Run Companies*. New York: Harper-Business.

Peterson, S. J. and Spiker, B. K. 2005. "Establishing the positive contributory value of older workers: A positive psychology perspective." *Organizational Dynamics*, 34:153–167.

Pew Research Center. 2012. "Fewer, Poorer, Gloomier. The Lost Decade of the Middle Class." *Pew Social and Demographic Trends*, August 12.

Pew Research Center. 2010. "Decline of Marriage and Rise of New Families." *Pew Social Trends*, November 2010.

Pew Research Center. 2007. "How Young People View Their Lives, Futures, and Politics: A Portrait of 'Generation Next.'" January 9. Available at http://people-press.org/files/legacy-pdf/300.pdf.

Pine, B. J. and Gilmore, J. H. 1999. *The Experience Economy*. Boston, MA: Harvard Business Press.

Pitt-Catsouphes, Marcie and Matz-Costa, Christina. 2008. "The multi-generational workforce: Workplace flexibility and engagement." *Community, Work & Family*, 11(2):215–229.

Poelmans, Stevens and Chinchilla, Nuria M. 2001. "A Concern for 21st Century Business: Family Friendly Policies." *IESE Report*. December. Retrieved March 15, 2013 at www.ee-iese.com/84/pdf84/afondo1.pdf.

Porter, M. 1985. *Competitive Advantage: Creating and Sustaining Superior Performance*. New York: Free Press.

Pugh, S. D. and Dietz, J. 2008. "Employee engagement at the organizational level of analysis." *Industrial and Organizational Psychology*, 1:44–47.

[PWC] PricewaterhouseCoopers. 2006. PWC 9th Annual Global CEO Survey. "Globalization and Complexity: Inevitable Forces in a Changing Economy."

Ray, Rebecca L. 2011. "CEO Challenge Reflections: Talent Matters." *The Conference Board, Executive Action Report*, No. 364.

Reich, Robert. 2001. *The Future of Success*. New York: Knopf.

Reeves, Martin and Deimler, Mike. 2011. "Adaptability: The new competitive advantage." *Harvard Business Review*, July–August.

Rhoades, L. and Eisenberger, R. 2002. "Perceived organizational support: A review of the literature." *Journal of Applied Psychology*, 87:698–714.

Robbins, S. P. and Judge, T. A. 2008. *Organizational Behavior, 13th Edition*. Upper Saddle River, NJ: Pearson Education, Inc.

Robinson, S. L.; Kraatz, M.; and Rousseau, D. M. 1994. "Changing obligations and the psychological contract: A longitudinal study." *Academy of Management Journal*, 37:137–152.

Robinson, S. L. and Morrison, E. W. 2000. "The development of psychological contract breach and violations: A longitudinal study." *Journal of Organizational Behavior*, 21(5):525–546.

Rothbard, N. P. 2001. "Enriching or depleting? The dynamics of engagement in work and family roles." *Administrative Science Quarterly*, 46(4):655–684.

Rotter, J. B. 1966. "Generalized expectancies for internal versus external control of reinforcement." *Psychological Monographs: General and Applied*, 80(1):1–28.

Rousseau, D.; Ho, V. T.; and Greenberg, J. 2006. "I-deals: Idiosyncratic terms in employment relationships." *Academy of Management Review*, 31(4):977-1004.

Rousseau, D. M. 1995. *Psychological Contracts in Organizations: Understanding Written and Unwritten Agreements.* Thousand Oaks, CA: Sage.

Sahadi, Jeanne. 2007. "Flex-time, time off: Who's getting these perks." *CNN Money*. June. Retrieved May 16, 2012 at www.money.cnn.com/2007/06/25/pf/work_life_balance/index.htm.

Saks, A. M. and Ashforth, B. E. 1997. "A longitudinal investigation of the relationships between job information sources, applicants perceptions of fit, and work outcomes." *Personnel Psychology*, 50(2):395–426.

Salter, Chuck. 2007. "Calling JetBlue." *Fast Company*, December 19.

Schaufeli, W. B.; Bakker, A.; and Salanova, M. 2006. "The measurement of work engagement with a short questionnaire: A cross-national study." *Educational and Psychological Measurement*, 66:701–716.

Schaufeli, W. B.; Salanova, M.; Gonzalez-Roma, V.; and Bakker, A. B. 2002. "The measurement of engagement and burnout: A two sample confirmatory factor analytic approach." *Journal of Happiness Studies*, 3:71–92.

Schmidt, Bryon. 2010. "Introduction to Business Analytics and Optimization: Smarter Decisions for Optimized Performance." Presentation at *IBM Information ON Demand*. Retrieved May 14, 2013 at www-950.ibm.com/events/wwe/ca/canada.nsf/vLookupPDFs/6_Business_Analytics_&_Optimization_-_Smarter_decisions_for_optimized_performance_-_Byron_Schmidt/$file/6%20Business%20Analytics%20&%20Optimization%20-%20Smarter%20decisions%20for%20optimized%20performance%20-%20Byron%20Schmidt.pdf.

Schneider, B. (1987). "The people make the place." *Personnel Psychology*, 40(3):437–453.

Schneider, B.; Macey, W. H.; Barbera, K. M.; and Martin, N. 2009. "Driving customer satisfaction and financial success through employee engagement." *People & Strategy*, 32:22–27.

Schoemaker, Paul J. H. 1995. "Scenario planning: A tool for strategic thinking." *Sloan Management Review*, Winter:25–40.

Schoemaker, Paul J. H. and van der Heijden, Cornelius A. J. M. 1992. "Integrating scenarios into strategic planning at Royal Dutch/Shell." *Planning Review*, 20(3):41–46.

Schroeck, Michael; Shockley, Rebecca; Smart, Janet; Romero-Morales, Dolores; and Tufano, Peter. 2012. "Analytics: The Real-World Use of Big Data." *IBM Institute for Business Value*. Downloaded at www-935.ibm.com/services/us/gbs/thoughtleadership/ibv-big-data-at-work.html.

Schwab, Klaus. 2012. "The Global Competitiveness Report 2011–2012." *World Economic Forum*. Geneva, Switzerland.

Shamir, B. 1991. "Meaning, self, and motivation in organizations." *Organization Studies*, 12(3):405–424.

Shamir, B.; House, R. J.; and Arthur, M. B. 1993. "The motivational effects of charismatic leadership: A self-concept based theory." *Organization Science*, 4:577–594.

Sheldon, K. M. and Elliot, A. J. 1999. "Goal striving, need-satisfaction, and longitudinal well-being: The self-concordance model." *Journal of Personality and Social Psychology*, 76:482–497.

Shore, L. M. and Shore, T. H. 1995. "Perceived organizational support and organizational justice," in R. S. Cropanzano and K. M. Kacmar (Eds.), *Organizational Politics, Justice, and Support: Managing the Social Climate of the Workplace*. Westport, CT: Quorum, 149–64.

Sirkin, Harold L.; Hemerling, James W.; and Bhattacharya, Arindam K. 2008. "Globality: Competing with Everyone from Everywhere for Everything." New York: Hachett Book Group. Cited in knowledge@wharton, September 22, 2008.

Smith, Gregory P. 2012. "Managing Generation X & Y." Retrieved March 2012 at www.chartcourse.com/articlegenx.html.

[SHRM] Society for Human Resource Management. 2008a. "Workforce Readiness Weekly Survey." February. Retrieved from www.shrm.org/surveys.

SHRM and WSJ.com/Careers. 2008. "Critical Skills Needs and Resources for the Changing Workforce." June. Retrieved from www.shrm.org/surveys.

SHRM Foundation. 2010. "Rebuilding the Talent Value Proposition for What's Next." Retrieved March 30, 2012 at www.shrm.org/about/foundation/research/Documents/2010%20TL%20Onsite%20Program-%20FINAL.pdf.

SHRM Foundation. 2008b. "Seeing Forward: Succession Planning at 3M." Retrieved May 4, 2013 at www.shrm.org/about/foundation/products/Pages/SeeingForwardDVD.aspx.

SHRM Workplace Forecast. 2011. "The Top Workplace Trends According to HR Professionals." February. Retrieved at www.shrm.org/research/futureworkplacetrends/documents/11-0014wpf_posting_6.pdf.

Sommers, Dexie and Franklin, James C. 2012. "Employment Outlook: 2010–2020. Overview of Projections to 2020." *Bureau of Labor Statistics Monthly Labor Review*, January.

Steiner, Christopher. 2012. *Automate This: How Algorithms Came to Rule Our World*. New York: Penguin Books.

Sterling, Robert. 2007. "Boeing Frontiers." Retrieved February 27, 2013 at www.boeing.com/news/frontiers/archive/2007/february/mainfeature.pdf.

Stone, Brad. 2012. "My life as a TaskRabbit." *Bloomberg Businessweek*, September 13.

Thomas, K. W. and Velthouse, B. A. 1990. "Cognitive elements of empowerment: An 'interpretive' model of intrinsic task motivation." *Academy of Management Review*, 15(4):666–681.

Tkaczyk, Christopher. 2013. "Marissa Mayer breaks her silence on Yahoo's telecommuting policy." *CNN Money*. Retrieved June 8, 2013 at http://tech.fortune.cnn.com/2013/04/19/marissa-mayer-telecommuting/.

Toossi, Mitra. 2012. "Employment Outlook 2010–2020." *Bureau of Labor Statistics, Monthly Labor Review*, January.

Toossi, Mitra. 2002. "A Century of Change: The U.S. Labor Force, 1950–2050." *Bureau of Labor Statistics, Monthly Labor Review*, 125:15–28.

Top500. 2012. "Top 500 List of Supercomputers." Retrieved January 4, 2012 at www.top500.org/list/2012/11/.

Towers Perrin. 2006. "Winning Strategies for a Global Workforce." *HR Services Executive Report*. Retrieved September 29, 2012 at www.towersperrin.com/tp/getwebcachedoc?webc=HRS/USA/2006/200602/GWS.pdf.

Training Magazine. 2001. "Chevron: Transferring best practices." July 1. Retrieved March 20, 2013 at www.trainingmag.com/article/chevron-transferring-best-practices.

Transamerica Center for Retirement Studies. 2012. "13th Annual Retirement Survey." Retrieved January 4, 2013 at www.transamericacenter.org/resources/tc_center_research.html.

Tsui, A. S.; Pearce, J. L.; Porter, L. W.; and Tripoli, A. M. 1997. "Alternative approaches to the employee-organization relationship: Does investment in employees pay off?" *Academy of Management Journal*, 40:1089–1121.

Tushman, Michael L. and O'Reilly, III, Charles A. 2002. *Winning Through Innovation: A Practical Guide to Leading Organizational Change and Renewal, Revised Edition.* Boston: Harvard Business School Press.

Ulrich, L. B. 2006. "Bridge employment." In J. H. Greenhaus and G. A. Callanan (Eds.), *Encyclopedia of Career Development*, 1:49–51, Thousand Oaks, CA: Sage.

United Nations Department of Economic and Social Affairs. 2011. "World Population Prospects: The 2010 Revision." New York: Population Division.

United Nations Conference on Trade and Development. 2010. "World Investment Report 2010." New York: United Nations.

U.S. Census Bureau. 2012. "Statistical Abstract of the United States." Retrieved April 21, 2012 at www.census.gov/compendia/statab/2012/tables/12s1009.pdf.

U.S. Census Bureau. 2011. "Current Population Survey 2011." Retrieved April 21, 2012 at www.census.gov/hhes/socdemo/education/data/cps/2011/tables.html.

U.S. Census Bureau, Population Division. 2009. "Annual Estimates of the Resident Population by Sex, Race, and Hispanic Origin for the United States: April 1, 2000 to July 1, 2008." May 14. Washington, DC: U.S. Census Bureau.

U.S. Census Bureau. 2008a. "America's Families and Living Arrangements." Retrieved April 6, 2010 at www.census.gov/population/www/socdemo/hh-fam/cps2008.html.

U.S. Census Bureau. 2008b. "An Aging World."

Van Ark, Bart. 2011. "Is Income Slowing Down Growth?" *The Conference Board*, 22(3), December.

Walsh, J. P.; Meyer, A. D.; and Schoonhoven, C. B. 2006. "A future for organization theory: Living in and living with changing organizations." *Organizational Science*, 17:657–671.

Wang, Wendy and Taylor, Paul. 2011. "For Millennials, Parenthood Trumps Marriage." *Pew Research Center*, March.

Watson, D.; Clark, L. A.; and Tellegen, A. 1980. "Development and validation of brief measures of positive and negative affect: The PANAS scales." *Journal of Personality and Social Psychology*, 54:1063–1070.

Watson Wyatt. 2009. *Driving Results Through Continuous Engagement: 2008/2009 WorkUSA Survey Report*. New York: Watson Wyatt.

Welch, Jack. 2001. *Straight from the Gut*. New York: Warner Books.

Whitener, E. M.; Brodt, S. E.; Korsgaardj, M. A.; and Werner, M. 1998. "Managers as initiators of trust: An exchange relationship framework for understanding managerial trustworthy behavior." *Academy of Management Review*, 23:513–530.

Wiener, Y. 1982. "Commitment in organizations: A normative view." *Academy of Management Review*, 7:418–428.

Willcocks, L. P and Lacity, M. 2009. *The Practice of Outsourcing: From IT to BPO and Offshoring*. London: Palgrave.

Williamson, O. E. 1981. "The economics of organization: The transaction cost approach." *American Journal of Sociology*, 87:548–577.

Wilson, E. O. 1998. *Consilience: The Unity of Knowledge*. New York: Random House, Inc.

Wilson, Jill H. 2009. "Trends in U.S. Immigration." Metropolitan Policy Program at Brookings. Miami, FL, March 24.

WorldAtWork, 2009. *Telework Trendlines*. Scottsdale, AZ.

Index

Numerics

21st century workforce, characteristics of
  baby boomers, 41-42
  contract human capital, 53-58
  diversity, 49-51
  educational disparities, 51-53
  Generation X, 42-43
  Generation Y, 43-45
  marriage and family life, 46-49
  multigenerational, 40-46
  traditionalists, 41
2008 financial crisis, 34-35
2012 Engagement 2.0 Employee Study (Aon Hewitt), 142

A

"A" positions (employee engagement framework), 239
absorption, 95
achieving success in the "new normal," strategic planning, 215-218
ADEA (U.S. Age Discrimination in Employment Act), 79
affective commitment
  identification, 111
  as measure of engagement, 110-111
affinity groups, 193-194
age waves across labor force, 45-46
alienation as cause of burnout, 98
aligning work environment with employee competencies, 231-232
  Nestlé on the Move program, 232
Allen, Frederick, 172
alternative work arrangements, 53
  contract firm employees, 55
  independent contractors, 54
  offshore employees, 55-58
  on-call workers, 54
  outsourced employees, 55-58
  strategic partnerships, 55
analyzing employee engagement results, 240-249
  data collection methods, 241
  problems with
    benchmarking results against other companies, 245-246
    failing to separate drivers from measures and outcomes, 242-243
    focusing on number of questions, 243-244
    invalid linkages between results and financial outcomes, 247-249

X-Y-Z